Law and the Legal System – An Introduction

Samuel Mermin

Professor of Law
University of Wisconsin

LITTLE, BROWN AND COMPANY
BOSTON   **1973**   **TORONTO**

Acknowledgment of permission to reprint
previously published material appears
on pages xi-xiv.

Published simultaneously in Canada
by Little, Brown & Company (Canada) Limited

PRINTED IN THE UNITED STATES OF AMERICA

In memory of

Charles and Nechame Mermin
John J. Mermin
Arthur F. Mermin, Esq.

CONTENTS

Chapter 2. The Illustrative Case
(Initial Aspects)

Chapter 3. Further Aspects of the Case: The Statute

Chapter 4. Further Aspects of the Case:
The Precedents

Chapter 5. Further Aspects of the Case:
The Constitution

Postscript

Appendix: Tips on Some Mechanics of Law Study

ACKNOWLEDGMENTS

I should like to acknowledge the courteous permission extended by the following publishers, journals, and authors to quote from their works:

George Allen & Unwin Ltd.—from *The State in Theory and Practise* by Harold J. Laski. Copyright 1935 by Harold J. Laski, © 1963 by Frida Laski.

The American Assembly—from Wahlke, "Organization and Procedure" in Heard, ed., *State Legislatures in American Politics* (1966). From Barrett, "Criminal Justice: The Problem of Mass Production"; Hazard, "After the Trial Court—The Realities of Appellate Review"; and Rosenberg, "Court Congestion: Status, Causes and Proposed Remedies," in Harry W. Jones, ed., *The Courts, the Public and the Law Explosion* (1965). From Huntington, "Congressional Responses to the Twentieth Century," in David B. Truman, ed., *The Congress and America's Future* (1965).

American Bar Association Journal—from American Bar Association, *Code of Professional Responsibility and Canons of Judicial Ethics* (1969); Fuller and Randall, "Report of the Joint Conference on Professional Responsibility," 44 A.B.A.J. 1159 (1958); Fuchs, "Lawyers and Law Firms Look Ahead—1971-2000," 57 A.B.A.J. 971 (1971); Medina, "Some Reflections on the Judicial Function," 38 A.B.A.J. 107 (1952); Oliphant, "A Return to Stare Decisis," 14 A.B.A.J. 71 (1928).

American Sociological Assn.—from Berkowitz and Walker, "Laws and Moral Judgments," 30 Sociometry 410 (1967), as reprinted in Friedman and Macaulay, *Law and the Behavioral Sciences* 209-210 (1969).

The Bobbs-Merrill Co., Inc.—from Berkowitz and Walker, "Laws and Moral Judgments," 30 Sociometry 410 (1967), as reprinted in Lawrence M. Friedman and Stewart Macaulay, *Law and the Behavioral Sciences* (1969). Copyright 1969 by The Bobbs-Merrill Company, Inc. Reprinted by permission. All rights reserved.

Bureau of National Affairs, Inc.—reprinted by permission from *Briefing and Arguing Federal Appeals*, by Frederick Bernays Wiener, copyright © 1961, 1967, by The Bureau of National Affairs, Inc., Washington, D.C.

Charles Warren Center for Studies in American History—from Hurst, "Legal Elements in American History," and Stevens, "Two Cheers for 1870: The American Law School," in Donald Fleming and Bernard Bailyn, eds., *Law in American History* (Cambridge, 1971). Copyright © President and Fellows of Harvard College.

Columbia Law Review—from Frankfurter, "Some Reflections on the Reading of Statutes," 47 Colum. L. Rev. 527 (1947), and Jones, "Statutory Doubts and Legislative Intention," 40 Colum. L. Rev. 957 (1940). Reprinted with permission of the Directors of The Columbia Law Review Association, Inc.

Crown Publishers—from *The Corrupt Judge* by Joseph Borkin. © 1962 by Joseph Borkin. Used by permission of Clarkson N. Potter, Inc. From *Timber Line* by Gene Fowler. © 1933 by Gene Fowler. Used by permission of Crown Publishers, Inc.

Curtis Publishing Co.—from Ribicoff, "Doesn't Congress Have Ideas of Its Own?" 237 Sat. Eve. Post 6 (1964). © 1964 The Saturday Evening Post, Indianapolis, Indiana.

Doubleday & Co., Inc.—from Berger, *Equality by Statute* (rev. ed. 1967).

Paul A. Freund—from Freund, *On Understanding the Supreme Court* (1949).

Harcourt Brace Jovanovich, Inc.—from Holmes, *Collected Legal Papers* (1920).

Harvard Law Review—from Hart, "The Power of Congress to Limit the Jurisdiction of Federal Courts: An Exercise in Dialectic," 66 Harv. L. Rev. 1362 (1953); Schwartz, "Legal Restriction of Competition in the Regulated Industries: An Abdication of Judicial Responsibility," 67 Harv. L. Rev. 436 (1954); Note, "Developments in the Law," 76 Harv. L. Rev. 983 (1963); Note, "The Right to Privacy," 4 Harv. L. Rev. 193 (1890). Copyrights 1953, 1954, 1963, 1890, respectively, by The Harvard Law Review Association.

Indiana Law Journal—from Cohen, "Judicial 'Legisputation' and the Dimensions of Legislative Meaning," 36 Ind. L.J. 414 (1961); Field, "The Advisory Opinion—An Analysis," 24 Ind. L.J. 203 (1949).

Lawyers Guild Review—from Pekelis, "The Case for a Jurisprudence of Welfare," Lawyers Guild Rev. 611 (1946). Reprinted from Lawyers Guild Review with permission from the successor publication, National Lawyers Guild Practitioner, Box 673, Berkeley, CA 94701.

Little, Brown and Co.—from Hurst, *The Growth of American Law: The Law Makers*. Boston: Little, Brown and Company, copyright 1950.

Soia Mentschikoff Llewellyn—from Llewellyn, *The Bramble Bush* (Oceana ed. 1951).

MacMillan Publishing Co., Inc.—from M.R. Cohen, "Fictions," in 6 *Encyclopedia of the Social Sciences* 228 (1931). Copyright 1931 by The MacMillan Company.

Modern Law Review—from Stone, "The Ratio of the Ratio Decidendi," 22 Mod. L. Rev. 597 (1959). Published by Carswell Co. Ltd., Toronto.

New York Academy of Medicine—from Cardozo, B.N.: Anniversary Discourse: "What Medicine Can Do for Law," Bull. N.Y. Acad. Med.

5:7, 581-607 (1929). Reproduced by permission. Address given Nov. 1, 1928, reprinted in Margaret Hall, ed., *Selected Writings of Benjamin Nathan Cardozo* (1947).

New York County Lawyer's Assn.—from Cardozo, "The Home of the Law," address given at the dedication of the new home of the N.Y. County Lawyer's Assn., May 26, 1930, reprinted in Margaret Hall, ed., *Selected Writings of Benjamin Nathan Cardozo* (1947).

The New York Times—from Humphrey, "To Move Congress Out of Its Rut," N.Y. Times, April 7, 1963 (Magazine). © 1963 by The New York Times Company. Reprinted by permission.

New York University Law Review—from Bloustein, "Privacy as an Aspect of Human Dignity: An Answer to Dean Prosser," 39 (No. 6) N.Y.U.L. Rev. 962 (1964). Reprinted by permission of the New York University Law Review.

Prentice-Hall, Inc.—from Huntington, "Congressional Responses to the Twentieth Century," in David B. Truman, ed., *The Congress and America's Future* (1965).

Fred B. Rothman & Co.—from Cohen, "Judicial 'Legisputation' and the Dimensions of Legislative Meaning," 36 Ind. L.J. 414 (1961). From Field, "The Advisory Opinion—An Analysis," 24 Ind. L.J. 203 (1949). From address by Hand, delivered before the Juristic Society of the University of Pennsylvania Law School, June 1930, in Dillard, ed., *Spirit of Liberty*, second edition; reprinted with permission from University of Pennsylvania Law Review, Nov. 1930 (Vol. 79, pp. 1-14). From Fuller, "American Legal Realism," 82 U. Pa. L. Rev. 429 (1934). From Jaffe, Book Review (M. H. Bernstein, *The Independent Agency— A New Scapegoat: Regulating Business by Independent Commission*), 65 Yale L.J. 1068 (1956). Reprinted by permission of The Yale Law Journal Company and Fred B. Rothman & Company from The Yale Law Journal, Vol. 65, pp. 1068, 1071, 1074.

Albert M. Sacks—from Hart and Sacks, *The Legal Process* (tentative mimeograph ed. 1958).

Stanford Law Review—from Franklin, "A Constitutional Problem on Privacy Protection: Legal Inhibitions on Reporting of Fact," 16 Stan. L. Rev. 107, 134-135 (1963). Copyright © 1963 by the Board of Trustees of the Leland Stanford Junior University. Reprinted by permission.

Time/Life Syndication Service—from Whipple, "Three Months' Ordeal in Open Boats," Life, Nov. 10, 1952, at 156. Copyright: A. B. C. Whipple, Life Magazine, © 1952 Time Inc.

University of Chicago Press—from Hand, "How Far Is a Judge Free in Rendering a Decision?" presented May 14, 1933 in Law Series I of National Advisory Council on Radio in Education. Hand's part in program reprinted with permission of University of Chicago Press which published it. Copyright 1935 by the University of Chicago Press.

University of Illinois Law Forum—from Schaefer, "The Advocate as a Lawmaker: The Advocate in the Reviewing Courts," 1956 U. Ill. L.F. 203, 210.

University of Pennsylvania Law Review—from address by Hand, delivered before the Juristic Society of the University of Pennsylvania Law School, June 1930, in Dillard, ed., *Spirit of Liberty*, second edition; reprinted with permission from University of Pennsylvania Law Review, Nov. 1930 (Vol. 79, pp. 1-14). From Fuller, "American Legal Realism," 82 U. Pa. L. Rev. 429 (1934).

University of Wisconsin Press—from Mermin, *Jurisprudence and Statecraft* (Madison; The University of Wisconsin Press). © 1963 by the Regents of the University of Wisconsin. Pp. 111-112.

. Vanderbilt Law Review—from Fordham and Leach, "Interpretation of Statutes on Derogation of the Common Law," 3 Vand. L. Rev. 438 (1950).

Viking Press, Inc.—from *The State in Theory and Practice* by Harold J. Laski. Copyright 1935 by Harold J. Laski, © 1963 by Frida Laski. Reprinted by permission of The Viking Press, Inc.

Virginia Law Review—from Kalven, "The Dignity of the Civil Jury," 50 Va. L. Rev. 1055 (1964).

West Publishing Co.—from Corbin, *Contracts* (1963); Prosser, *Handbook of the Law of Torts* (4th ed. 1971).

Wisconsin Law Review—from Auerbach, "Some Thoughts on the Hector Memorandum," 1960 Wis. L. Rev. 183; Mermin, "Computers, Law and Justice," 1967 Wis. L. Rev. 43; Zick, "Liability Without Fault in the Food and Drug Statutes," 1956 Wis. L. Rev. 641.

Yale Law Journal Co.—from Jaffe, Book Review (M. H. Bernstein, *The Independent Agency—A New Scapegoat: Regulating Business by Independent Commission*), 65 Yale L.J. 1068 (1956). Reprinted by permission of The Yale Law Journal Company and Fred B. Rothman & Company from The Yale Law Journal, Vol. 65, pp. 1068, 1071, 1074.

Yale University Press—from Cardozo, Lecture 2, "The Methods of History, Tradition and Sociology," in Margaret Hall, ed., *Selected Writings of Benjamin Nathan Cardozo* (1947).

PREFACE

A word about how and why this book was born. As a beginning law student in the 1930s, I deplored the lack of any kind of orientation period. Hence, when after ten years as a government lawyer I went into teaching, one of the first courses I welcomed doing was an introduction-to-law course. I have taught such a course for more than two decades in a law school and several times in a political science department. I still believe there is great value in such a one-semester course.

The present book, however, aims to fulfill the same need in a more abbreviated fashion. During these years of teaching, I have been asked for such an abbreviated text by a variety of people. They were: (1) college students considering the possibility of going to law school; (2) "prelaw advisors" in colleges; (3) parents (usually lawyers) desirous of having their college-age children exposed to what law study is about; (4) citizens desiring to gain a not too painful understanding of the functioning of our legal system; (5) beginning law students. Some of them had seen books on "what every citizen should know" about leases, auto accidents, probate, etc., or surveys or exposés of the legal profession, or books of massive readings including cases and extracts from books and articles, or a civics book type of exposition that was either too dull and detailed or so simplified as to have substantial utility only for those (e.g., foreigners) quite unfamiliar with our legal institutions. These people were looking for something else.

They wanted a short expository analysis, giving some perspective on the system as a whole, couched in simple language, but not avoiding the difficult problems posed by the system. They wanted, I believe, a discussion of what the law is trying to do, what factors affect the success of its efforts, and the nature and interrelationships of the system's institutions.

And the beginning law students additionally wanted, before plunging into their case courses, a brief grounding in fundamentals and some tips on effective law study. The students wanted these things even if they were taking an introduction-to-law course (not offered, by the way, in all law schools), since some fundamentals to assist in coping with their other courses were needed at the outset rather than later.

I had been thinking of writing a book that would meet these varied demands, when it developed that the materials being used for a one-semester introduction course at my law school had become somewhat outdated; there was no time for a thorough revision, and a suitable substitute could not be agreed on. Thus was born the idea of filling the gap with the kind of book I had been contemplating — a short text that could be read by law students before regular classes began.

The experiment, which used a preliminary version of the present book in the fall of 1972, proved successful enough to warrant the book's publication. Although we used the book in an intensive week prior to regular classes and offered no introduction course, the book might also be used as a supplement to such a course. Alternatively, the student might be asked to read the book on his own, prior to commencement of regular classes or during the first few weeks of classes. Whatever system is used will, I think, be preferable to having the unoriented student embarked on law study, as he so often does today, in a climate of bewilderment and frustration.

The plan of the book is simple and readily explained. The long first chapter provides a jurisprudential perspective by discussing the law's dependence on the social environment, the law's social functions, the social limits on the law's efficacy, and the inescapable role of values in legal judgment. This part of the book also presents the law as a *system*, describing not only some salient characteristics and problems of each of the law's agencies (courts, legislatures, administrative and executive agencies) but also the functioning interrelationships and techniques of these agencies. Some of this chapter may seem elementary to you, but I have no way of knowing which of my audience has more than the average layman's knowledge of our legal system, gained perhaps through a sophisticated political science course on the subject. In the succeeding chapters I deal with various aspects of a case that was litigated in the federal courts of South Carolina in the '60s involving the law of privacy, and I supplement these aspects of the case with background notes designed to canvass the problems raised by the case and to present relevant background information about our system.

Thus, the second chapter presents the pleadings, the trial court and appellate court opinions in the litigated case, and a glimpse of the lawyer's appellate briefs, together with a discussion of appellate advocacy. There is then a background note on mainly procedural materials to aid your understanding of how the court process works. The note deals with requirements for starting a lawsuit, including the difficult problem of "standing" to sue; why the case is in a federal court; some relations between state and federal courts; significance of the "motion to dismiss" filed in the case; nature of our "adversary system" of litigation, etc. A further note provides a background in the substantive law of privacy.

The third chapter presents another aspect of the case — i.e., the court's treatment of the South Carolina statute — and discusses some basic issues of interpretation raised thereby. The background notes deal with further aspects of statutory interpretation and with the role of statutes in relation to common law.

Next come those aspects of the case involving the court's handling of case precedents. The text analysis of this process, together with the succeeding background note, treat some fundamental features of the Anglo-American precedent system.

The fifth chapter discusses a constitutional issue the defendant might have raised but didn't: whether the state statute violated the freedom of expression protected by the

Fourteenth Amendment. The background note goes on to discuss four basic features of our constitutional jurisprudence.

Briefly treating some miscellaneous topics not previously discussed, the Postscript discusses (1) the future of the legal profession, (2) legal education, and (3) law and other disciplines.

The Appendix deals with some bread-and-butter questions of the entering law student, such as: how to summarize an assigned case; how to prepare for class; what to do in class; how to cope with law examinations. An examination question and a suggested answer are included.

I am grateful to my nine colleagues who experimented with me last year in the teaching of these materials and shared with me their experiences in so doing. I profited also from the painstaking review and comment by Emeritus Professor William Gorham Rice and by Lora N. Mermin. Mrs. Ruth Wright of the University of Wisconsin Law School staff labored skillfully and patiently in processing the manuscript of both the preliminary and the present edition, with able assistance from Mrs. Violet Moore.

S.M.

Madison, Wisconsin
January 1973

*Law and the Legal System
an Introduction*

CHAPTER 1

Some General Observations on Law and the Legal System

A. THE LAW-IN-SOCIETY PERSPECTIVE

People specializing in a particular study area tend after a time to think of their area as being at the center of the universe. You have perhaps seen the humorous drawing of a New Yorker's view of the United States — in which the Eastern seaboard dominates the map, while the Midwest, mountain States, and Far West are an almost undifferentiated glob of shrunken territory off to the left. When your life is bound up with the law, you may tend to think of it as hovering over everything else, like some "brooding omnipresence in the sky."

But if you were a student of society as a whole, bent on assessing the roles of all factors in social life, law would assume a more subordinate role. You would think of society as molding the law. You would say that society shapes people's attitudes and ideals. You would say these in turn shape the kinds of courts, legislatures, and other legal institutions we have, and the kinds of conduct ("law-abiding" or otherwise) that people engage in. If you were a Marxist sociologist you would lay particular stress on how legal and other aspects of the society are shaped by the "means of production" and economic class interest.

Even the non-Marxist, however, recognizes the vital role of economic interest and the material conditions of life in influencing the law. The Supreme Court itself can be cited on this point. In 1943, when the Court was dealing with a damage suit by an injured railroad worker who (the railroad argued) had "assumed" the risk of injury on the job, the Court talked about the development, in the preceding century, of this "assumption of risk" doctrine. Recognizing that the doctrine was based on a judicially *implied* provision in the employment contract, the Court said the doctrine was "a judicially created rule which was developed in response to the general impulse of common law courts at the beginning of this period to insulate the employer as much as possible from bearing the 'human overhead' which is an inevitable part of the cost — to someone — of the doing of industrialized business. The general purpose behind this development in the common law seems to have been to give maximum freedom to expanding industry."[1] Many have agreed with this assessment.[2]

Or consider the following history of judicial interpretation of an insurance policy clause. Not long after invention of the airplane there was commonly an exclusion clause in accident and life insurance policies, under which the insurance company was not to be liable for injuries or death resulting from the policyholder's "participation in aeronautics." In the 1920s and early 1930s, court decisions were to the effect that a *passenger* came within the exclusion clause; he had, by virtue of being a passenger, "participated" in aeronautics.[3] But a shift in judicial opinion to the opposite view occurred in the next two decades. Why? The courts were simply taking account of the enormously expanded role of aviation since the early cases, and the consequently broader social impact of adverse decisions on the status of passengers. A court in 1942 put it this way: " 'Participating in aeronautics' in 1913 is far different in its meaning than is 'participating in aeronautics' now or in 1929. . . . The law is a living thing that must keep [pace] with the people and conditions it regulates."[4]

1. Tiller v. Atlantic Coast Line R. Co., 318 U.S. 54, 58-59 (1943).

2. Among those works suggesting similar explanation of the "assumption of risk" doctrine — or of a subdoctrine, the "fellow servant rule" (under which the employee was said to have impliedly assumed the risk of injury by a fellow employee's negligence) — are Levy, The Law of the Commonwealth and Chief Justice Shaw 178-181 (1957): Bohlen, "Voluntary Assumption of Risk," 20 Harv. L. Rev. 14, 31 (1906); Friedman and Ladinsky, "Social Change and the Law of Industrial Accidents," 67 Colum. L. Rev. 50, 51-58 (1967). For opposing argument see Pound, "The Economic Interpretation of the Law of Torts," 53 Harv. L. Rev. 365, 373-380, 382 (1940); Burdick, "Is Law the Expression of Class Selfishness?" 25 Harv. L. Rev. 349, 354-371 (1912).

3. See, e.g., Bew v. Travelers' Ins. Co., 95 N.J.L. 533, 112 A. 859 (1921); Travelers' Ins. Co. v. Peake, 82 Fla. 128, 89 So. 418 (1921); Meredith v. Business Men's Accident Assn., 213 Mo. App. 688, 252 S.W. 976 (1923); Head v. New York Life Ins. Co., 43 F.2d 517 (10th. Cir. 1930).

4. Wells v. Kansas City Life Ins. Co., 46 F. Supp. 754, 758 (D.N.D. 1942), aff'd, 133 F.2d 224 (8th Cir. 1943). For a summary of the development of the law in these insurance cases, see Annot. 45 A.L.R.2d 462 (1956).

In general,

One can plausibly correlate factors in the material environment in America with developments in American law, law enforcement, and public attitudes towards law. For instance, the fact of abundant land permitted a legal policy of liberal disposition of the public domain; led to habits of wastefulness, ultimately requiring legislation on conservation; and promoted an American tendency to thumb one's nose at legal authority (one could, if necessary, move on.) A difference in the availability of water, as between the arid western states and the eastern states, correlates with clear differences in the legal doctrines governing the use of water in the various states. Although the Supreme Court held in 1825 that the federal admiralty and maritime jurisdiction extended only to tidewater, it overruled itself in 1851, recognizing explicitly that the effects of the invention of the steamboat and settlement of the Mississippi Valley upon commerce on navigable streams made it necessary that the federal jurisdiction apply to all navigable waters. Technological change in such fields as printing and telegraphy produced new legal problems, in areas of trademark and copyright, libel, and freedom of speech. Urbanization, the coming of the automobile, mass production, meant new problems for legal solution, and new doctrines in auto negligence law, legislation on health, safety, fair dealing, employer-employee relations, monopolies, and many other subjects. Technological change also affected law enforcement: it made enforcement in some ways more difficult (e.g., the auto provided a fast means of escape) but in many ways easier (officials had not only fast transport and quick communication, but many scientific weapons of crime detection).[5]

The social environment of law of course includes more than material conditions. It includes the force of particular *ideas* and *ideals* — which may be part of a general, contemporary "climate of opinion," or of the current "legal culture." It includes the intellectual and charismatic force exerted by particular people — the "greats" among the judges, legislators, administrators, and advocates. All of these factors, along with miscellaneous others, like sheer accident, human inertia, human greed, and human ignorance, play their parts in making law what it is.

Much of this was epitomized in 1881 on the first page of Holmes's *The Common Law*. The book was one of the first

   5. Auerbach, Garrison, Hurst, and Mermin, The Legal Process 85-86 (1961). For concise elaboration of the dependent role of law, see Hurst, The Growth of American Law 3-19, 439-446 (1950).

attempts to afford a unifying perspective on the mass of technical, seemingly inconsistent, and confusing doctrines in Anglo-American judge-made law. The often-quoted passage reads:

> The life of the law has not been logic: it has been experience. The felt necessities of the time, the prevalent moral and political theories, intuitions of public policy, avowed or unconscious, even the prejudices which judges share with their fellow-men, have had a good deal more to do than the syllogism in determining the rules by which men should be governed. The law embodies the story of a nation's development through many centuries, and it cannot be dealt with as if it contained only the axioms and corollaries of a book of mathematics.

Law, in turn, as I shall later more fully suggest, plays its part in shaping the social environment. True, some laws, when they run too much against the grain, are ineffective. But it can hardly be denied that the Supreme Court decisions on, let us say, abortion, school segregation, and obscenity, or congressional statutes on welfare, labor relations, or wage-price-rent controls, or executive decisions on such matters as the Vietnam War (coupled with court decisions not to interfere) have substantially affected the nature of our lives.

The most common mistake of one in the early stages of studying law is to forget this social setting of the law — this *interaction* between society and law.

B. FUNCTIONS OF LAW

Let me now explore one general aspect of this relation: what does law *do* for people in our society — or, putting it in terms of what the legal agencies are supposed to do or are trying to do (sometimes successfully), what are the social functions of our law?

You probably think first about the *dispute-settling* function. We do tend to think first about the courts and their business of settling disputes. These may be disputes between private parties, or between a private party and a government unit or official, or between different government units or officials. Many government administrative agencies also engage in adjudicative dispute-settling. But it is worth remembering that private individuals functioning in the area of labor arbitration and commercial arbitration already account for a larger number of dispute settlements per year than do all the courts of the nation. Here too, however, the courts play a role — they can be called on to enforce the arbitration award, and sometimes to enforce an agreement to arbitrate. ·

Another function we tend to think of right away is *maintaining order*, through the bulk of criminal law, against violence or aggravated harm to persons or property, by the threat of the penalties of imprisonment and/or fines. This of course includes the policing function as well as the court's role in trials and sentencing, and the operations of other officials such as prosecutors and parole and probation personnel. Maintaining order also involves protection (through sedition, treason, and related laws) against that extreme threat to order, the violent overthrow of government. Thus the law legitimates certain uses of force by government but not (save for exceptional circumstances) by private parties.

But there is much more to our legal system than settling disputes and maintaining order. For one thing, the legal system constitutes a *framework within which certain common expectations about the transactions, relationships, planned happenings, and accidents of daily life can be met* (and this force for predictability and regularity can itself be viewed as a species of maintenance of order). We expect that those who have suffered personal injuries — particularly those who were without fault — will be compensated for their injuries under the laws of tort; that those who have made promises will be held to their promises (or, if not, be required to make recompense) under the laws of contract; that those who own property can get the law to enforce their expectations that they have exclusive rights in it and are free to dispose of it as they wish. All of these expectations have to be somewhat qualified, since the rights involved — especially those of property — have been subjected to conditions and exceptions. That is, the nature of the expectations is partly a product of conditioning by the legal system — thereby illustrating what I referred to before as the interaction of law and society.

There are functions of another sort, that can be seen in both constitution and statute. There are provisions aimed at *securing efficiency, harmony, and balance in the functioning of the government machinery.* Here I am thinking of the constitutional separation of powers by which specific kinds of power are allocated to specific branches of government with an attempt to avoid undue concentration in any one branch. And I think of other provisions for planning the affairs of government — statutes like the Full Employment Act and government reorganization acts — and the fiscal planning represented by budgets for the raising (taxation, borrowing) and spending of public money. I think of a different kind of planning, too, exemplified by zoning and other land use controls, conservation laws, and environmental protections. I think also — because the legal machinery requires maintaining legal skills for its maintenance — of provisions governing the qualifications of lawyers, judges, and other government officials for their respective vocations. There are, moreover, measures that build into the system, agencies to make continuing assessments and proposals for improvement of the system — e.g., the state legislative councils and judicial councils, the commissioners on uniform state laws, the federal judicial conferences and the Administrative Conference of the United States.

In the Constitution can be seen another vital function of our law: *protection of the citizen against excessive or unfair government power.* I refer mainly to the Bill of Rights — to such basic rights as freedom of speech, press, and religion, the right to privacy and against unreasonable searches and seizure, the privilege against self-incrimination, the right of jury trial for crime. Remember that the "due process" clause has been construed by the courts to assure both fair *procedure* and freedom from arbitrariness in the *substance* of government requirements. A standard of equality of treatment applies to the states through the equal protection clause of the Fourteenth Amendment and is, to some uncertain extent, applicable to the federal government through the due process clause of the Fifth Amendment. Remember also that included in the due process protection against both governments are property rights, as well as life and liberty.

Our legal system is concerned, too, with *protecting people against excessive or unfair private power*. In addition to antitrust law protection against private monopolistic power are a number of specialized protections. For example, an employer's power is curbed by laws like those compelling the payment of minimum wages, or prohibiting discrimination in employment, or compelling collective bargaining with unions; a corporation's power in the sale of its securities is curbed by SEC requirements. Analogous restrictions apply through a host of regulatory laws and administrative commissions on both federal and state levels.

Somewhat overlapping in function with these laws are some that are aimed at *assuring people an opportunity to enjoy the minimum decencies of life* by protecting their economic and health status. These functions have been more prominent in the later history of our society. I have in mind laws on unemployment insurance, social security, Medicare, public housing, welfare, and antipoverty programs, as well as older statutes like those on bankruptcy and garnishment. I would also include measures for psychic health. By that I mean not only government services for the poor who are mentally ill, but also measures attempting to eliminate various external sources of psychic distress: laws and decisions discouraging discrimination, giving redress for injuries to reputation and invasions of privacy, enlarging opportunities for recreation, and reducing the pollution of air, water, and landscape.

One other point: is there any sense in which it is true that law has an *ethical or moral function*? The answer, I think, is definitely yes. Most of the functions already mentioned have a clear ethical dimension. Thus, in settling disputes, the law aims at a result that is fair and socially desirable. A good deal of the criminal law carries out ethical precepts of conduct — many of which are in the Ten Commandments. In tort law, many of the principles concerning either negligent or intentional infliction of injury may be traced to the principle of the Golden Rule. The obligation to keep one's promises is an ethical obligation. Similarly, the agencies I mentioned as being concerned with improving the legal system have had as goals not only increased efficiency but also more socially desirable results. Ethical or humanitarian motivation has been at least one of the sources of the mentioned legislation aimed at raising the standard of living of the disadvantaged and legislation protecting people against unfair exercise of public or private power. Much legislation and general legal principle uses explicitly ethical terms in laying down standards of conduct — phrases like "good faith," "not profiting by one's own wrong," "fair and equitable," "unjust enrichment." The Constitution itself, as we have seen, speaks in terms of equality and (as a judicial interpretation of "due process") fairness.

Hence it is altogether misleading to say, as some have said, that legal duties have nothing to do with moral duties. Those who do say it are addressing themselves to a situation in which, it is said, a moral duty but not a legal duty exists. For example, a blind stranger is starting to cross the street. You are beside him and without harm to yourself can avoid his walking into an automobile by simply grabbing his arm. You don't do so, and he is injured. Generally in America the law says you are not liable for damages. Your inaction in these circumstances was, legally, not "negligence." The court might say: you had an ethical or moral duty but not a legal duty. But this does not mean that the law is here indifferent to ethical or moral duties. It means that the law here chooses a different ethical duty from that which a moralist is likely to choose, and does so on the assumption that it will better serve the public welfare.

Thus, the judges are in effect saying this: one ought not to have to respond to damages here, because one ought not to have legal obligations that (1) strongly limit our basic ideal of individual freedom of action (including our freedom to do nothing) by requiring affirmative action in an emergency situation where it is not clear that the average man would so act, especially in the absence of a known requirement to do so; (2) are very difficult to administer because of the vagueness of the rule, and because of the difficulty arising where more than one spectator is at hand, i.e., which one has the duty? and if all have, won't they get in each other's way? (3) apply in the kind of emergency situations where people tend to freeze or panic. In short, the judges are saying that it is *unfair* to impose a legal duty in this situation. You may disagree with the reasoning, but you can't say the law is being indifferent to ethical or moral duties. In its concern with standards of conduct, the law is honeycombed with "ought" propositions that purport to be rationally based. After all, the law is not an end in itself; it is a means for the achievement of social ends. Even the Sabbath, it has been said, was made for man, not man for the Sabbath.

Perhaps you tend to think of a judge's decision as value-free, i.e., as flowing strictly and logically from the unequivocal requirements of statute or judicial precedent. This, as Chapter 4 tries to make clear, and as my earlier quotation from Holmes suggests, is a delusion. Of course, the requirements of logical and factual truth are not irrelevant to a judicial decision. The judge does want his facts to be true, and wants his decision to be logically consistent with a reasonable view of the requirements of constitution, statute, and judicial precedent. But notice that I speak of a *reasonable view* of the requirements; for they are not free from ambiguity. Within the range of freedom allowed for his choice of that reasonable view (and I suspect it is a larger range than you presently suppose), he is concerned with questions like fairness and social reasonableness of the result. This is why an astute legal scholar has said that judicial decisions are not true or false, they are good or bad.[6]

6. F. S. Cohen, Ethical Systems and Legal Ideals 32-33 (1933; Cornell ed. 1959).

C. LIMITS OF LAW

Given some such list of law's functions as I have set out — and other lists could be compiled, shorter or longer, or couched in different categories[7] — an interesting question is, how far can these functions go? What kinds of specific barriers have been encountered in the attempt to fulfill these functions? What, in other words, are the major "limits on effective legal action," to use the phrase of Roscoe Pound? By this I don't mean legal limits like those set by the constitution. I am concerned rather with the important nonlegal or practical limits, which are rooted, you might say, in the human condition — though I shall occasionally refer to the constitution as well.

1. SOCIAL CONDITIONING

One outer limit, of course, arises from an already mentioned fact: the social conditioning of law. In other words, if basic socioeconomic conditions and interests have a shaping influence on the law, one cannot expect the law to

7. Thus, Professor Hurst observes that within the limits of the ideal of "constitutionalism," law's functions in American history were (1) embodying the "legitimate monopoly of force" and claiming "as a corollary, the right to appraise the legitimacy of all private forms of power," (2) emphasizing "regular and rational procedures," as well as "some level of rationality in the substance of public policy," (3) "allocat[ing] scarce economic resources . . . by taxing and by spending" and indirectly by "public borrowing and also by the standards by which it regulated behavior (as when by setting standards for marketing food, it required a certain level of capital investment by food dealers)." Hurst, "Legal Elements in United States History," in Fleming and Bailyn, eds., Law in American History 3-6 (1971). Llewellyn thought that the "law-jobs" consisted of: "cleaning up . . . grievances and disputes"; "channeling conduct . . . so that, negatively grievances and disputes are avoided, and, positively, men's work is geared into team-play"; "re-channeling along new lines"; "allocation of that *say* which in case of doubt or trouble is to go, and . . . the procedures for making that say an official and binding say"; "producing a net organization and direction of the work of the whole group or society, and in a fashion which unleashes incentive"; "building and using techniques and skills for keeping the men and machinery of all the law-jobs on their jobs and up to the jobs." Llewellyn, "On the Good, the True, the Beautiful in Law," 9 U. Chi. L. Rev. 224, 253 (1942); "The Normative, the Legal, and the Law Jobs," 49 Yale L.J. 1355, 1373-1400 (1940). Summers

turn around and completely transcend those conditions and interests. No one, in a society with the kind of private property substructure that America now has, expects that Congress will in the foreseeable future pass a National Communization of Property Act destroying and replacing that substructure.

This is not to say that gradual legislative restrictions on private property rights have not occurred and will not occur. Some of these occurrences I have mentioned in discussing the function of law. They have occurred in spite of the fact that legislators' economic interest is generally viewed as closer to that of the "Establishment" than to the classes that were principal beneficiaries of the legislation. The same can be said of the role played by, and economic affiliations of, the judges. Because judges have so often been charged with economic class bias, the following counterweight from a prominent student of the Supreme Court deserves consideration:

A crude economic interpretation of the judicial office ignores too many elements of character. The taking of the robe, an experience at once emancipating and humbling, is apt to dissolve old ties and to quicken the sense that there is no escape from that judgment of one's successors which is called history.

The record of the Court supplies many cautions against the generalization that the lawyer is father to the judge. It was a successful lawyer for shipping interests, Henry Billings Brown, who as Mr. Justice Brown delivered a memorable dissent in the income-tax cases: ". . . the decision involves nothing less than a surrender of the taxing power to the moneyed class. . . . I hope it may not prove the first step toward the submergence of the liberties of the people in a sordid despotism of wealth." . . . It was [a] railroad lawyer, Joseph P. Bradley, who as Mr. Justice Bradley protested against the use of the due-process clause to review the regulation of railroad rates by the states, and who would have permitted the states to regulate interstate rates until Congress assumed the responsibility. And it was Harlan F. Stone, whose record in

---

and Howard recognize seven functions of law: helping to (1) promote human health, including a healthy environment, (2) reinforce the family and protect private life, (3) keep community peace, (4) protect basic freedoms, (5) secure equality of opportunity, (6) recognize and order private ownership, (7) exercise surveillance and control over persons in positions of power. Summers and Howard, Law, Its Nature, Functions and Limits 440 (2d ed. 1972).

sustaining the validity of social legislation needs no comment, who had written in 1916 by way of commentary on Herbert Spencer's "The Sins of Legislators" that "Spencer's vigorous warning furnishes food for thought and will perhaps inspire with caution the zealous advocates of such sweeping legislative changes as are involved in the many proposals for the various types of pension law, and minimum wage statutes, and modern legislation of similar character." The list could be extended. . . .[8]

Yet when all such cautionary qualifications have been made, it remains true that "the business of a legal system is to make the postulates of a society work. It would be remarkable indeed if it could be so worked as to secure their fundamental transformation."[9] Thus one aspect of the first of the law's limits that I am listing is that basic change in the socioeconomic structure is, to put it mildly, neither easily nor quickly achieved through legal agencies. This is as true of drastically different legal systems — Soviet, Chinese, or Cuban — as it is of ours.

2. *POPULAR HABITS, ATTITUDES, IDEALS*

A second limit that comes quickly to mind is that the law dare not get too far away from popular attitudes, habits, and ideals in the various situations that keep coming up in everyday life. I shall deal below with a number of these affirmative habits, attitudes, and ideals. But bear in mind also the strong negative tendency — which Professor Hurst has called "drift" or "inertia" — that seems to be a more potent factor in explaining law's role in our history than most of us have realized.[10]

a. Racial Prejudices

Thus the difficulties with enforcing racial desegregation stems largely from strongly entrenched popular attitudes or habits on the part of a substantial segment of the population, particularly in the South. It is possible — but far from

8. Freund, On Understanding the Supreme Court 45-47 (1949).
9. Laski, The State in Theory and Practice 177 (1935).
10. Hurst, Law and Social Process in United States History, c. 2 (1960).

easy — for the law to help change those racial attitudes, and I shall later comment on some basis for optimism in this respect.

b. Opposition to Sumptuary Restraints

Racial prejudice is of course not the only illustration of this second limit. Liquor prohibition was contrary to the entrenched attitudes of so many people that it led to widespread violation and big-time racketeering, and eventually had to be repealed. But remember, in comparing the law's retreat in the case of liquor prohibition with its relative lack of retreat in the case of prohibiting segregation, that the opposition to liquor prohibition was pretty widespread rather than particularly concentrated in one geographical region of the country. Nor did liquor prohibition have a determined national enforcement; enforcement was very spotty indeed. Nor was it backed by the moral force of providing equality of opportunity for a long-suffering race. Experience with marijuana prohibition seems to be developing in a fashion somewhat resembling the experience with liquor prohibition: penalties are being drastically reduced, and ultimate legalization is probable in the absence of new evidence of the drug's harmfulness.

c. Opposition to Excessive Rigor: The Death Penalty

Consider another example, this time from further back in history. In eighteenth-century England, you may remember, the penalty imposed for various crimes — even the minor crimes like pickpocketing and other petty theft — was death. In the later eighteenth century and the early nineteenth century, as the opposition to the severity of these penalties developed more strongly, an interesting thing happened. Judges and juries started circumventing these penalties. The law had diverged too much from the general attitudes of the people. So judges interpreted the statutes in a very peculiar way in order to get the particular defendant out of the reach of the particular statute, when a normal reading of the statute would apply to him. The jury would also come in with strange verdicts. It would come in with acquittals when the normal observer of the evidence would assume that this was a case of guilt. Sometimes the jury would merely postpone the day of reckoning. For instance, there was a well-known case involving a defendant who was charged with stealing a pair of trousers, an act to which the death penalty applied. The jury ultimately came in with a verdict of manslaughter. It knew that the judge would set aside the verdict as not making sense. At least a little time was gained, and this defendant might or might not be prosecuted again.[11]

In our day, we have seen a rather analogous inability of the death penalty to operate effectively — this time because a substantial segment of public sentiment was finding the penalty too cruel not merely for certain relatively minor offenses but for major offenses, typically murder. Witness the protracted delays in executions, the executive commutations to life sentences; the seemingly greater tendency of appellate courts in capital cases to find that reversible errors had been committed in the trial; a seemingly greater jury tendency in capital cases to convict of an offense less than the charged offense; and finally, the two climactic decisions of 1972: The Supreme Court of California's decision that the death penalty violated the state constitution as a "cruel or unusual punishment,"[12] and the United States Supreme Court's somewhat limited decision that the imposition and carrying out of death sentences under statutes giving juries discretion over when the death penalty should be applied violated the Federal Constitution's prohibition against "cruel and unusual punishment."[13] Two of the Supreme Court majority of five took the all-out position that the death penalty itself was "cruel and unusual punishment." The other three based their position on the arbitrary or discriminatory manner (or

11. J. Hall, Theft, Law and Society 138 (1935). For various instances of circumventions by judges, prosecutors, and juries, of death penalties for minor transgressions, see id. at 118-141.

12. California v. Anderson, 6 Cal. 3d 628, 493 P.2d 880, cert. denied, 406 U.S. 958 (1972).

13. Furman v. Georgia, 408 U.S. 238 (1972).

infrequency and hence nondeterrence) of imposition, under the statutes which gave juries a choice as to imposition; they did not express themselves against a mandatory death penalty.

You will note I referred to "a substantial segment of public sentiment" against the death penalty rather than to public opinion as a whole. The Supreme Court decision indeed represents the *unusual* instance of a strong legal change being made by a *court* where popular sentiment for the change does *not* represent a strong majority. The dissenters in the case argued strenuously that the Court's about-face in its constitutional interpretation of cruel and unusual punishment (limited though the decision was, as I have described above) was an inappropriate, "legislative" act — because it was in the face of recent as well as traditional state and federal legislative approval of the penalty and its administration through jury discretion, and in the face of sharply divided public opinion.

d. Opposition to Excessive Rigor: Jury Moderation and Compassion; Prosecutor Moderation

I have mentioned the jury's role. Let me now say something more about that. The oft-noted observation that juries exert a moderating influence on the rigors of the law seems accurate, though exaggerated. Elaborate studies by the University of Chicago Law School show that in about 17% of criminal cases, the jury acquitted when the judge would have convicted; and in convictions in capital cases, the discretion whether to assess the death penalty was exercised against the death penalty slightly more by the jury than by the judge.[14]

The Chicago studies show the jury as a moderating force in civil cases too. Take the usual personal injury case, e.g., involving an auto accident, where the rule is that the injured plaintiff has the burden of proving the negligence of the defendant. The Chicago studies suggest that the jury, in fact, in spite of the rule I mentioned, tends to resolve the doubts it has about the defendant's negligence in favor of the injured plaintiff. I am assuming, of course, that it is a case of some

14. Kalven and Zeisel, The American Jury 62, 436 (1966).

doubt. It is true that the jury still brings in verdicts against the injured plaintiff in cases of clear absence of negligence on the part of the defendant. But it seems that the jury tends to resolve the doubts it has in the controversial, fairly evenly balanced cases in favor of the plaintiff, whereas this rule of the burden of proof would seem to mean that they would have to resolve doubts in favor of the defendant. What we mean by saying that the plaintiff has the burden in this personal injury suit is that he has to prove and convince by a *preponderance* of the evidence. (In a criminal case, the plaintiff, i.e., the prosecution, has the burden of proving its case beyond a reasonable doubt.)

Other things have been found to be true about the actual operation of juries, as distinct from the theory, in these personal injury cases. For example, there is a rule in most states to the effect that if the injured plaintiff was himself negligent (what the law terms "contributory negligence") and this negligence contributed substantially to the injury that he suffered, such a plaintiff is barred from recovery. His own contributory negligence prevents his recovery of damages, even though the defendant was negligent. That is a pretty harsh rule and it doesn't even take cognizance of the relative amount of negligence as between the plaintiff and the defendant. It simply says that if the plaintiff's negligence also contributed to the injury, he cannot recover. A few states, with Wisconsin as a leader, have a more enlightened attitude than that. They have what we call the "comparative negligence" rule. But even in the majority states you tend to find the jury in fact operating on a comparative negligence basis. That is to say, what the jury seems to be doing in a case where it feels that the plaintiff's own negligence contributed to his injury is this: it brings in a verdict with reduced damages for the plaintiff rather than a verdict for the defendant as would have been proper under the judge's instructions. It is another example of the "law in action" differing from the "law in books."

However, you should not assume that the moderating or nullifying role of juries in civil cases represents much greater sympathy for the plaintiff than would be shown by the judge if he were deciding the case. The Chicago studies show that in 80% of the personal injury cases, the judge agreed with the jury's determination as to who should win (the same percentage as in criminal cases). However, "The judge disagrees with the jury because he is more pro-plaintiff about as often as the jury disagrees with him because it is more pro-plaintiff." And looking "simply at the 44% of the cases where both decide for the plaintiff, we find considerable disagreement on the level of damages. In roughly 23% the jury gives the higher award, in 17% the judge gives the higher award and in the remaining 4% they are in approximate agreement. More important, however, is the fact that the jury awards average 20% higher than those of the judge."[1][5]

Sometimes, in criminal cases, instead of the jury being in the role of potential moderator or nullifier it is the prosecutor who is. He too is sensitive to popular attitudes, and he acts accordingly. Witness, for example, the well-known reluctance to prosecute sexual behavior that violates stautory prohibitions like those against adultery or fornication.

e. Desire for Government Noninterference with Privacy and with Conduct Not Injurious to Others; the "Mill Principle"

As a matter of fact, the state legislative prohibitions in the field of sexual behavior may eventually be generally modified in line with this general reluctance of the prosecutor, when you consider the position taken by the influential American Law Institute. It worked for many years on a model penal code, and completed its labors in 1964. The code has not yet been generally adopted, but it has affected the thinking of legislatures in a good many states. Here is what the Commentary of the code says in explaining the lack of prohibition against fornication and adultery: "The Code does not attempt to use the power of the state to enforce purely moral or religious standards. We deem it inappropriate for the

15. Kalven, "The Dignity of the Civil Jury," 50 Va. L. Rev. 1055, 1065 (1964).

government to attempt to control behavior that has no substantial significance except as to the morality of the actor. Such matters are best left to religious, educational, and other social influences. Apart from the question of constitutionality which might be raised against legislation avowedly commanding adherence to a particular religious or moral tenet, it must be recognized, as a practical matter, that in a heterogeneous community such as ours, different individuals and groups have widely divergent views of the seriousness of various moral derelictions."[16] The code does prohibit prostitution, certain lewd exposures in public, and sex relations involving force, fraud, or females that are underage or mentally incapable.

Such attitudes in this area of consensual sex conduct seem to me to be a particular illustration of a more encompassing attitude, strongly held by large numbers of people and in even larger proportion among young people. I have in mind the drawing of a circle around certain kinds of conduct as being "private" — conduct which the law shouldn't stick its nose into in order to promote one view of morality, or further the defendant's own good, as distinguished from the purpose of protecting other people from harm. John Stuart Mill expressed this quite common attitude when he said in the first chapter of his essay "On Liberty": "The object of this essay is to assert one simple principle, as entitled to govern absolutely the dealings of society with the individual by way of compulsion and control, whether the means used be political force in the form of legal penalties, or the moral coercion of public opinion. That principle is that . . . the only purpose for which power can be rightfully exercised over any member of a civilized community, against his will, is to prevent harm to others. His own good, either physical or mental, or moral, is not a sufficient warrant."[17]

16. ALI Model Penal Code, Commentary at 207 (Tent. Draft No. 4, 1955). This commentary is made applicable by Article 213 of the Proposed Official Draft of the code (1962).

17. Mill, Utilitarianism, Liberty, and Representative Government 72-73 (Everyman ed. 1910).

Such a principle extends far beyond the field of sexual behavior. On the basis of this principle, for instance, it could be argued that a state could not compel a person to accept for his own good a life-preserving blood transfusion he didn't want; or compel mental health treatment for the harmlessly insane; or compel participation in an air raid drill, or the wearing of seatbelts by autoists and helmets by motor-cyclists; or prohibit personal use or consumption (or posses-sion for personal use or consumption) of alcohol, drugs, or obscene material; or prohibit abortions, particularly early abortions.

How have the courts treated the Mill principle? They have not often come squarely to grips with it in the sense of accepting or rejecting the principle as such. Where a court has upheld a statute that might arguably be viewed as violating the Mill principle, the decision has generally been based not on a rejection of the principle but rather on the idea that the prohibited conduct *did* threaten harm to others. (This is not quite the same as holding that *only* in cases of such harm will the statute be upheld.) And when a statute that might arguably be viewed as violating the Mill principle was *invalidated*, this has generally been for reasons other than application of the Mill principle.[18] The six numbered paragraphs below (and a few paragraphs after the sixth) give a sketch of contemporary judicial attitudes in a number of situations that pose a Mill principle type of issue or something related to it.

(1) Thus, consider the *upholding* of hard drug statutes and liquor prohibition statutes aimed at possession and consump-tion. They were upheld for reasons like these: The user might well cause economic and other harm to his dependents; he might well engage in crime against others to pay for an expensive drug habit; prohibiting use or possession was a necessary supplementary means of enforcing the clearly valid prohibitions against manufacture and sale. (Interestingly,

18. See generally Note, "Limiting the State's Police Power: Judicial Reaction to John Stuart Mill," 37 U. Chi. L. Rev. 605 (1970).

some early liquor cases in the states had cited the Mill
principle and gone the other way.)

(2) The harm basis for upholding prohibitions on marijuana as distinguished from hard drugs is not as easy to
sustain. But so far the courts have been willing to say that the
legislature could reasonably have found that the necessary
harm existed.[19] Some modification of this conclusion
occurred in the 1972 Report of the National Commission on
Marijuana and Drug Abuse headed by former Pennsylvania
Governor Shafer, when it declared that "experimental or
intermittent use of this drug carries minimal risk to the
public health," and public health officials should concentrate
on "the small minority of heavy, long-term marijuana users
who are exposed to a much greater relative risk of impaired
general functioning in contemporary America . . ." However,
the commission was "concerned that social influences might
cause those who would not otherwise use the drug to be
exposed to this minimal risk and the potential escalation of
drug-using patterns. For this group we must deglorify,
demythologize, and de-emphasize the use of marijuana and
other drugs." The commission expressed concern that the
small proportion of heavy, long-term users (about 2%) would
increase with a sudden legalization of the drug. Hence it
recommended "only a decriminalization of possession of
marijuana for personal use on both the State and Federal
levels. The major features of the recommended scheme are
that production and distribution of the drug would remain
criminal activities, as would possession with intent to
distribute commercially; marijuana would be contraband
subject to confiscation in public places; and criminal sanctions would be withdrawn from private use and possession
incident to such use, but, at the state level, fines would be
imposed for use in public."[20]

19. See, e.g., People v. Stark, 175 Colo. 59, 400 P.2d 923 (1965);
Commonwealth v. Leis, 355 Mass. 189, 243 N.E.2d 898 (1969).
20. Excerpts from the Report appear in the N.Y. Times, March 23, 1972, at 1,
col. 5.

(3) So far, too, courts have found a sufficient social harm-prevention basis for existing prohibitions against forni-cation, adultery, and other deviations from orthodox sexual mores.[21] Here there is assumed to exist a government power (perhaps religiously inspired originally) to protect public morals and thereby, it is argued, preserve the social fabric.[22] The American Law Institute, however, was persuaded that sex offense legislation, with the few exceptions previously indicated, does not appropriately and sufficiently serve to prevent such social harms as illegitimacy, disease, and undermining of the marriage institution.[23]

(4) The motorcycle helmet laws have usually been upheld with involved reasoning on social harm, e.g., that helmets (a) prevent accidents involving injury to others which could result if the cyclist loses control when hit in the head by wind-blown objects, such as road pebbles catapulted by a vehicle's tires; (b) keep accident insurance costs from rising; (c) prevent the situation where cyclists with head injuries put a burden on ambulances and hospitals and medical services, and may even (themselves or their dependents) become public charges. Some of these cases mentioned the Mill principle, and for the above reasons, as to social harm, found it not to apply adversely to the statutes.[24]

(5) As I have said, the cases *invalidating* a statute that might be viewed as violating the Mill principle don't generally do so on the ground of that principle. An occasional case, however, has done so — e.g., a few minority motorcycle helmet cases, stressing that the statutory purpose was protecting the operator's personal safety rather than the safety of others.[25]

21. See State v. Lutz, 57 N.J. 314, 272 A.2d 753 (1971); State v. Barr, 110 N.J. Super. 365, 265 A.2d 817, rev'd on other grounds, State v. Clark, 58 N.J. 72, 275 A.2d 137 (1971); State v. Ronek, 176 N.W.2d 153 (Iowa 1970); Rhinehart v. Washington, 70 Wash. 2d 649, 424 P.2d 906 (1967), cert. denied, 389 U.S. 832 (1967); People v. Roberts, 256 Cal. App. 2d 488, 64 Cal. Rptr. 70 (1967); Note, supra note 18, at 622 n.78.

22. See Note, supra note 18, at 622-623.

23. See discussion in ALI Model Penal Code at 204-210 (Tent. Draft No. 4 1955).

24. Note, supra note 18, at 614-617.

25. People v. Fries, 42 Ill. 2d 446, 250 N.E.2d 149 (1969); American

(6) However, a number of cases have invalidated statutes or rules that had *some* grounding in a rationale against public harm, where the harm was deemed too dubious or insubstantial to justify impairment of the constitutional "privacy" right involved. They are thus not illustrative of the "pure" Mill principle, but are related enough and important enough to be mentioned here. For example, the Supreme Court in 1965 invalidated a Connecticut prohibition as applied to married persons, against use of contraceptives, on the ground that it was an invalid invasion of marital privacy.[26] The rationales of the many opinions in the case were diverse. What interests us here is this common thread in the opinions of the majority: the proposition that a state policy of discouraging illicit sex relations by banning contraceptive use could not justify a prohibition so broad as to cover use by married persons. The Court in 1972 went farther by invalidating a Massachusetts prohibition against *distribution* of contraceptives to *unmarried* persons.[27] Four justices felt that once the privacy right in this context had been recognized by Massachusetts for married people, the Constitution's equal protection clause required its recognition for unmarried people. Two other justices joined in reversing the conviction on the ground that the particular type of contraceptive distributed by the defendant hadn't been shown to be harmful; if it had, the state's police power could, they thought, override the privacy right.

On the ground of privacy and the ground of interference with First Amendment rights of freedom to receive information and ideas, the Supreme Court in 1969 invalidated a Georgia statute prohibiting the knowing possession of obscene films, as applied to possession of obscene films intended for viewing in the privacy of defendant's home.[28] The Court thought that the existing state of knowledge with respect to socially harmful consequences of the prohibited conduct gave no support to the prohibition. Earlier cases had

Motorcycle Assn. v. Davids, 11 Mich. App. 351, 158 N.W.2d 72 (1968).

26. Griswold v. Connecticut, 381 U.S. 479 (1965).

27. Eisenstadt v. Baird, 405 U.S. 438 (1972).

28. Stanley v. Georgia, 394 U.S. 557 (1969).

suggested that a valid prohibition against obscene material need *not* depend on a showing of the danger of *antisocial conduct by those exposed* to such material; that so long as the material was obscene, it had no First Amendment protection against prohibition. But that was said, the Court now explained, in a context of distribution of obscene material to the *public*, where there was a *potential* for *some kinds* of public harm, since the material might "fall into the hands of children" or "intrude upon the sensibilities or privacy of the general public."[29] Those factors were not sufficiently present in the Georgia case.

As for the blood transfusion cases, they usually upheld an adult, mentally competent individual's right to refuse the transfusion, at least where no minor children were involved. The emphasis, however, was on religious freedom — the refusal of the transfusion having generally been based on religious grounds.[30]

Consider, finally, the 1973 landmark Supreme Court decisions in the abortion cases. The Court steered a middle course. It rejected the argument that a woman's right to privacy and freedom of action with respect to her own body justified a decision to abort a fetus at any time and under any circumstances. Society's concern for the woman's health, and for the life of the later-stage fetus, permitted some regulation after the first trimester of pregnancy. Thus, for the first three months, "the abortion decision and its effectuation must be left to the medical judgment of the pregnant woman's attending physician." During this period, said the majority, the established medical fact is that the danger of the mother's death from an abortion is less than that attaching to normal childbirth. This is no longer true of abortion during the next period, i.e., from three months to the "viability" stage (viability occurring at six or seven months, when the fetus "presumably has the capability of meaningful life outside the mother's womb"). Hence, from the three-month point on, a state may regulate the abortion procedure so as to protect

29. Id. at 567.
30. Note, supra note 18 at 623.

maternal health. "Examples of permissible state regulation in this area are requirements as to the qualification of the person who is to perform the abortion; as to the licensure of that person; as to the facility in which the procedure is to be performed . . .; as to the licensing of the facility; and the like." Finally, from the point of "viability" on, the state may effectuate its interest in "potential life," and "may go so far as to proscribe abortion during that period except when it is necessary to preserve the life or health of the mother."[31]

I think it is fair to say, in brief, that there is a widely shared attitude — not as yet fully reflected by the law in all situations — against government interference with conduct which either involves *no* probable and substantial harm to others, or which falls within an area of "privacy" deemed worthy of legal protection even where *some* kinds of public harm from the conduct may be probable. This constitutes one of the limits that lawmaking, to be effective, must reckon with. It is one example of the limits I lumped together into my second category, namely the "popular attitudes, habits, and ideals in the various situations that keep coming up in everyday life."

f. Desire for Other Freedoms

Obviously the desire for privacy is not the only kind of freedom urge that operates as a limit on law in our society. Nor is it the only attitude that has been given constitutional protection. The Constitution protects, against undue governmental invasions, one's life, one's liberties, and one's property, as well as assuring equal protection of the laws. Should government press too far against such ideals as freedom and equality, it will be reminded through popular resistance, if not through court decision, that these ideals set limits to the law's possibilities. Unfortunately, it would unduly lengthen this book to explore, as I have done in the case of "privacy," some court attitudes on such limits.[32]

31. Roe v. Wade, 409 U.S. 817 (1973).

32. But you can get a good idea of the nature of, and legal limits on, a variety of other freedoms or strong claims made by Americans, in Dorsen, ed., The Rights

g. Attitudes on Importance of "Fault" or "Blame"

There are some additional attitudes or ideals that seem to me so pervasive as to necessarily put limits on the lawmaker, though they are so obvious as to perhaps escape attention. One is the general acceptance of the notion of "fault" or "blame," and the feeling that the innocent should be treated differently from those who are at fault or worthy of blame. This point may seem self-evident, but you will encounter many instances of difficulties arising from its neglect.

As one example, consider the proposals made by some responsible students of criminal law that the insanity defense should be abolished because of difficulties in interpreting and administering the defense. They point to the fact that psychiatrists are in disagreement on the issue of insanity, with many of them asserting that they are no better equipped than the layman to answer the kinds of questions put to them as witnesses in an insanity case; that some defendants take unfair advantage of the defense; that the defense is too ambiguous to justify sending Defendant A to an institution for treatment of mental illness and Defendant B, whose overt homicidal conduct was the same, to prison or the gas chamber. These critics urge that the trial should merely determine whether the defendant did what he is accused of doing. After a finding of guilt, his mental condition then and now would be considered, on the issue of proper "disposition," by getting answers to questions like: "Is he treatable? Is he dangerous? Is he deterrable?" Perhaps the chief obstacle to adopting this proposal is the sentiment that one who was incapable of avoiding the doing of what he did, or of knowing that what he did was wrong, should not be blamed for doing it. He should not be subjected to the same stigma of guilt through a criminal conviction as the person who did have the capacity to control himself and appreciate the wrongfulness of his conduct. It would arouse a widely shared

---

of Americans (1970). Also, I shall be saying more about privacy problems in Chapter 2, pages 197-202, and Chapter 5, pages 270-272.

sense of injustice. Even a dog, Holmes reminded us, distinguishes between being kicked and being stumbled over.

The proposed reform encounters, therefore, one of law's powerful limits and is unlikely to receive any near future acceptance.

Much the same point is illustrated by the limits on the possibility of extending "strict liability" in criminal law. This needs a little explanation. The typical crime involves a certain culpable mental element, as for instance the intent to kill, the intent to take away another's property without his consent, or carelessness that is gross enough (in relation to the circumstances known by defendant) to amount to criminal negligence. The typical tort, too, involves culpability or fault, as for instance the intent to assault, the intent to defame, or negligence (by which is meant the failure to abide by the standard of conduct which would have been followed by a "reasonable man" in the circumstances involved).

In the tort field there have developed some areas of "strict liability," i.e., liability *without* fault. One example is the workmen's compensation system under which the worker injured on the job files his claim with an administrative agency and collects compensation on the basis of a governmentally prescribed schedule of benefits. He does not have to assert the employer's negligence, or his own freedom from contributory negligence. The financial structure varies, but a common system is for the compensation payments to be made by the insurance company with which the employer has insured himself. Another illustration of strict liability in tort is the field of "products liability." Suppose you were personally injured in an auto accident because your steering wheel had a defect which was unknown to you and which was there when the car left the factory. If you can prove these facts to the satisfaction of the jury, then under the developing law of recent years you would be able to recover damages from the manufacturer without proving negligence on his part.

In neither of these tort fields has there been very strong criticism of the fact that liability was being imposed in the absence of fault. We have, in recent decades, been increasingly sympathetic to the injured worker and injured consumer; the negligence standard in both fields has not worked out satisfactorily for plaintiffs; the employer and manufacturer defendants are in a better position to shoulder the loss, and can protect themselves by insurance. Moreover, under the strict liability standard they are not going to jail and are free from the stigma of a criminal conviction. "It's only money" they are paying out, in insurance premiums, and the added costs can probably be reflected in their selling prices.

There are similar practical reasons for the growing success of the movement for "no-fault" auto accident insurance — under which at least certain economic losses from accidents (medical expenses, loss of work income) would be recovered under the victim's own insurance policy, regardless of who was at fault. A mounting concern over the difficulties, delays, and inequities of the prevailing "fault" system has made people receptive to such an alternative system (of which there are many varieties) that promises to be cheaper and to make recoveries more rapid and certain.[33]

The situation is quite different when you are dealing with strict criminal liability. Criminal liability without fault has existed on the outer edge of criminal law but it has been a growing edge, with a tendency of the laws to extend beyond such standard categories as food and drugs, liquor, conservation, and traffic regulation.[34] The sense of injustice that I earlier described with respect to the insanity defense operates here too, and is mirrored in the call by scholars for a halt to the spread of strict criminal liability, and in the willingness of courts to reject the idea that imprisonment can ever be

33. See O'Connell, The Injury Industry (1971); N.Y. Insurance Dept. (Report to Gov. Rockefeller), Automobile Insurance . . . for Whose Benefit? (1970); U.S. Dept. of Transportation, Motor Vehicle Crash Losses and Their Compensation in the U.S. (1971); Prosser and Wade, Torts — Cases and Materials 631-651 (1971); Kimball, "Automobile Accident Compensation Systems — Objectives and Perspectives," 1967 U. Ill. L. Forum 370; Bombaugh, "U.M.V.A.R.A.: Key to Reform of Accident Reparations," 50 A.B.A.J. 45 (1973).

34. See ALI Model Penal Code, Commentary at 141-145 (Tent. Draft No. 4, 1955).

imposed on a strict liability basis, and in the forthright position of the American Law Institute that: "Crime does and should mean condemnation and no court should have to pass that judgment unless it can declare that the defendant's act was wrong. This is too fundamental to be compromised. The law goes far enough if it permits the imposition of a monetary penalty in cases where strict liability has been imposed."[35]

Even where a statute seems to permit imposition of criminal liability without fault (i.e., because it is silent on the required mental element; very rarely does a statute explicitly authorize imposition of criminal liability without fault) some studies show that the same feeling I have described about the necessity of a fault element strongly influences the actual administration and enforcement of the statute. Thus, a study of Wisconsin's food and drug regulations shows that "prosecution under them takes place *only when the defendant has demonstrated subjective fault* by showing a conscious intent to violate, or, at least, a wilful heedlessness in failing to respond to repeated warnings. However, the liability without fault character of these provisions is still of prime importance . . . because the necessity of proving guilty knowledge or intent to the satisfaction of a court or jury would in many instances present an insurmountable burden to the department and greatly hinder efforts at control and regulation. This would be true even in many cases of conscious and advertent violation."[36] (Emphasis added.)

h. The "Rule of Reason" Ideal

The final attitude or ideal I wish to point to is something that underlies many of the points I have already made (and even some of those I shall make later). Looking back, for instance, at my examples of people resisting law that strikes

---

35. Id. at 140. See scholars cited after the quotation; see also Commonwealth v. Koczwara, 397 Pa. 575, 155 A.2d 825 (1959); Morisette v. United States, 342 U.S. 246 (1952).

36. Zick, "Liability Without Fault in the Food and Drug Statutes," 1956 Wis. L. Rev. 641, 654-655.

them as *overly* severe, or *unduly* encroaching on people's "private" conduct, or *unreasonably* hampering the exercise of strong and pleasurable human drives: these bespeak a "rule of reason." That is, people generally expect legal standards to be reasonable. Laws and decisions that depart too far from this common expectation create enforcement problems and the danger of a spreading disrespect for law. Even in the most complex bodies of doctrine in any legal field, the lawmaker is constantly trying to avoid overstepping the boundaries of the rule of reason, and you will get guidance through some jungles by remembering that. "The main underlying purpose" of the law of contracts, said one of its most respected students, Arthur Corbin, is to attempt "the realization of reasonable expectations that have been induced by the making of a promise."[37] "The common thread woven into all torts," said the prominent torts scholar, William Prosser, "is the idea of unreasonable interference with the interests of others."[38] And when *official* unreasonableness becomes gross enough it runs afoul of barriers within the law itself, such as the Constitution's "due process" protection against arbitrariness.

3. *HUMAN FRAILTIES IN EMERGENCIES*

I come now to a third type of limit — one which is set by human frailties in moments of great stress.

(a) For example, the law tends to deal rather leniently with some kinds of criminal conduct that are impelled by a sense of overwhelming necessity. You have no doubt heard of the famous American criminal case involving the lifeboat, adrift on rough seas, that was leaking and so overcrowded that the first mate thought it imperative to throw some people overboard in order to lighten the load and thereby save the lives of others, rather than lose the lives of all. This was a case in about mid-nineteenth-century, in a lower

37. 1 Corbin, Contracts 2 (1963).
38. Prosser, Handbook of the Law of Torts 6 (4th ed. 1972).

federal court.[39] The ship *William Brown* with 65 passengers and a crew of 17 had hit an iceberg off Newfoundland. About half the passengers went down with the ship. And so perhaps did a noble maritime tradition. For while the facts are not altogether clear, it seems that the captain and crew got out first. At least we know that all of them, together with the other half of the passengers, managed to get into a "long boat" and a "jolly boat." In the long boat, where the relevant action occurred, there were 9 crew members and 32 passengers. Acting pursuant to the first mate's orders to spare the women and not part husband from wife, the crew threw over most of the male adults. Next morning the long boat was sighted by a ship, and all on board were saved.

The sole defendant in the criminal prosecution was a crew member named Holmes; the first mate and the other participating crew members could not be located. The moderating influence on the law exerted by the fact that the situation was one of emergency stress is seen first in the fact that the grand jury refused to indict for murder, but rather charged manslaughter. Moreover, the trial jury which came in with a guilty verdict of manslaughter recommended mercy, and the prison sentence finally imposed by the judge on Holmes (who had already waited nine months in jail) was only six months. The judge's instructions to the jury had said that the law recognized a defense in terms of "necessity," applying to extreme situations as in defending oneself against mortal attack, where the "peril [is] instant, overwhelming, leaving no alternative but to lose our own life or to take the life of another person." But this defense would not apply where "the slayer" not only wasn't attacked by others but was "under . . . obligation to make his own safety secondary to the safety of others," as the defendant sailor was, said the judge, in relation to the passengers. Where action need not be instantaneous, the drawing of lots would be a fair procedure,

39. United States v. Holmes, 26 F. Cas. 360 (No. 15,383) (C.C.E.D. Pa. 1842). Further on the Holmes situation, see Cahn, The Moral Decision 61-71 (1955); Hicks, Human Jettison (1927).

the judge thought, among those "in equal relation"; the sailor's obligation to the passengers, however, would have made that alternative unavailing here. In a 1928 address, Supreme Court Justice Cardozo, then a New York Court of Appeals judge, discussed the Holmes case in his distinctively ornate style (which you will come to recognize instantly upon reading a court opinion authored by him):

There is no rule of human jettison. Men there will often be who, when told that their going will be the salvation of the remnant, will choose the nobler part and make the plunge into the waters. In that supreme moment the darkness for them will be illumined by the thought that those behind will ride to safety. If none of such mold are found aboard the boat, or too few to save the others, the human freight must be left to meet the chances of the waters. Who shall choose in such an hour between the victims and the saved? Who shall know when masts and sails of rescue may emerge out of the fog?[40]

Note how confounding are the issues in a case like this, how unanswered are the questions that persist: what basis was there for the judge's finding an "obligation" in the sailor that would not, in this situation, reside in a passenger? How realistic was it to assume that for passengers (those in "equal relation") in so exigent a situation the drawing of lots should be required? How does the drawing of lots compare, in fairness, with sailor Holmes's order (described by his lawyer as "the clear dictate of humanity") to spare the women and not to separate man and wife? Should Holmes's order have been different if the passengers included children, a dying man, male and female prisoners being transported to a place of execution, a world-famous male scientist or top political leader or Olympic record-holder? Is there a "natural law" principle (and if so, should the criminal law follow it here) that under no circumstances shall an "innocent" life be deliberately taken in order that another, or even a greater number, shall live? Should the kind of situation in the Holmes case be viewed as governed by the practices applicable in a "state of nature," i.e., outside the bounds of organized society, on the theory of Holmes's lawyer that "All

40. Hall, ed., Selected Writings of B. N. Cardozo 390 (1947).

became their own lawgivers. . . . Every man on board had a right to make law with his own right hand"?

There was an analogous British case,[41] equally famous and even more horrendous. This was the case of four seamen who were in an open boat on the high seas, 1600 miles from the Cape of Good Hope, having had to abandon a yacht in a storm. After drifting for eighteen days, and after seven days without food and six days without water, two of them agreed, with the third dissenting, that the fourth seaman — a youth of 17 or 18 who lay helpless, extremely weakened by famine and the drinking of seawater — should be killed for sustenance the next day if help hadn't yet arrived. And kill him they did, next day. All three of them fed on his body for four days before being picked up by a passing vessel. The two ringleaders were prosecuted for murder. The jury found that probably all would have died within the four days had not the three men fed on the body; that probably the youth would have died first anyway. The jury left it to the court to determine whether it was murder. The judge so held, rejecting the idea that "necessity" could justify taking an innocent human life. He referred to the "awful danger of admitting the principle which has been contended for." "Who is to be the judge of this sort of necessity? By what measure is the comparative value of lives to be measured?"

However, the death sentence he imposed was commuted by the crown to six months. So you see, again, the persistence of this feeling that when you consider the frailties of the human being in the kind of overwhelming stress that these individuals experienced, the letter of the law ought to be moderated at some stage of the legal process.[42]

This English case is the famous one, as far as cannibalism *ex necessitate* is concerned. But there are some interesting

41. Regina v. Dudley and Stephens, L.R. 14, Q.B.D. 273, 15 Cox Crim. Cas. 624 (1884).
42. Further on the type of situation presented in this English case, see McCormick, Blood on the Sea (1962); Gibson, The Boat (1953) (a World War II episode); Fuller, "The Case of the Speluncean Explorers," 62 Harv. L. Rev. 616 (1949) (imaginary case and opinions).

ones in this country, not all of which were immortalized in court opinions. One involved the Donner party, trapped by early snow in what is now known as the Donner Pass in the high Sierras. Some survivors of the disaster fed on the bodies of some of the dead, as Bernard De Voto has vividly described.[43] Murder and subsequent cannibalism by a Utah gold hunter, Frank Packer, in Colorado in 1873 drew a sentence of hanging by Judge Gerry in 1883 — of which Gene Fowler contributes a memorable vignette:

Although Judge Gerry delivered what was considered the most eloquent hanging speech in Western court history, an apocryphal sentence is the one that persists, and by which this scholarly gentleman's name still lives. . . . Larry Dolan, who had a grudge against Packer, attended every session of the trial. Between times, Larry filled himself to the larynx with "Taos Lightning". . . . Just as the fluent Judge Gerry began a classical pronouncement of doom, Larry let out a cheer and fell from a bench. Then he rose, and ran drunkenly to his favorite saloon, bellowing like ten Apis bulls of Egypt:

"Well, boys, ut's all over; Packer's to hang. The Judge, God bless him . . . p'intin' his tremblin' finger at Packer, so ragin' mad as he was, he said: 'They was siven Dimmycrats in Hinsdale County, but you, yah voracious man-eatin' son of a bitch, yuh eat five of thim! I sintince ye t' be hanged by th' neck until y're dead, dead, dead; as a warnin' ag'n reducin' the Dimmycratic popalashun of th' State.' "[44]

I can't resist telling one more tale, of the same macabre genre. The whaleship *Essex* was rammed and sunk in the Pacific in 1820 by an enormous whale, and this incident became the climax of Herman Melville's *Moby Dick*. What happened after the sinking — which Melville didn't write about — was this: Of the three lifeboats that were launched, one was lost; on the other two, after lengthy ordeals of storm and famine, cannibalism was practised on the bodies of a few who had died. On one boat the men were also driven to kill one of their number, after drawing lots. The victim was the cabin boy, a nephew of the master of the *Essex*, Captain Pollard, who was in the same lifeboat. "There is a Nantucket

---

43. DeVoto, The Year of Decision: 1846, at 386-387 (1943). Cannibalism following an Andes plane crash is described in Read, Alive (1974).

44. Fowler, Timber Line 37 (1933). After reversal and a second conviction, Packer received a life sentence, and was pardoned after 18 years. Id. at 38.

legend that when a reporter from the mainland came out to the island to interview [Captain Pollard] on his last birthday, the reporter closed the interview with the personal remark that he was distantly related to one of the Essex' crew. 'You remember him, of course,' he added. 'Remember him,' the old man cackled. 'Hell, son, I et him!' "[45]

There was apparently no prosecution in this case. Where prosecution did occur in the other cases mentioned, we have seen that the courts typically refused to recognize a "necessity" defense as such, but punishment tended to be lenient. "The law falters and averts her face and sheathes her own sword when pronouncing judgment upon creatures of flesh and blood thus goaded by the Furies."[46] (Yes, that was Cardozo again.) Judge Gerry's treatment of Frank Packer doesn't fit this description, but not all the facts of the case are clear; and further data presented by Gene Fowler might suggest that the multiple killings were unnecessary and connected with a robbery motive.

Though the states today would rarely be found recognizing a necessity defense where the defendant had taken an innocent, human life (as distinct from, say, theft or destruction of another's property), the American Law Institute's Model Penal Code is willing to go further by recognizing for all crimes a "choice of evils" provision. This recognizes as a defense the defendant's belief in the necessity of his conduct where "the harm or evil sought to be avoided by [the defendant's] conduct is greater than that sought to be prevented by the law defining the offense charged," unless this defense would be inconsistent with a legislative purpose appearing elsewhere in the state's statutes.[47]

(b) Related to this necessity defense is a classic defense in terms of "duress" or coercion. The Model Penal Code, for instance, recognizes this defense where there was coercion

45. Whipple, "Three-Month Ordeal in Open Boats," Life, Nov. 10, 1952, at 156.
46. Hall, ed., supra note 40, at 390.
47. ALI Model Penal Code §3.02 (Proposed Official Draft 1962); id., Commentary at 5-10 (Tent. Draft No. 8, 1958).

against the defendant by use or threatened use of unlawful force against the person — force which a person of reasonable firmness in his situation would have been unable to resist.[48]

(c) Some other related situations: you are doubtless familiar with the fact that some rather frequently occurring stressful circumstances will mitigate an intentional killing so as to prevent its classification as "murder." If the circumstances amount to "self-defense," there is a complete defense to the alleged crime. If the defendant were not acting in self-defense but his intentional killing can be shown to have been done "in the heat of passion" and upon "sufficient provocation," then under many homicide statutes these stressful circumstances would mitigate the crime from murder to "voluntary manslaughter."

(d) A highly stressful situation of still a different sort is that of euthanasia or mercy-killing — involving, for example, the terminal cancer patient who is in great pain which cannot be relieved by drugs (or can be relieved only by a fatal dosage) and which impels the defendant to commit euthanasia. Here the letter of the law is still against the act, through a legislative prohibition either against murder or against assisting a suicide. But the letter of the law is being moderated by leniency in the administration of the law. There have been a number of cases where a jury acquittal was based upon a defense in terms of temporary insanity, or a defense that the conduct of the defendant had not actually *caused* the death. You may remember the much-publicized English trial of Dr. John Bodkin Adams several years ago, skillfully described in Sybille Bedford's book.[49] The defense was in terms of causation — i.e., that his conduct had not caused the death. The reason why the jury was able to acquit on that ground was that the judge's instruction said: if the administration of the drug by the doctor merely had the effect of hastening the death so that it occurred on Monday

48. ALI Model Penal Code §2.09 (Proposed Official Draft 1962); id., Commentary at 2-16 (Tent. Draft No. 10, 1960).
49. Bedford, The Trial of Dr. Adams (1958).

rather than on Tuesday, this could not be viewed as the *cause* of the death. That is a pretty lenient instruction on what constitutes cause. Here you have an illustration of a judge, not just a jury, showing compassion in this situation. And there have been other mercy-killing cases where, after a jury verdict of guilty, the judge was lenient in the sentence. So, too, there have been cases where after a substantial sentence has been imposed, the executive has shown clemency by reducing it very considerably.

There is an opinion in a euthanasia case, by the highly respected Judge Learned Hand of the federal Court of Appeals for the Second Circuit (which sits in New York), together with a dissenting opinion by the equally renowned Judge Jerome Frank, that are important enough to merit consideration at some length. Judge Hand set out the basic facts as follows:

The District Attorney, on behalf of the Immigration and Naturalization Service has appealed from an order naturalizing the appellee, Repouille. The ground of the objection in the district court and here is that he did not show himself to have been a person of "good moral character" for the five years which preceded the filing of his petition. The facts were as follows: The petition was filed on September 22, 1944 and on October 12, 1939, he had deliberately put to death his son, a boy of thirteen, by means of chloroform. His reason for this tragic deed was that the child had "suffered from birth from a brain injury which destined him to be an idiot and a physical monstrosity malformed in all four limbs. The child was blind, mute and deformed. He had to be fed; the movements of his bladder and bowels were involuntary, and his entire life was spent in a small crib." Repouille had four other children at the time towards whom he has always been a dutiful and responsible parent; it may be assumed that his act was to help him in their nurture, which was being compromised by the burden imposed upon him in the care of the fifth. The family was altogether dependent upon his industry for its support. He was indicted for manslaughter in the first degree; but the jury brought in a verdict of manslaughter in the second degree with a recommendation of the "utmost clemency;" and the judge sentenced him to not less than five years nor more than ten, execution to be stayed, and the defendant to be placed on probation, from which he was discharged in December 1945. Concededly, except for this act he conducted himself as a person of "good moral character" during the five years before he filed his petition. Indeed, if he had waited before filing his petition from September 22, to October 14, 1944, he would have been admitted without question.[50]

Judge Hand went on to say that, under prior decisions of the court, the statutory "good moral character" requirement was to be decided by the "generally accepted moral conventions current at the time." He acknowledged that ascertaining these conventions was extremely difficult "in the absence of some national inquisition, like a Gallup Poll." He thought many people would be willing, in some matters of deep personal conviction, to defy the law; "few of us exact of ourselves or of others the unflinching obedience of a Socrates." But he was unwilling to give decisive weight to the sympathetic attitude shown by the jury and judge in Repouille's criminal case, since "a similar offender in Massachusetts . . . although . . . not executed, was imprisoned for life." So on the basis of the best guess he could make about current moral conventions, he concluded that "only a minority of virtuous persons would deem the practise morally justifiable, while it remains in private hands, even when the provocation is as overwhelming as it was in this instance." Therefore, disagreeing with the trial judge, he ordered the petition for naturalization dismissed, but "without prejudice to the filing of a second petition."

The decision was concurred in by Augustus Hand (Learned's cousin), but Judge Jerome Frank dissented. He argued first that the statute contemplated as a standard not the opinions of the whole public but rather "the attitudes of ethical leaders." But since prior decisions had already ruled against that interpretation, he addressed himself to the ascertainment of public opinion by declaring that

in any case such as this, where we lack the means of determining present-day public reactions, we should remand to the district judge with these directions: The judge should give the petitioner and the government the opportunity to bring to the judge's attention reliable information on the subject, which he may supplement in any appropriate way. All the data so obtained should be put on record. On

50. Repouille v. United States, 165 F.2d 152 (2d Cir. 1947).

the basis thereof, the judge should reconsider his decision and arrive at a conclusion.

Notice, first of all, that the treatment of Repouille by the criminal court and by this court does not represent an exception to the point I have been making. The criminal court did show leniency at every stage: the grand jury had indicted for manslaughter in the first degree instead of murder; the jury convicted of manslaughter in the second degree with a recommendation of utmost clemency; the judge's sentence of five to ten years was suspended and Repouille was merely put on probation. Moreover, in the naturalization case, the majority's decision was only super-ficially tough; they knew, and mentioned in the opinion, that Repouille's application after the decision would be successful because of expiration of the statutory five-year period. Nor did the Massachusetts case referred to by Judge Hand represent an exception to my point. In that case, the governor had gotten his executive council to approve a reduction of sentence from death to life imprisonment; and (a couple of years after the Repouille decision) a new governor got approval of his council, by a 6 to 3 vote, to reduce the sentence to six-years-to-life, thereby resulting in the prisoner's immediate parole.[51]

Notice also the difference in the attitudes of Judges Hand and Frank toward ascertaining public opinion on the "good moral character" issue. Hand was willing to depend on his best guess; Frank said actual evidence of public opinion should be taken. It so happened that just prior to the decision a Gallup "national inquisition" *had* occurred, in which the question, "When a person has incurable disease, should doctors be allowed to end his life painlessly if requested by patient and family?" was answered yes by 37% of those queried — with much variation on the basis of age, sex, economic status and education.[52] A question put in

51. Newsweek, Jan. 17, 1949, at 24-25.
52. See Note, "Judicial Determination of Moral Conduct in Naturalization Hearings," 16 U. Chi. L. Rev. 138, 141-142 (1948); 11 Public Opinion Q. 477 (1947).

terms of the Repouille situation would presumably have drawn an even smaller percentage of approval, so Hand probably guessed right.

But Frank's approach rides the wave of the future as far as poll evidence is concerned. Such evidence is relatively new and there are certain obstacles to be hurdled in the law of evidence, but a widening variety of such evidence is being accepted as valid, when the witness is a qualified expert who explains the method and theory of his polling procedures. Poll evidence is obviously pertinent where a defendant seeks a change of venue (place of trial) on the ground that community opinion is inflamed against him. An interesting use of poll evidence in a breach of contract case involving a question rather analogous to the "good moral character" issue in the Repouille case was this: A movie screenwriter had a contract with a Hollywood studio in which he agreed to conduct himself with due regard to public conventions and morals, and not do anything tending to bring himself into public disgrace, ill will, or ridicule. He thereafter refused, on the ground of his Fifth Amendment privilege against self-incrimination, to answer questions before the House Committee on Un-American Activities concerning his alleged affiliation with Communists. In the breach of contract suit, the court received in evidence an opinion poll conducted by an expert pollster in Muncie, Indiana, indicating that about 67% of those polled thought such a refusal to testify showed the witness to be a Communist or Communist sympathizer.[53] A lawyer-sociologist team of Nebraska researchers has laid in a stock of poll evidence with potential use by courts and legislatures, by assessing public opinion on a number of issues in the field of domestic relations: e.g., parents' right to transfer custody of the child without

53. This case together with numerous others, in a striking variety of situations, is covered in Annot., "Admissibility and Weight of Surveys or Polls of Public or Consumers' Opinion, Recognition, Preference, or the Like," 76 A.L.R.2d 619 (1961). There is a good discussion of problems encountered in the use of such evidence in Zeisel, "The Uniqueness of Survey Evidence," 45 Cornell L.Q. 322 (1960).

supervision, their right to control a child's earnings, the child's duty to support indigent parents, etc.[54]

It is important to understand, however, that such an ascertainment of community values is not the final word on what the law ought to be. In the Repouille case, it was treated as the final word (as against the views of "ethical leaders" or the court's personal views) because the naturalization statute was construed to require just that. Congress was viewed as requiring the court to adopt the *public's* view of what constituted "good moral character." In the absence of such legislative direction, the wise court takes the public's view into account but does not necessarily reflect that view. Even a legislator (who is regarded as more directly responsible to a constituency than is a court) is ideally responsible to his own conscience when that conflicts with his constituency's desires, as President Kennedy (then senator) tried to remind us in his 1955 book, *Profiles in Courage.*

I can illustrate the point in still another way: When the above-mentioned Nebraska researchers expressed the hope that out of their study would come "a more reliable method than is now in use for those who seek to narrow the distance between lawmakers and their subjects," and seemed to be criticizing the Model Penal Code drafters for not consulting community opinion, this drew a response from a principal drafter of the code. The response was that the code was not trying "to 'narrow the distance between lawmakers and their subjects'; i.e., to make 'popular' law. On the contrary the Institute is trying to narrow the distance between lawmakers and such 'unpopular' people as psychiatrists and sociologists. We are engaged in making rational, useful law which we hope can be popularized by education."[55]

The point, as I've already suggested, is even more pertinent to the operation of a court — though obviously a known

54. Cohen, Robson, and Bates, Parental Authority: The Community and the Law (1958).
55. Schwartz, "Ascertaining the Moral Sense of the Community: A Comment," 8 J. Legal Ed. 319-320 (1955).

preponderance of public opinion would weigh very heavily in the deliberations of both legislator and judge. You can see how the point that I've been making about stressful situations (out of which grew the discussion about the court's active or passive role in relation to public attitudes about those situations) dovetails with the earlier point about the law's inability to get too far out of line with public attitudes. At the close of this section on limits of law, I shall have more to say, by way of summary, on the law's capacity. to *effectively change* people's attitudes and behavior.

Returning then to the main point for which the euthanasia cases have been used here — the limits put by stressful situations upon the law's effectiveness — you may well ask: Well, then, why doesn't the law openly recognize a right of mercy killing? Why does it cling to the principle that a defendant's worthy motives may be considered in mitigation of penalty but not as a complete defense? Apparently for the same reason that it doesn't condone the other types of conduct under stress that I have already mentioned: the fact that great practical difficulties and dangers would arise from even such a limited recognition of the right to kill.

4. *DIFFICULTIES AND RISKS IN ADMINISTRATION*

What I have just mentioned in fact represents a fourth general limit on what the law can do, namely, the fact that difficulties and risks in the administration of an otherwise desirable right may make the granting of the right more harmful than beneficial. In the case of euthanasia, what are these risks and difficulties? Consider the much-discussed legislative proposal in England to allow a doctor to administer euthanasia in the presence of another doctor or lawyer or nurse, upon the patient's consent, obtained in writing, in the presence of two witnesses; and two other doctors having concurred that it is a fatal and incurable disease. Now, are we not justifiably troubled by the realization that a patient who is crazed with pain is not in a position to freely give consent, and if he is not in such an extremity then he is not likely to give consent? Also, should we not worry over whether a miraculous cure may not be discovered shortly after the killing? And might this procedure be an entering wedge for other less defensible killings — for instance, of the senile or the mentally defective? And should the law ignore the strong moral and religious objections to suicide and to assisting in suicide? You may not find these considerations weighty enough, but so far they have led the law to say "no" to euthanasia.[56]

In this particular instance, the possibility of fraudulent abuse of the right would have perhaps been largely avoided by the various safeguards that I mentioned in the proposed law. The possibility of fraudulent abuse has, however, been stronger in certain other areas where the law has been unwilling to recognize an otherwise desirable right. For instance, there has been a well-established rule (departed from in a few exceptional situations) that you cannot recover damages for nonintentional but negligent infliction of mental suffering alone. That is, in the absence of a physical impact upon the plaintiff who, for instance, suffered emotional shock as an eyewitness to injury done to another, there would be no recovery. Court attitudes have been shifting,[57] particularly in the case of a plaintiff who had been in the zone of danger at the time of the injury. But what has underlain the "impact rule"? Principally, it has been the fear that the right of recovery would be too readily subjected to fraudulent abuse. The suffering testified to by plaintiffs might be wholly imaginary but disproof would be difficult, and the partial safeguard that comes from there having been some physical injury would be lacking.

---

56. For pros and cons and information in the euthanasia controversy, see Williams, The Sanctity of Life and the Criminal Law 311-350 (1957); Silving, "Euthanasia: A Study in Comparative Criminal Law," 103 U. Pa. L. Rev. 350 (1954); Kamisar, "Some Non-Religious Views Against Proposed Mercy-Killing Legislation," 42 Minn. L. Rev. 969 (1958); Williams, " 'Mercy-Killing' Legislation — A Rejoinder," 38 U. Colo. L. Rev. 178 (1966); Morris, "Voluntary Euthanasia," 45 Wash. L. Rev. 239 (1970).

57. Prosser, supra note 38, at 328-333; Kalven, "Tort Watch," 34 Am. Trial Lawyers J. 12-29 (1972).

Courts have sometimes changed their minds on whether the problem of proof and disproof presented too much difficulty — as is apparent from the shift in judicial attitudes I referred to in the previous paragraph. Another illustration is in the fact that since 1946 one case after another has repudiated the long-standing rule that a child cannot recover damages for injury suffered (while in the mother's womb) as the alleged result of negligent injury inflicted on the mother.[58]

However, another kind of claim by a child, based also on the consequences (after his birth) of alleged misconduct occurring prior to his birth, has not fared so well. Courts have thus far rejected a child's attempt to recover damages against his unwed father who had induced the mother to engage in sexual relations by fraudulent promise of marriage, thereby depriving the child of a claimed "right to be a legitimate child, to have a normal home, to have a legal father, to inherit from his father, to inherit from his paternal ancestors, and for being stigmatized as a bastard." A main concern of the Illinois court rejecting the claim was that to recognize the alleged right would open wide the "doors of litigation" to all persons "born into the world under conditions they might regard as adverse."[59] This, then, is another practical difficulty that gives the courts concern: the feared swamping of the courts with litigation. Sometimes called the "floodgates" argument, it is one which you will often encounter in court opinion rejecting novel claims.

Sometimes the difficulty or danger that is involved in recognizing a right is that an exercise of the right — even an exercise that does not represent a fraudulent abuse — would place a possibly intolerable burden on other people. This might be illustrated by the blind man situation described in Section B of this chapter. That is, why hasn't American law

58. Prosser, supra note 38, at 335-338.
59. Zepeda v. Zepeda, 41 Ill. App. 2d 240, 190 N.E.2d 849 (1963), cert. denied, 379 U.S. 945. See also Williams v. State, 18 N.Y.2d 481, 223 N.E.2d 343 (1966); Note, "Compensation for the Harmful Effects of Illegitimacy," 66 Colum. L. Rev. 127 (1966).

yet recognized a right to recover against you for failing to come to the rescue of a stranger when you could have done so without much risk to yourself? Apparently because of the fear that the burden imposed by such a right might be too heavy — particularly considering the fact that you may readily panic in such emergency situations, and that the situations in which there will be a duty to act have not been clearly defined. Our prevailing morality barely makes us our blood-brother's keeper; it hasn't yet made us a stranger's keeper. I must point out, however, that there has been strong moral criticism of this position of the law. It seems to me that a judicial change of mind — like that which occurred in the field of prenatal injuries I mentioned above — is likely to occur here.[60]

5. "INTERNAL" DISPUTES

I move to another category, but it's not wholly a separate one. It involves in part the kind of practical considerations already treated in the previous category, together with privacy considerations that were also involved in an earlier category. I am thinking of the situations involving the internal affairs of nonprofit associations, like families, fraternal societies, religious groups, unions. In some instances, especially where the group has monopolistic or other great power and the action it takes towards a member — let us say a union's expulsion of a member — can have great impact on him, the law has been willing to step in and avoid injustice. But you can see why, in general, the law stays its hand. Not only are there constitutional restraints to worry about,[61] but

60. For discussion of the law on this point, see Prosser, supra note 27, at 340-343; Rudolph, "The Duty to Act: A Proposed Rule," 44 Neb. L.J. 499 (1965); Feldbrugge, "Good and Bad Samaritans: A Comparative Survey," 14 Am. J. Comp. L. 630 (1967); Note, 52 Colum. L. Rev. 631 (1952); Franklin, "Vermont Requires Rescue: A Comment," 25 Stan. L. Rev. 51 (1973).

61. For instance, religious freedom under the First Amendment has been successfully invoked against legislative intervention in the internal affairs of religious societies. See, e.g., Kedroff v. St. Nicholas Cathedral of the Russian Orthodox Church in North America, 344 U.S. 94 (1952). And, "Since the First

a court's inquiry into, and interpretation of, a group's rules
and practices "may lead it into what Professor Chafee has
called the 'dismal swamp,' the area of its activity concerning
which only the group can speak with competence"[62] — not
to mention the difficulties encountered when the court tries
to provide appropriate remedies.

Take just one example, the family. Some family disputes
are obviously not appropriate for resolution by a court. The
wife who complains, for instance, that her husband no longer
exhibits affection, can hardly get a court to order a husband
to exhibit affection, or even get a court to order a wayward
husband to live under the same roof. The same goes for
certain other family disputes. For example, in 1959 the
Supreme Court of Alabama considered a case in which a
father was seeking a court injunction to restrain his wife,
with whom he was living, from sending their child to a public
school — the father desiring that the child go to a parochial
school. The court decided that it shouldn't interfere at all. It
pointed out that the case didn't involve a question concerning custody of the child, incident to a separation or divorce,
"but simply whether a court of equity should settle a
difference of opinion between parents as to what is best for
their minor child when the parents and the child are all living
together as a family group." "It seems to us," said the court,
that "if we should hold that equity has jurisdiction in this
case, such holding will open wide the gates for settlement in
equity of all sorts and varieties of intimate family disputes
concerning the upbringing of children. The absence of cases
dealing with the question indicates a reluctance of the courts
to assume jurisdiction in disputes arising out of the intimate
family circle. It does not take much imagination to envision

Amendment and due process clauses appear to guarantee to individuals the right
to associate freely, such intervention might be challenged on constitutional
grounds as an interference with the protected sphere within which groups are free
to act as they wish and, in particular, to choose their own members." Note,
"Developments in the Law: Judicial Control of Actions of Private Associations,"
76 Harv. L. Rev. 983, 990-991 (1963).

62. Id. at 991.

the extent to which explosive differences of opinion between parents as to the proper upbringing of their children would be brought into court for attempted solution. . . . Considerations of policy and expediency forbid a resort to injunctive relief in such a case."[63]

I have by now given you numerous instances in the present category and the preceding one — where the law has been unwilling to recognize certain rights because of its anticipation of adverse consequences. But sometimes it is more than a matter of anticipation. Sometimes, after a right has been recognized, the abuses of it are discovered to be so acute as to call for the withdrawal of that right. This is what happened in some states, like Wisconsin, which have passed statutes abolishing a right to damages for so-called heartbalm — where there had been, for example, a breach of promise to marry. A New York statute some thirty-five years ago declared in its introductory section as follows (and I think this explanation would go for many other states which have passed similar statutes):

> The remedies heretofore provided by law for the enforcement of actions based upon alleged alienation of affections, criminal conversation, seduction and breach of contract to marry, having been subjected to grave abuses, causing extreme annoyance, embarrassment, humiliation and pecuniary damage to many persons wholly innocent and free of any wrongdoing, who were merely the victims of circumstances, and such remedies having been exercised by unscrupulous persons for their unjust enrichment, and such remedies having furnished vehicles for the commission or attempted commission of a crime and in many cases having resulted in the perpetration of frauds, it is hereby declared as the public policy of the state, that the best interests of the people of the state will be served by the abolition of such remedies . . ."[64]

You must be familiar with other areas where it has been argued that a similar withdrawal of rights or obligations should occur because of the practical difficulties and dangers which have flowed from their recognition. I think, for

63. Kilgrow v. Kilgrow, 268 Ala. 475, 479, 108 So. 2d 885, 888 (1959).
64. N.Y. Laws 1935, c. 263.

instance, of the withdrawal of the legal obligation to refrain from gambling, as was done in Nevada. This has been defended on the ground that criminal prohibition of gambling simply drives gambling underground and results in the same kind of corruption and gangsterism that once resulted from liquor prohibition. Similar arguments are heard about existing criminal laws on narcotics — that is, that the system raises the price of the illegal drugs, induces addicts to commit crimes in order to buy the high-priced drugs, and fails to get addicts to seek or to obtain effective treatment. The suggested alternative is to abolish punishment of the users, set up a system of distribution through doctors who may dispense controlled doses to addicts as well as attempt cures, require record-keeping, and prohibit distribution through other than authorized channels. This rough description of what has been the British system of narcotics control illustrates, by the way, that the difficulties encountered in using one of the law's sanctions might be obviated not by a complete lifting of legal controls but by simply using an alternative form of control, in this case a kind of licensing system. Strong arguments have been made that the high economic and social costs of marijuana law enforcement makes reasonable a repeal of the all-out prohibition and replacement by a system permitting sales through licensed dealers under a control system analogous to liquor control.[65] As I mentioned earlier, the National Commission on Marijuana and Drug Abuse hasn't been willing to go quite that far.

The same point is illustrated by reference to the problem of intrafamily disputes, already mentioned. While the court, as I said, will not order a man to exhibit love for his wife, or live under the same roof with her, the law does give the wife certain other remedies — like divorce, or support money.

So, while it is true that difficulties, costs, risks, and impracticalities are considerations that may bar the establishment or continued recognition of a particular right or obligation, it is also true that some alternative right or

65. See, e.g., Kaplan, Marijuana — The New Prohibition (1970).

obligation not involving such considerations can sometimes be substituted.

6. *THE PROBLEM OF KNOWLEDGE*

Now finally let me suggest another broad limit on what the law can accomplish: the limit which is imposed by the relative lack of reliable scientific knowledge.

Reliable knowledge is of course important to a lawman producing an enactment or decision, since he is interested in knowing what are the probable consequences of the enactment or decision. Knowledge of this kind is notoriously limited.

What about the kind of scientific knowledge that would enable the *fact finder* in a dispute to accurately reconstruct the happenings that gave rise to the dispute? We are here dealing with what Max Radin once called one of the two "permanent problems of the law" (the other permanent problem being the determination, and the public's prophesying the determination, of the "just" decision).[66] Jerome Frank, in his popular book *Courts on Trial*, in 1950 vigorously demonstrated the many pitfalls that lie in the path of the fact finder, among them the uncertainty over the credibility of witnesses. The law would *like* to have a surefire method of testing the truth of a witness's testimony; but lie-detector evidence is generally *inadmissible* in court, partly because of unreliability. In this instance, though, the main reason for inadmissibility may be not inherent unreliability but the fear that the trier of facts, whether judge or jury, will tend to give an infallibility to the evidence that it doesn't deserve.[67]

At the other end of the spectrum you have scientific knowledge which is not only admissible but is *conclusive*, as in the case of negative blood test evidence in a paternity case. That is, if the blood types of the child and the alleged father

---

66. Radin, "The Permanent Problems of the Law," 15 Cornell L.Q. 1 (1929).
67. McCormick, Evidence §207 (2d ed. 1972).

are of certain kinds — for instance, the father is AB type and the child is O type — then science says the alleged father *cannot* be the actual father. One judge put it this way: that on the basis of the scientific evidence, the defendant could no more be the father of this child than a dog could be the father of a cat. That is how utterly conclusive this evidence is deemed to be. I am not talking now about scientific evidence that this man is *possibly* the father. That kind of test evidence generally wouldn't even be admissible. But if the expert testimony is to the effect that this man *cannot* be the father because of these two blood types, then in most states that would be regarded as conclusive evidence, no matter what the testimony of the woman in the case is about his being the father.

But it is interesting that even where this kind of virtually absolute scientific knowledge exists, some features of the legal system can serve to undermine the normal legal consequence of such knowledge. I am referring to the powerful role of the initial fact finder, whether jury or judge, and to the special consequence that statutes may have.

Consider, for example, why Charlie Chaplin in 1946 lost a paternity suit brought against him in California.[68] The jury chose to believe the girl's testimony rather than the blood test evidence which, according to the scientists, showed he could not have been the father. It happened that the California statutes had *not* laid down a mechanical rule that negative blood-test evidence (as I have described it above) would absolve the defendant of the paternity charge.

A rather similar case was similarly decided in Wisconsin in 1957.[69] It had some additional features worth analyzing. And it would deserve quotation if only to illustrate that one who dons the judicial robes need not simultaneously shed his sense of humor and style. A husband, who had married in 1950, was appealing from that part of a divorce decree which adjudged him to be the father of his wife's child born in 1954, and which ordered him to pay support money. The

---

68. Berry v. Chaplin, 74 Cal. App. 2d 652, 169 P.2d 442 (1946).
69. Prochnow v. Prochnow, 274 Wis. 491, 80 N.W.2d 278 (1957).

basic facts and commentary thereon in Justice Timothy Brown's majority opinion were as follows:

In February, 1953, Robert began his military service. When he came home on furloughs which he took frequently in 1953, he found his wife notably lacking in appreciation of his presence. Although he was home on furlough for eight days in October and ten in December, after August, 1953, the parties had no sexual intercourse except for one time, to be mentioned later. In Robert's absence Joyce had dates with a man known as Andy, with whom she danced in a tavern and went to a movie, behaving in a manner which the one witness who testified on the subject thought unduly affectionate. This witness also testified that Joyce told her that Robert was dull but that she and Andy had fun. She also said that a few days before Friday, March 12, 1954, Joyce told her she had to see her husband who was then stationed in Texas, but must be back to her work in Milwaukee by Monday.

On March 12, 1954, Joyce flew to San Antonio and met Robert there. They spent the night of the 13th in a hotel where they had sex relations. The next day, before returning to Milwaukee, she told him that she did not love him and was going to divorce him. Her complaint, alleging cruel and inhuman treatment as her cause of action was served on him April 8, 1954. On September 16, 1954, she amended the complaint to include an allegation that she was pregnant by Robert and demanded support money.

The child was born November 21, 1954. Before trial two blood grouping tests were made of Mr. and Mrs. Prochnow and of the child. . . . The experts by whom or under whose supervision the tests were conducted testified that each test eliminated Robert as a possible parent of the child. . . .

The trial judge found the fact to be that Robert is the father of Joyce's child. The question is not whether, on this evidence, we would have so found: what we must determine is whether that finding constituted reversible error.

Sec. 328.39(1)(a), Stats. commands: "Whenever it is established in an action or proceeding that a child was born to a woman while she was the lawful wife of a specified man, any party asserting the illegitimacy of the child in such action or proceeding shall have the burden of proving beyond all reasonable doubt that the husband was not the father of the child . . "

. . . The wife's conduct with Andy on the few occasions when the witness saw them together can justly be called indiscreet for a married woman whose husband is absent, but falls far short of indicating adultery. Indeed, appellant did not assert that Andy is the real father but left that to the imagination of the court whose imagination, as it turned out, was not sufficiently lively to draw the inference. Cynics, among whom on this occasion we must reluctantly number ourselves, might reasonably conclude that Joyce, finding herself pregnant in February or early March, made a hasty excursion to her husband's bed and an equally abrupt withdrawal when her mission was accomplished. The subsequent birth of a full-term child a month sooner than it would usually be expected if caused by this copulation does nothing to dispel uncharitable doubts. But we must acknowledge that a trial judge, less inclined to suspect the worst, might with reason recall that at least as early as the preceding August, Joyce had lost her taste for her husband's embraces. Divorce offered her freedom from them, but magnanimously she might determine to try once more to save the marriage: hence her trip to Texas. But when the night spent in Robert's arms proved no more agreeable than such nights used to be she made up her mind that they could live together no more, frankly told him so and took her departure. The medical testimony concerning the early arrival of the infant does no more than to recognize eight months of gestation as unusual. It admits the possibility that Robert begat the child that night in that San Antonio hotel. Thus, the mother swears the child is Robert's and she knew, in the Biblical sense, no other man. Robert, perforce, acknowledges that it may be his. Everything else depends on such reasonable inferences as one chooses to draw from the other admitted facts and circumstances. And such inferences are for the trier of the facts.

The majority opinion went on to stress that this being a child born to a married woman (a different situation from that in the many cases like the Chaplin case), the already quoted statute put the burden on the person asserting illegitimacy, *to prove beyond a reasonable doubt* that the husband was not the father. This had not been done, without the blood test evidence. And that evidence, in turn, could properly be viewed by the trial court as insufficient to meet the burden, because another statute (the blood test statute) had *not* made the negative type of blood test evidence *conclusive*. Some other states' statutes had done so, but this legislature had chosen merely to say that such negative evidence "shall be receivable in evidence." Said the majority:

No doubt in this enactment the legislature recognized that whatever infallibility is accorded to science, scientists and laboratory technicians by whom the tests must be conducted, interpreted and reported retain the human fallibilities of other witnesses. . . . When the trial judge admitted the Prochnow tests in evidence and weighed them against the testimony of Mrs. Prochnow he went as far in giving effect to them as our statute required him to do. Our opinions say too often that trial courts and juries are the judges of the credibility of witnesses and the weight to be given testimony which conflicts with the testimony of others for us to say that in this case the trial court does not have that function.

The dissenting justices thought that even though the statute didn't make the negative paternity evidence conclusive, *the statute was not intended to prevent the court from ruling that such evidence was in itself conclusive.* The courts had the power to rule, as a matter of the law of evidence formulated in the light of undisputed scientific fact, that such negative blood test evidence was conclusive.[70] (Nor had there been any evidence to show that these particular blood tests were not carried out by qualified experts.) The majority, on the other hand, thought the court shouldn't declare such an evidentiary rule and strongly intimated it would be inconsistent with the statutory scheme: the statute *was intended to prevent the court from ruling that such evidence was in itself conclusive*; a legislature which had "pointedly refrained" from adopting the conclusive-evidence standard of other state statutes wanted to let the fact-finder weigh the negative paternity evidence along with all other evidence, and to preserve the fact finder's primacy in the weighing of evidence and judging the credibility of witnesses. So that here when the trial judge found the wife's testimony rendering the scientific evidence doubtful enough to prevent the husband from fulfilling his burden of proof beyond a reasonable doubt, the appellate court should not treat this as reversible error.

70. The dissent said in part: "This court has frequently held that the testimony of a witness or finding of a jury which is contrary to unquestionable physical situations or common knowledge is of no weight in favor of the side it is invoked to support. . . . Thus, it is frequently held in negligence cases that testimony as to location, speed, and the like must give way to physical facts established by uncontradicted testimony. For instance, if verified skid marks show that a car traveled on the left side of the road when and after the brakes were applied sufficiently to slide the wheels, no weight can be given to testimony of the driver and his passengers that he was at all times in the right-hand traffic lane. . . . Courts should not shut their eyes to advances in science which conclusively establish a fact, by simply repeating the age-old maxim that the credibility of witnesses is for the trier of fact." 274 Wis. at 502.

You can see, then, why I asserted earlier that even where firm scientific knowledge exists, it may not carry the day — because of special factors, e.g., as in this case, the weight to be given to findings of the original fact-finder, and the special role that a statute may play. (Incidentally, after this Wisconsin decision, the legislature did amend the statute so as to make negative blood test evidence conclusive.)

Now to get back to the point about the scientific knowledge spectrum: on one end, you have lie detector evidence, which the courts usually don't even admit into evidence. On the other end, you have this negative blood test evidence for paternity, with the law tending to say nowadays that the evidence is absolutely conclusive. In between, you have all kinds of things. For instance, you have psychiatric testimony. That, as you know, is admitted in evidence, but its weight will depend on many factors, including the expert's qualifications and persuasiveness and how persuasive the psychiatrist is on the other side (you generally do have psychiatrists testifying on both sides). Most expert or scientific evidence that the law is dealing with falls, like psychiatric evidence, somewhere between the two extremes I have indicated.

This is true, for instance, of the opinion poll evidence that I referred to in connection with the Repouille euthanasia case. It is also true of the social psychologist evidence that figured in the 1954 Brown v. Board of Education school desegregation decision of the Supreme Court.[71] Because that decision is often referred to — and (I think) erroneously, as being *based* on sociological evidence — as well as for other reasons, I think I should take a little time here to give you some information about the case.

The courtroom testimony by psychologists for the plaintiff school children in the Brown case centered around some "doll tests." Sixteen black children — ages 6 to 9 — had been asked questions about the drawings of a white doll and a black doll, identical except for skin color. These questions

71. 347 U.S. 483 (1954).

were asked: (a) Show me the doll you like best, or that you'd like to play with (10 chose the white doll); (b) Show me the doll that looks bad (11 chose the black doll, 1 chose the white doll, the remaining 4 were silent); (c) Show me the nice doll (9 chose the white).

The witness-stand interpretation of these answers by psychologist Kenneth Clark for the plaintiffs was that the black child accepts a "negative stereotype" about himself.

However, Edmond Cahn has argued with considerable force that the questions asked were ambiguous. The child might select what he "likes," or "likes to play with," or the "nice" doll, on the basis of what he is accustomed to; and most dolls are white. "Bad" might have been interpreted similarly, i.e., as not a customary type of doll (or might have been considered as the doll who'd been naughty and hence more fun to play with and rebuke; or might have been treated as referring to the remaining dolls, by process of elimination, after the preceding question had been answered).[72]

Again, psychologist Clark's interpretation could be disputed when he described as an "evasion of reality" the children's answers to the last of the following questions: (d) Give me the doll that looks like a white child (16 picked the white doll); (e) Give me the doll that looks like a colored child (16 picked the black doll); (f) Give me the doll that looks like you (7 picked the white doll). Cahn here again points to ambiguities: "looks like you" in what respect? The child might not have been thinking of color but of other likenesses. I.e., since they found the white dolls "nice," perhaps it was this niceness they were identifying with, not the color.

There are other difficulties. Not only was the sampling not shown to be adequate, but the tests did not purport to isolate the *effect of school segregation* on the children's answers. Indeed, another study by psychologist Clark had shown that

72. Cahn, "A Dangerous Myth in the School Segregation Cases," 30 N.Y.U.L. Rev. 150 (1955).

black children's preference for white dolls *decreased* as their
ages went from 4 years to 7 years, yet these latter years are
when they are attending school.[73] And still another Clark
study had shown Northern black children even more pro-
nounced in their preference for the white doll — apparently
tending to refute the notion that school segregation causes
this preference.[74]

Thus the psychological evidence presented in the Brown
case was not strong. Remember, however, that the Supreme
Court opinion did not rely on or even cite this evidence.
Neither did it refer to a lengthy appendix to plaintiff's
Supreme Court brief, entitled "The Effects of Segregation
and the Consequences of Desegregation: A Social Science
Statement," signed by more than thirty leading scholars,
including sociologists, anthropologists, psychologists, and
psychiatrists. What it did cite in its now famous footnote 11
were several articles and books (most of which had been
included in the authorities cited in the above appendix)
dealing with the opinions of social scientists on the effects of
school segregation. These seemed not to be cited as the *basis*
of the Court decision but rather as corroborating it. That is,
after stating that school segregation had a detrimental effect
on school children, and after quoting the finding of the
Kansas court (in one of the four cases being heard together
by the Supreme Court) to the same effect, the Court stated,
"Whatever may have been the extent of psychological
knowledge at the time of Plessy v. Ferguson,[75] this finding is
amply supported by modern authority." And footnote 11
was appended to this statement.

Cahn made a further argument, namely that the use of
social science evidence in these cases was dangerous. However
appropriate such evidence might be in cases of socioeconomic
regulation, he asserted, it should not be the basis for
determining the scope of our "fundamental" rights, such as

---

73. Garfinkel, "Social Science Evidence and the School Segregation Cases,"
21 J. Politics 37 (1959).
74. Ibid.
75. 163 U.S. 537 (1896).

equal protection of the laws. These rights, he argued, shouldn't depend on whatever happens to be current fad among social scientists; future social scientists may have illiberal, "racist" notions.

But note: (1) Scientific evidence, whether the case involves economic regulation or civil liberties, *can't be kept out*, if relevant to the issues, and presented by properly qualified experts, and not regarded as too misleading to the trier of fact by its aura of scientific infallibility (cf. lie detector evidence). (2) How much *weight* is to be given the evidence will depend on the facts of each case: on how careful the analyses and the experimentation or survey or testing; how qualified and persuasive the expert; how widely accepted the assumptions. (3) This doesn't mean that the court's common-sense evaluations of fundamental rights, e.g., of what is unequal protection of the laws, will be automatically eliminated. It means that where common sense does not speak strongly and unequivocally, the court will be *more inclined* to rely on carefully prepared scientific evidence. The Supreme Court in the Brown case was more inclined to cite what it called the "supporting authority" from social scientists because there had been a past difference of opinion on the basis of commonsense evaluation, regarding constitutionality of racial segregation. In Plessy v. Ferguson (the precedent which had upheld racial segregation in transportation) the Court as a matter of common sense hadn't thought that segregation produced unequal protection. In fact the Court there made some assertions that made it almost imperative for the plaintiff's lawyers in Brown to introduce psychological material designed to refute the assertions. Thus, the Court in Plessy had said that segregation *doesn't* stamp the colored race with a badge of inferiority; that the colored race has merely put that construction on it. It had also asserted that "social prejudice" and "racial instincts" *cannot* be overcome by legislation. The psychological testimony and the collected social science opinion in the appendix were directed at refuting these assertions — as well as showing that school segregation didn't fulfill a reasonable educational purpose, and that under certain conditions, desegregation could be accomplished without undue conflict or violence.

I don't wish to underestimate the difficulties in obtaining reliable social science evidence. The Commission on Obscenity and Pornography expended an enormous and careful effort in the preparation of the research reports that ultimately underlay its finding that empirical evidence shows no causal relation between exposure to pornography and antisocial behavior. But a minority report stressed that "conclusively proving causal relationships among social science type variables is extremely difficult if not impossible. Among adults whose life histories have included much exposure to pornography, it is nearly impossible to disentangle the literally hundreds of causal threads or chains that contributed to their later adjustment or maladjustment. Because of the extreme complexity of the problem and the uniqueness of the human experience it is doubtful that we will ever have absolutely convincing scientific proof that pornography is or isn't harmful . . ."[76]

But in spite of such difficulties, as I have already suggested, it seems the part of wisdom not to ignore social science evidence, but rather to proceed cautiously, keeping pace with its reliability. "We cannot turn back the clock. Social scientists are with us for good, and are going to remain in the very midst of government. . . . Judges may and should become acquainted with the various non-legal disciplines. But because of the variety of these disciplines, and of the variety of their judicial tasks, they will always remain intelligent *laymen*, as far as these disciplines are concerned. And intelligent lay control . . . seems the best defense against the tyranny of experts. . . ."[77]

76. Report of Commissioners Hill and Link, concurred in by Commissioner Keating, in Report of the Commission on Obscenity and Pornography 489 (Bantam ed. 1970).
77. Pekelis, "The Case for a Jurisprudence of Welfare," Lawyers Guild Rev. 611, 625-626 (1946).

7. *A PERSPECTIVE ON THE LIMITS*
OF LEGAL EFFECTIVENESS

Looking back now on the various limits that I have mentioned, the rather obvious moral is: it is silly to automatically respond to a social problem by saying "There Oughtta Be a Law" — without careful investigation into the limits that may apply.

On the other hand, it is silly to automatically respond by another slogan, that "You Can't Legislate Morality" or "You Can't Change Human Nature by Law" — because law does play an affirmative, a deterrent, and an educative role, getting people to act in a way that without the law they might not act, and to have attitudes that without the law they might not have.

Let me elaborate a little bit on this. Early in this chapter, I pointed out how the criminal law embodies moral precepts aimed at influencing people's attitudes and behavior. Can it really be argued that this attempted influence is ineffective; that when most of us respect and obey the criminal laws we are adopting attitudes and behavior that we would adopt even in the absence of the promulgation and enforcement of those laws? Many years ago in Boston during a policemen's strike, there was a good deal of looting of the stores going on, and in most cases the looting was done by youths who had never done anything like that before. The inference is that the law had helped to keep them in line, and that once the policemen were removed they felt they could get away with indulging in this activity.[78]

Andenaes[79] has pointed to a similar phenomenon during an English policemen's strike, and another during the period in 1944 when the Germans had arrested the Danish police force and substituted an unarmed watch corps. He has referred to instances in this country where criminal activity

78. See M. R. Cohen, Reason and Law 49 (1950).
79. Andenaes, "The General Preventive Effects of Punishment," 114 U. Pa. L. Rev. 949 (1966).

closely correlated with the degree of enforcement activity. And he reminds us that when the Norwegian drunken driving prohibition — the penalty for violation of which was an automatic year's revocation of driver's license and generally a minimum 21-day jail penalty — was strictly enforced, it seems to have changed people's habits and attitudes. I tried to show earlier that when penalties get too severe, obstacles may be created by prosecutors, juries, and judges. But within that outer limit, it seems true that the commission or noncommission of at least some kinds of conduct that is presently labeled criminal is closely related to the existence and degree of enforcement of legal prohibitions on that conduct, and sometimes to the severity of the known penalties. This is more likely to be true where the conduct is typically preceded by some rationalistic calculation of risks. But even in the case of less calculating conduct, the law is an important background factor, helping to shape moral inhibitions that exert some counterforce against the pressures for antisocial conduct.[80]

That is, the very fact that certain conduct is known to be prohibited by law exerts a morally inhibiting pressure — surely for some people and for some kinds of conduct, and perhaps for most people and most kinds of conduct. "Studies of public opinion show, says Hadley Cantril, that after the adoption of certain laws and policies there is a rise in public opinion favorable to these actions. Cantril offers as a 'law' of public opinion: 'When an opinion is held by a slight majority or when opinion is not solidly structured, an accomplished fact tends to shift opinion in the direction of acceptance.' "[81]

A 1964 study, comparing attitudes toward school desegregation existing in 1942 and in 1956 (the Supreme Court school desegregation decision having been in 1954) and then

80. See Andenaes, "General Prevention — Illusion or Reality," 43 J. Crim. L.C. & P.S. 176, 179-180 (1952); Hawkins, "Punishment and Deterrence: The Educative, Moralizing and Habituative Effects," 1969 Wis. L. Rev. 550; Berkowitz and Walker, "Laws and Moral Judgments," 30 Sociometry 410 (1967), as reprinted in Friedman and Macaulay, Law and the Behavioral Sciences 200-201 (1969).

81. Berger, Equality by Statute 219 (rev. ed. 1967).

in 1964, reported substantial rises for both of the later years in the proportion of favorable attitudes; and the Southern attitudes were found to "vary according to the degree of integration existing in a given area," with the official desegregation measures occurring before the change in attitude.[82] Involved in this example is a related phenomenon: the conforming *behavior* of others, especially those in one's own peer group, and even one's own conforming behavior, may tend to generate the appropriate approving *attitude*. I am reminded here of an experiment reported in the memoirs of a British scientist, Sir Francis Galton. He had wondered why certain idols, in spite of their being ugly and grotesque, were worshipped by primitive peoples, and whether hc could induce such an attitude in himself. He selected a grotesque picture of Punch, set it up in a room of his house, and daily went through a ritual of obeisance and prayer before it. After several months he found to his surprise that he was experiencing a feeling of awe and reverence. He would catch himself turning toward the picture when he passed the room, with an impulse toward bowing and worship.

To get back to the study of desegregation attitudes: I am not saying that studies of attitudinal changes in the context of *other* laws and/or other circumstances are bound to come out the same way, or that law is the most significant variable affecting such changes. Rather, in the cautious words of a 1967 study: "There appears to be a comparatively small but nevertheless significant tendency for *some* people to alter their views of the morality of *some* actions in accord with laws specifying that these actions are legal or illegal. Knowledge of the existence of these laws, however, does not have as much effect in changing the moral judgments as knowledge of a consensus of opinions among one's peers."[83] (Emphasis added.)

---

82. Hyman and Sheatsley, "Attitudes Toward School Desegregation," 211 Sci. Am. (July 1964), as reprinted in Schwartz and Skolnick, Society and the Legal Order 487-488, 490-491 (1970).

83. Berkowitz and Walker, "Laws and Moral Judgments," as reprinted in Friedman and Macauley, supra note 80, at 209-210. See also id. at 212-214.

Further on the racial problem, there are plenty of factors in addition to peer influence that can work *against* an accord between attitudes and legal requirements. For example, provocation from violent elements in the civil rights movement seems sometimes to have diminished favorable attitudes. So too, lack of positive support from prestigious sources can act as a negative factor — as when President Eisenhower declined to back the Supreme Court's 1954 decision with a strong moral stand. His position was that the decision was the law of the land and had to be enforced, but he pointedly declined to defend the court decision in moral terms. President Kennedy in the beginning of his administration had a similar attitude, though he changed eventually to a more positive position. It was particularly important, I think, to get this national executive support for the decision at the crucial early stage when a drastic social change was being initiated by law. Its absence helped to fan the flames of resistance in the South even more than did President Nixon's go-slow position in the late 1960s and early 1970s.

So I repeat that the question of what limits apply to the law's accomplishment of desirable goals isn't answered by mechanical application of any slogans, like "There Oughtta Be a Law" or "You Can't Change Human Nature by Law." Each problem stands on its own feet. You have to investigate the significant facts in the particular problem and ask the questions relevant to the limits that may operate on the effectiveness of the proposed law or the proposed decision. Some relevant questions and considerations are:

(a) What is the strength of the values or attitudes or drives with which the law in question is inconsistent? (Here, as with questions later on, we must ask whether there is reason to think that the strength varies with different classes of individuals.) The problem is obviously greater, for instance, where human drives and widely enjoyed pleasures are involved, like sex, alcohol, and other drugs. The problem is also complicated by the fact that reinforcement of or opposition to attitudes, drives, etc. may be received: (1) from the rest of an individual's value system, including his general attitude toward conforming to the law (but if he has a strong proclivity both for the conduct prohibited and for conformity with law generally, then heaven help him); (2) from the values and attitudes of others in the society nationally, regionally, and locally, including molders of opinion such as newspapers, educators, clergy, the president, etc., and those in his peer group; (3) from his belief that the prohibited conduct works no serious harm to others. Also pertinent would be the question whether situations of great stress could be expected to occur to such an extent that the legal requirement couldn't be influential, and judges and juries could be expected to be lenient.

(b) What techniques would be used to establish and enforce the prohibition or requirement in question? (1) Legislatures, courts, executives, and administrative agencies don't all have the same prestige, though perhaps the ranking is different on different subjects and in different places. For instance, there are those who believe that a congressional statute, implementing the Fourteenth Amendment and requiring racial desegregation in the schools, would have had greater public acceptance than the Supreme Court's decision. (2) Is time allowed for a transition period, and does such allowance make acceptance more likely, or less so? The Supreme Court used this technique in the school segregation case by allowing the decision to be implemented by the policies of the local district courts, using "all deliberate speed." Some argue that the technique in this instance was less effective in gaining acceptance of the decision than the Court's issuance of its own plans for prompt desegregation would have been. (3) Would enforcement personnel be really committed, or are they likely to be tolerant, apathetic, or corrupt? (4) Would enforcement be hampered for lack of complainants? This is a factor which, together with lack of enforcement enthusiasm, is important in the case of "crimes without victims," like prostitution, gambling, fornication, drugs, consensual homosexuality. (5) Would the law's expected benefits be outweighed by the costs, practical difficulties, and risks in administering it — such as possibilities of fraud or other abuse, difficulties of proof, a flood of litigation, interference with internal affairs of private groups, etc.? In this connection, will the objections to one form of legal sanction be obviated by resorting to another form?

(c) To what extent do we have the knowledge necessary to answer not only (1) the fact questions relevant to the consequences and desirability of the proposed law, but also (2) all of the other questions? The more you study the law's problems, the more you will appreciate the significance of our relative lack of the necessary reliable knowledge. The law must continue to make impossible demands on a social science that too often is insufficiently developed to give clear and conclusive answers.

D. AGENCIES AND TECHNIQUES OF LAW

By "legal agencies" I mean the judicial, legislative, executive, and administrative agencies that carry out the official business of law. Consider first the nature of the judicial agency.

1. *THE COURTS*

a. Structure

I'll begin with the structure of the court system, and confine myself on this point to the state courts, since Chapter 2 will have occasion to discuss the structure of the federal court system.

Each state has a triple-layered hierarchy of courts. On the bottom are those dealing with the petty cases where small monetary amounts or minor criminal penalties are involved. In a nonurban area, the judge of such a court is likely to be called a justice of the peace, and his job might be only a part-time one. In the cities he is likely to be called a magistrate or a judge and might be attached to a specialized court like police court, traffic court, small claims court. These petty or "inferior" courts are generally not "courts of record"; they make no detailed record of the proceedings beyond the identification of parties, lawyers, and disposition of the case. The procedure may be rather informal. The losing party may appeal to the next level of court, but it is not what we usually mean by appeal, since it typically involves a completely new trial rather than appellate review of the record made in the lower court (there will usually have been no such record there).

This next level of court would be known as a "trial court of general jurisdiction," authorized to hear civil and criminal cases generally. Unlike the petty court, it is a court of record; its procedure is quite formal; it is not confined to, and indeed is usually prevented from entertaining, the petty cases. It is called perhaps most often a "district" court or "circuit" court, though in some places it has such other names as "superior court" or "court of common pleas." (New York State creates a special confusion by calling it the "supreme court" — which elsewhere of course means the highest appellate court — and recognizing both this trial part of its supreme court and an appellate part which is an intermediate court, the final appeals court being called the New York Court of Appeals.) Besides the trial court of general jurisdiction — or, in some states, departments or divisions thereof — there are specialized courts like those handling probate matters, or divorce and other domestic relations issues, or juvenile problems.

The trial court of general jurisdiction, as I've indicated, exercises *some* appellate jurisdiction when it takes "appeals" from the petty courts. But I've said that those appeals are usually heard as completely new trials (trials "de novo"). To a limited extent, the trial court of general jurisdiction also exercises the more usual form of appellate jurisdiction — for instance, it may be authorized to review *administrative agency* decisions on the record made before the administrative agency, as distinguished from holding a trial *de novo*. In such a case the agency fact-findings, while not conclusive, will be upheld by the court in the absence of arbitrariness.

Third and uppermost in the hierarchy are the appellate courts. In most states, there is only one appellate court, and that is the highest court of the state. It hears appeals from the judgments of the trial courts of general jurisdiction, and either affirms or reverses, or occasionally modifies, the judgment. There are some cases in which a litigant seeks to control the trial court's action not by waiting to take an appeal from its judgment but by seeking directly in the highest court an "extraordinary writ" directing the lower court to do something (e.g., grant a change in the venue or place of trial, or justify its order holding someone in allegedly illegal custody) or refrain from doing something (e.g., from continuing to exercise jurisdiction in a case).

In about a third of the states, there are intermediate appellate courts. Their role varies in the different states. A state may provide that the appeal from a trial court goes to this intermediate court, and that a further appeal is then permissible, after unfavorable judgment, to the highest court. The state may say that in some other classes of cases (deemed more serious) the losing party in the trial court can skip the intermediate court and appeal directly to the highest court. In still other cases, the appeal from the trial court may be allowed only to the intermediate court, and an additional appeal to the highest court is either not allowed or allowed only for special reasons, or is left to the discretion of the highest court to allow. This limited-review type of provision is being increasingly suggested as a means of coping with the overburdened dockets of the states' highest courts.

A prerequisite for review by the United States Supreme Court of the decisions of the highest state court that is empowered to decide the particular case is that the case comes within the "judicial power of the United States" as outlined in the Constitution. However, Congress in the exercise of its constitutional power to determine the appellate jurisdiction of the Supreme Court has made most such review discretionary — known as review by writ of certiorari. The Court's review of a state court decision can be demanded as a matter of *right,* according to Congress, only where a state court has held a federal law or treaty invalid, or upheld a state law against the claim that it violates the Federal Constitution, laws, or treaties.

b. Selected Operational Problems

Turning from the structure of the courts to aspects of their functioning, I'll confine myself to only three such matters, and will have to deal with them sketchily: (1) court delay, (2) selection and tenure of judges, and (3) the limited role of the court itself in the disposition of litigation.

(1) Court Delay

The problem we hear most about today is delay. It is not exactly a new problem. "Hammurabi denounced it; Shakespeare immortalized it: Hamlet, compiling his dolorous list of the burdens of men, sandwiched the 'law's delay' between the 'pangs of dispriz'd love' and the 'insolence of office.' English chancery delay made Bleak House one of the best know edifices in English literature and made Dickens a leading law reformer. Paradoxically, German court delay, scholars tell us, led Goethe to give up the law for letters."[84] But never before has there been such a pervasive concern over the problem, coupled with concerted efforts to find solutions.

One type of delay is caused not by the court system but by the lawyers: the court is ready for trial but the lawyers want postponement. Lawyers often feel unable to meet the date set for trial because of conflicting dates for other trials or other legal business. (This would be somewhat less of a problem if trial litigation were not such a specialty, concentrated in the hands of a fraction of the total bar.) Similarly, a Pittsburgh study showed that in more than half of the randomly picked cases, lawyers added more than a year to disposition of the case, by tardiness in filing papers. Although many cases are negotiated and settled by the parties after filing suit and long before possible trial, many others that could be so handled are delayed in settlement until close to trial or after the first day of trial, in order to put bargaining pressure on the other side — as well as, in some instances

---

84. Rosenberg, "Court Congestion: Status, Causes and Proposed Remedies," in Jones, ed., The Courts, The Public and the Law Explosion 30 (1965).

perhaps, in order for the lawyer to collect a fee for a day in court.[85]

The measures proposed for dealing with delay include tightening up the permission for postponements, and other devices aimed at lawyer-caused delay.[86] But principally, reforms are aimed at reducing court-system delay. One general approach is to reduce the volume of cases to be handled by courts. A way of accomplishing this is to shift some types of cases to administrative tribunals: what has already been done in the area of workmen's compensation has long been recommended for auto accident cases, which are largely responsible for court congestion and delay. Another kind of shift away from the courts for the auto cases would be through the "no-fault" plans now gaining considerable support, under which the major costs suffered in most auto accident cases would be compensated by insurance policies without the necessity of a court suit.[87]

A second approach to court-system delay is to increase the man-hours spent in judging. Thus, proposals are being considered to increase the number of judges, and/or to make judges put in a longer workday, and with shorter vacations, and/or to use pseudojudges. By the latter I mean something like "auditors" and "arbitrators" for auto cases, such as have been used in Massachusetts and Pennsylvania — their determinations being subject to possible (but in practice infrequent) review by a regular judge; or the use of that kind of nonjudicial personnel for handling pretrial conferences with the litigants.[88]

Still another approach has been to promote a more efficient administration of judicial business. This may involve shifting cases from overly busy courts to less busy ones; judicial appointment of impartial medical experts where the

85. In support of this paragraph, see Rosenberg, supra note 84, at 35-37.

86. Rosenberg, supra note 84, at 45; Mermin, "Computers, Law and Justice," 1967 Wis. L. Rev. 43, 50-51.

87. See studies cited in note 33 supra.

88. In support of this paragraph, see Rosenberg, supra note 84, at 41-42, 51-54.

extent of plaintiff's injuries are to be disputed by the parties' opposing experts — an appointment which often helps induce settlement; saving time by encouraging waivers of jury trial in civil cases, or by speeding up the process of jury selection, or getting the state to abolish the jury in state civil cases (University of Chicago studies suggest that a juryless trial is about "40% less time-consuming than a jury trial of the same case,"[89] or putting it the other way, a jury trial is 1 2/3 times as long);[90] employing modern managerial methods, including computers, to streamline the administration of the docket; and two additional techniques, the advocacy of which has been somewhat dampened by recent studies: the greater use of pretrial conferences, and the "split trial."

These last two techniques deserve a separate word. The pretrial conference between the judge and the opposing lawyers has long been viewed as salutary. It is a preview of the case that helps clarify and simplify the issues. And it has been thought to shorten the trial and facilitate a settlement of the case without trial. The latter two effects are now subject to some doubt, as a result of empirical studies. The larger cases, in particular, resist settlement in spite of pretrial. Trials were found to be no shorter because of pretrial, yet the conferences do absorb an appreciable amount of the judge's time; so these would seem to be a negative contribution toward solving the problem of delay. To be weighed against this is the improved quality of the trial where there had been a pretrial conference — apparently because the conference had improved the lawyer's understanding of problems to be met and methods to be followed. Also to be pondered is the fact that plaintiff's recoveries were found to be higher when there had been a pretrial. After these facts had been revealed by the Columbia Project for Effective Justice in a study which had been requested by Chief Justice Weintraub of New

89. Kalven, "The Dignity of the Civil Jury," 50 Va. L. Rev. 1055, 1059 (1964).

90. Kalven's translation of the first form of statement to the second gives him the mathematically erroneous figure of 1 1/2 rather than 1 2/3. Id. at 1059-1060 n.12.

Jersey, the New Jersey Supreme Court changed its rule requiring pretrial conferences in personal injury suits, and made the conference optional in auto accident cases.[91]

Now the "split trial." In such a trial, instead of evidence being admitted on both the liability issue and the damage issue, there is no evidence admitted on damages until after there has been a determination of liability. This can save considerable time (some say about 20% of total trial time, some say "substantially less"), because (1) juries in personal injury suits bring in verdicts of *no* liability about 40% of the time, and (2) even after a verdict of liability, the split-trial system might save time that would normally be spent on evidence of damages, since in some cases the defendant chooses to settle after the liability verdict — i.e., no evidence is taken on damages. And here, as in the case of the pretrial conference technique, studies showed an unexpected substantive effect of the procedural change. This time the effect was to favor the defendant — i.e., in split trials, there were substantially more verdicts of nonliability (probably because of the absence of the emotional impact on the jury, on the liability issue, that one might expect from evidence on damage suffered by the plaintiff).[92]

In short,

there is no acceptable evidence that any remedy [for delay] so far devised has been efficacious to any substantial extent. Only a few of the new measures have worked even to a modest extent, and some of them have been positively counter-productive on the efficiency scale. More important, many of them have had unsuspected side effects in changing the outcome of appreciable numbers of law suits.

A major lesson of this chronicle is that progress in coping with the old problem of court delay will have to come from marshalling relief measures in groups, not from a one-injection miracle cure. There is no such panacea.[93]

What about delay in *criminal* cases? There is congestion in the criminal courts in spite of significant trial-eliminating

91. In support of this paragraph, see Rosenberg, supra note 84, at 49-51.
92. In support of this paragraph, see Rosenberg, supra note 84, at 46-49.
93. Rosenberg, supra note 84, at 55.

factors, such as the fact that about three-quarters of the defendants plead guilty, and the fact most minor traffic offenses get disposed of by simple forfeiture of bail. One of the most tragic facts about criminal case delay is the impact on the indigent defendant, who waits in jail because he could not raise bail. Solutions involving a careful loosening of bail requirements are being experimented with.

But the delay problem in the criminal case is not so much the civil case problem of speeding up the court process between the time the initial papers are filed and the time the case is disposed of. Rather, one of the chief problems is how *more* time can be spent on the minor criminal cases that now may receive a minute or less of time per case in the assembly-line treatment of defendants who have pleaded guilty. An expansion in the number of minor criminal court judges seems imperative. It has been further suggested that some load can be removed from the criminal courts by (1) removing criminal penalties from some types of offenses and substituting other approaches such as civil monetary penalties; (2) expansion of "medical, psychiatric and other treatment facilities so as to reduce by cure the volume of persons processed through the criminal courts because of addiction to alcohol or drugs."[94]

Finally, what can be done about congestion and delay in the appellate courts? Among the many suggestions that have been made, let me select two for brief discussion. First is increasing the number of appellate judges. This could take the form of enlarging the highest court and/or creating or enlarging an intermediate appellate court (which most states still don't have). There are some limits here. Thus it has been observed that in California, "the number of intermediate appellate courts has been increased from three to five, and there has been an even greater increase in the number of judges sitting on those courts. To push the California development a few steps further, suppose that there were ten

94. Barrett, "Criminal Justice: The Problem of Mass Production," in Jones, ed., The Courts, The Public, and the Law Explosion 121-123 (1965).

or fifteen intermediate appellate courts in that state ten years hence. In such circumstances, what were once authoritative appellate tribunals, subject to occasional review by the Supreme Court of California, would have been converted into a judicial Tower of Babel. The proliferation of utterances could divest any one of these courts of significant authority."[9 5]

The other suggestion is to make some classes of cases not appealable at all. The analog of this device is now used in some states with intermediate appellate courts where the appeal to the highest court, for at least some classes of cases, is precluded or else left discretionary with that court. But extending this, in states with no intermediate appellate courts, to cases of appeal from the trial court to the highest state court, is going further than we presently seem prepared to go. It's not that the Constitution requires at least one appeal; it doesn't. But I think both the public and the profession do want a system of at least one appeal.[9 6]

An additional objection centers around criteria for the class of case which would be excluded from appeal. If, for instance, the criterion were on the basis of how much money was at stake in the lawsuit, or on the particular subject matter involved (e.g., auto accidents), this might be attacked on the ground that (1) importance of the legal points to be appealed has no necessary relation to money involved or subject matter, and (2) the criterion might be unconstitutionally discriminatory, denying to those excluded the "equal protection of the laws."

(2) Selection and Tenure of Judges

On the selection and tenure of judges, the practice in America falls into two groupings. The system for federal

95. Hazard, "After the Trial Court — The Realities of Appellate Review," in Jones, ed., supra note 94, at 81.

96. Id. at 83. On the recent proposal for a new National Court of Appeals to screen cases for which Supreme Court review is sought, see Editorial, 59 A.B.A.J. 139 (1973); Freund, "Why We Need the National Court of Appeals," 59 A.B.A.J. 247 (1973); Gressman, "The National Court of Appeals: A Dissent," 59 A.B.A.J. 253 (1973).

judges is *appointment* (by the president, with the advice and consent of the Senate) and *life tenure* ("during good behavior"). The system for state judges in a majority of the states is *election* and *limited tenure* (for a fixed period such as six years). Even in the states the earliest preference was for appointed judges, but populist currents after the 1830s swung the practice toward the elective system.

The two systems are not as different as they seem. The appointment system is based indirectly on the elective process (election of the appointing executive and of the legislative representatives who must, in most of the appointive states, approve). Conversely, the system of electing judges can be viewed as a system of de facto appointment: (1) In practical effect, judicial elections are usually perfunctory ratifications of "appointments," i.e., nominations by party leaders, except where judges run without party labels. (2) A large proportion of elections come after a vacancy (due to death or retirement of an elected judge) had been filled by interim appointments by the governor — and this means, in view of the tradition favoring election of a sitting judge, that the governor's interim nominee is generally elected at the subsequent election.

But while there are elements of both election and nomination in the two systems, a combination of the elements in a different kind of mix has been proposed for the states and is slowly gaining ground. Often referred to as "the Missouri Plan," it has long been supported by the American Bar Association and by the American Judicature Society. The plan involves: (1) initial appointment by the governor (not merely for vacancies in an elected term) from a panel of names submitted by a commission composed of representatives of the bar, judiciary, and the public; (2) the incumbent judge's running for election, after expiration of each term of years, but on his own record — i.e., not against any rival. The plan would normally be instituted by legislative action, but it has also been done by executive order of the governor, e.g., Governor Scranton of Pennsylvania in 1964 instituted such a system. His commission consisted of the president of the University of Pennsylvania, the president of Temple University, a prominent layman interested in the problem of court congestion, three lawyers, and a judge.

Why the dissatisfaction with the purely elective system? Primarily because of the beliefs that (1) the selection process doesn't pay primary attention to professional quality of the judges, (2) the public does not cast an intelligent vote in view of its limited knowledge of legal matters and of the qualifications of candidates, and (3) while in office the elected judge is more prone to allow improper political considerations to influence his judicial judgment, and as election time nears, feels the need to take time away from his judicial duties for campaigning or political fence-mending.

The federal judges, according to professional opinion, are of generally higher caliber than the state judges. This doesn't mean that no state judge measures up to the quality of the best federal judges. But it means that judges appointed to life-tenure judicial posts carrying substantially higher prestige and compensation, and screened by the president and the Senate with cooperation from an American Bar Association committee, are more likely to be quality judges than are state judges selected by currently orthodox methods. Some poor ones do slip through the screen — but fortunately, not because of any acceptance of Senator Hruska's deathless remark in defending President Nixon's abortive Supreme Court nomination of Judge Carswell: that mediocrity, too, deserves representation on the Court. There have been not only some mediocrities, there have been some actually corrupt federal judges. The most celebrated instance was that of Judge Manton of the Second Circuit Court of Appeals, who in 1939 was convicted of selling justice. It was he who argued, ingeniously and ingenuously, in his appeal to the Supreme Court, that "it serves no public policy for a high judicial officer to be convicted of a judicial crime. It tends to destroy the confidence of the people in the courts."[97] And it was he of whom Thomas Reed Powell observed that he was "the finest judge that money could buy." But as Hurst puts

97. Borkin, The Corrupt Judge 23 (1962).

it, "over the years the instances in which even a substantial charge of corruption was raised against federal judges were trifling." And "when all the state *causes célèbres* were added together their total, like that in the federal courts, was trifling," though there was as yet no comprehensive study of corruption in the state judiciary.[98]

In addition to being criminally prosecuted for his derelictions, a judge may of course be removed from office. But the process for federal judges, and generally for state judges, is the cumbersome one of impeachment by the legislature. In recent years, proposals have been made to allow removal by other means — e.g., on the federal level, through a statute allowing removal by a commission, for misbehavior such as gross neglect of judicial duties. The commentators have clashed over whether impeachment is constitutionally the exclusive method of removal, even for misbehavior other than the constitutionally specified "high crimes and misdemeanors."[99]

(3) Limited Role of the Court Itself in the Disposition of Litigation

Considering all the disputes that seem headed for resolution by courts (rather than by administrative agencies or arbitrators), to what extent is it the court's action that resolves those disputes? The answer is: to a small extent. A 1964 study of auto accidents in Michigan showed the following: of 86,100 cases of auto injuries in 1958, most of them (74,000) not only didn't go to court but were not even put in the hands of lawyers — i.e., 24,700 were settled by payment and 49,300 were dropped. Of the 12,100 in which lawyers were hired, only 4000 suits were filed in court. (4100 having been settled by payment and 4000 having been

98. Hurst, The Growth of American Law 142 (1950).
99. See Berger, "Impeachment of Judges and Good Behavior Tenure," 79 Yale L.J. 1475 (1970); Kurland, "The Constitution and the Tenure of Federal Judges: Some Notes From History," 36 U. Chi. L. Rev. 665 (1969); Stolz, "Disciplining Federal Judges: Is Impeachment Hopeless?" 57 Calif. L. Rev. 659 (1969).

dropped). Of the 4000 lawsuits, only 1400 went to the pretrial stage (400 having been dropped and 2200 having been settled by payment). Thereafter, only 500 went to trial (100 having been dropped and 800 having been settled by payment); and of these, 140 were terminated without payment, and 360 by settlement payment or pursuant to court judgment. There were only 80 appeals from judgments for or against liability.[100]

These figures should serve as an antidote to a natural tendency to exaggerate the role of the court judgment in the disposition of disputes. Rather, the court primarily exerts background pressure, by its costs and delays, towards disposition of disputes without any court judgment.

2. THE LEGISLATURES

The organization of legislatures has numerous aspects, only a few of which I can touch on here. As far as legislative sessions are concerned, the almost continuous character of the sessions of Congress contrasts with the more interrupted nature of legislative session in the states. Usually states' regular sessions occur every second year (sometimes with budget sessions in the off-year); and usually there are rigid limits on the length of both regular and special sessions. All of which makes it extremely difficult to cope in a deliberative way with the mounting volume of business.[101]

The pattern of state legislative leadership is modeled roughly on that of Congress, though the formal pattern does not always reveal the realities of power. The presiding officer in the lower house is an elected Speaker, and in the upper house is usually the lieutenant governor, who has been elected by statewide ballot. And there is an important "steering" committee that controls the timing of floor consideration of bills. But, "Whereas in Congress the informal

100. Conard, "The Quantitative Analysis of Justice," 20 J. Legal Ed. 1, 3 (1967); Conard, Morgan, Pratt, Voltz, and Bombaugh, Automobile Accident Costs and Payments 154-155 (1964).

101. Wahlke, "Organization and Procedure," in Heard, ed., State Legislatures In American Politics 137-139 (1966).

structure of party leadership provides much of the animating force behind legislative decisions made by formal leadership, party leadership in most state legislatures tends to be much more fluid and less influential."[102]

Composition of standing committees in the states is nowhere near as strongly dominated by seniority considerations as is the composition of congressional committees. The state committees are "on the average, more archaic in form, in terms of number, size and description of their jurisdiction, as well as less influential in the legislative process than their Congressional counterparts."[103] They have less power to block or alter legislative proposals, are less prone to hold full hearings, and seldom issue fully informative committee reports on bills.

This last is not the only deficiency in reporting at the state level. The printing of bills, floor proceedings, and committee hearings, as well as of committee reports, while excellent on the congressional level, is poor on the state level. Although the legislative chambers in about two-thirds of the states publish a daily journal during the sessions, these do not report the floor discussion or debate, or even summaries thereof, and often don't identify the members who made proposals for passage, amendment, and the like. Not only are committee reports and committee hearings not usually printed; in "many cases, committee records are not even maintained in typed or raw note form." Moreover, "about one-third of the American states do not provide legislators with printed copies of bills on which action is expected. Of these, some ten do not even provide mimeographed or any other form of copies of bills. Still fewer routinely print proposed amendments to pending bills. There is likewise considerable variation among legislatures in the character and quantity of information given legislators about the status of bills, including information about the calendar or agenda for any given legislative day."[104]

102. Id. at 140-141.
103. Id. at 143.
104. Id. at 136-137.

The importance of this deficiency in reporting is many-sided: (1) The knowledge that his activities are being identified and reported presumably would tend to make a legislator act more responsibly. (2) It would also of course tend to make him act more intelligently, since the availability to him of committee reports, etc. makes action on a more informed basis possible. (3) The information would be valuable to others too — not only to historians, but to courts that are called upon to interpret statutes. You will find that a statute's "legislative history" (e.g., the various drafts of the bill, the committee hearings, the committee reports, what was said on the floor), when available, often plays a significant role in its interpretation. Accordingly, the role of legislative history is much more important in cases involving federal, as distinct from state, statutes.

Another organizational aspect that should be mentioned is the physical and staff facilities. Again, Congress is well supplied with offices and with clerical and staff administrative and research assistance. But state legislators must work with surprisingly limited facilities: inadequate or no office space, inadequate or no clerical assistance, inadequate or no staff assistance.[105]

The Citizens Conference on State Legislatures published in 1971 more than seventy general recommendations for the reform of state legislatures,[106] as well as specific recommendations for each state. Among the general recommendations are: full hearings on major bills; publication of the hearings, of informative committee reports, and of the committees' votes; reducing the size of the legislature as well as the size and number of committees; improving the facilities and staff available to members and to committees; increasing legislators' compensation; appending to every bill introduced a statement by the author describing in layman's language what the bill is intended to accomplish; removing the restrictions on length of session so that within a biennial session the legislature can convene, recess, and reconvene for such

105. Id. at 135-136, 137.
106. Citizen's Conference on State Legislatures, The Sometime Governments 151-168 (1971).

periods as are necessary; establishing a representative citizens' commission to study (over a two-year period) legislative operations, facilities, and needs, and to recommend improvements; making provision for effective regulation of lobbyists and avoidance of legislative conflicts of interest; expanding the conduct of policy research, and requiring reports thereon, by standing committees during the period between sessions, under supervision of the legislative councils. The latter are the bipartisan bodies mentioned in the first part of this chapter in the discussion of the functions of law. They have already been instituted in most states for purposes of research and policy formulation — though they are seldom sufficiently funded to do the job that needs doing.

A further word on Congress. There are a number of things that undermine the stereotype of Congress as the effective source of national legislative power. The organization of Congress embodies such a dispersion of power among its committees as to weaken it for a national leadership role in legislation.[107] And compared to members of the executive bureaucracy, Congress is more "oriented towards local needs and small-town ways of thought. The leaders of the administration and of the great private national institutions are more likely to think in national terms."[108] In fact the executive's initiation, and shepherding through Congress, of its own legislative program has become a commonplace of national political life since World War II. Senator Ribicoff complained in 1964 that Congress "has surrendered its rightful place in the leadership in the lawmaking process to the White House. No longer is Congress the source of major legislation. It now merely filters legislative proposals from the President, straining out some and reluctantly letting others pass through. These days no one expects Congress to devise the important bills."[109]

Of course the Constitution itself contemplates a legislative role by the president not only in its provision for presidential

107. Huntington, "Congressional Responses to the Twentieth Century," in Truman, ed., The Congress and America's Future 18-22 (1965).

108. Id. at 15.

109. Ribicoff, "Doesn't Congress Have Ideas of Its Own?" 237 Sat. Eve. Post 6 (1964).

approvals and vetoes, but also in the provision for presidential messages recommending legislation. But the practice has
been not to stop with unimplemented recommendations.
Half a century ago, in the Budget and Accounting Act of
1921, the president was given the duty to propose an
executive budget; and executive initiative has spread since
then — with a push from FDR and Truman — to legislation
generally.[110]

With its legislative function reduced, what remains as
major functions of Congress? One is the service to constituents. Senator Humphrey wrote in 1963 that the "most
pressing day-to-day demands for the time of Senators and
Congressmen are not directly linked to legislative tasks. They
come from constituents."[111] The other major function is
"oversight" of the bureaucracy — the many ways in which
Congress attempts to control or influence the executive and
administrative agencies.

A catalog of the major techniques of "oversight" would be
something like this: Congress has a say in the appointments
to agencies. It may influence substantive policy through
control over the size of appropriations — for the agency's
work generally or for particular programs. It may put a short
expiration date on a statute, e.g., a year, so that hearings can
annually be held on whether agency policies are to be
approved through reenactment. Congress has this way and
many other ways of getting informed about what is going on
in the agencies: committee investigations; a statutory requirement of regular agency reports; committee hearings on
appropriations and other matters within the committee's
jurisdiction; the required publication in the Federal Register
of agency rules and regulations; and a watchdog committee
that might be established over the operations of an agency
generally, as in the case of the Atomic Energy Commission (a
state may have a committee for watching *all* agency rules and

110. Neustadt, "Politicians and Bureaucrats," in Truman, supra note 107, at
110-111.
111. Humphrey, "To Move Congress Out of Its Rut," N.Y. Times Magazine,
April 7, 1963, at 39.

regulations, as under Wis. Stats. § 13.56). Moreover, the existence of the standing "subject matter" committees, appropriations committees, and Committees on Government Operations, in both Houses, means that each agency has at least six committees which, while not watchdog committees, are capable of keeping in close contact with, and influencing, the agency's operations. Whether or not they are on such committees, members of Congress (acting usually in behalf of constituents) are known to intercede with and put pressure on the agencies. Finally, Congress may use statutory devices that reserve a power in a mere portion of Congress — a committee, or one House — to disapprove, let us say, an administrative regulation, or reserve power to act by congressional resolution (i.e., without presidential approval) to terminate a statute or override agency action taken thereunder. Statutory devices such as these have been criticized as unconstitutional, but the Supreme Court has not clearly spoken on this point.

3. *EXECUTIVE AND ADMINISTRATIVE AGENCIES*

I have referred in the previous section to the legislative role of the chief executive. But normally, of course, we think of the "executive" part of the government as "carrying out" or "executing" the law made by the legislature. Perhaps you think of tax officials, inspectors, licensing officers, policemen, prosecutors, motor vehicle commissioners, the president and his subordinates, the governor and his subordinates, etc.

There are really two main forms of the executive. There are, first, the departments, bureaus, and divisions (agriculture, labor, public health, tax, etc.) that report to the chief executive. There are secondly the "administrative agencies" — such as the Securities and Exchange Commission, National Labor Relations Board, Federal Trade Commission on the federal level; or the public service commission, workmen's compensation commission and zoning commission on the state level — that are semi-independent of the chief executive.

Either form of agency can exhibit a mixture of functions. In the first place, for executing or administering the law laid down by the legislature, the department or agency may be authorized by the legislature to exercise a *lawmaking* function (i.e., issue rules and regulations, with the force of law, that implement the statute) as, for instance, when the Treasury Department issues tax regulations, or the SEC issues rules regarding the sale of securities.

So too, both forms of executive agencies may exercise *judicial* functions. In the first form of agency, consider a law enforcement department: the prosecutor has to make some judgments that might be called "adjudicative," such as whether criminal proceedings should be brought, or whether the nature of the case, the condition of the office workload, and other factors justify substituting a lesser charge in return for a guilty plea to the lesser charge. The police, too, are constantly making instant adjudications when they determine whether the facts justify making an arrest. A Veterans Administration or a Social Security office adjudicates claims for pensions, though generally informally.

But it is the second form of agency — the "administrative agency" — that we are prone to recognize as more clearly exercising a judicial function. This seems to be because of the hearings held prior to adjudication of, let us say, whether an FTC cease and desist order, or an NLRB unfair labor practice order, should issue. They are hearings which in many respects resemble the hearing in a civil court proceeding. These administrative agencies are thus often called "quasi-judicial" agencies, as distinct from ordinary executive departments. But the dividing line is somewhat blurred: there are some executive departments, too, e.g., the federal Department of Agriculture, in which constituent bureaus hold hearings and issue adjudicative orders in the administration of statutes such as the Packers and Stockyards Act or Perishable Agricultural Commodities Act.

The chief executive too has more than strictly executive powers. His power to pardon, or commute sentences, represents essentially an adjudication that the facts in a particular case warrant leniency. He also has legislative power of a sort, since he can within certain limits issue Executive Orders, can approve or veto legislation, and can see that desired legislation is initiated. The federal executive is now responsible for most of the bills introduced and passed in Congress.

In terms of sheer volume of disputes handled, it is clear that executive and administrative agencies have become far more important than the courts. In a given recent year the federal district courts will have handled several thousand cases, but the federal agencies will have handled ten times as many, counting only those involving an oral hearing and verbatim transcript. If federal informal adjudications were counted, the annual number would run into the hundreds of millions and perhaps billions. And remember that the average state may have more than a hundred agencies with powers to adjudicate or issue rules (or both) with the force of law.[112]

It is not hard to see the advantages of lawmaking and enforcement by agencies. The legislature has neither the time nor the expertise to handle the detailed requirements of a regulatory scheme for a myriad of different industries with different and ever-changing problems, and to provide the continuous, day-to-day supervision that may be needed.

Could the legislature meet the lawmaking aspect of the problem by regulating in general rather than detailed terms? Of course, it sometimes does this. But it is an unsatisfactory technique: (1) it is unsatisfactory to the industry or other subject of the regulation because the vagueness gives unsatisfactory notice, and indeed would sometimes be unconstitutional on this account; (2) it, at any rate, tends to maximize the amount of litigation over the meaning of the standard.

As to the enforcement aspect of the problem, could the legislature leave it to the district attorney, or to aggrieved individuals, rather than administrative agencies, to bring court enforcement suits? Again, of course, it sometimes does

112. In support of this paragraph, see Davis, Administrative Law Text 4 (3d ed. 1972).

this. But it foregoes certain advantages of administrative agency adjudications and agency enforcement suits in court. The advantages here would be: quantitatively greater enforcement as a result of continuous supervision; qualitatively better enforcement because of the development of a uniform enforcement policy and because of specialized knowledge on the part of the plaintiff enforcers.

But while this expertise of the agencies is important, you should beware of attempts to exaggerate its extent and its value. Top members of administrative commissions and boards are not always experts in the field involved; and though there are experts on the staff, they are not always expert in the precise area of the agency's field (e.g., a power commission concerned with water power problems may have to hire an engineer whose expertise in water problems is acquired after rather than before the hiring). Moreover, agency experts, like other personnel of bureaucratic organizations, tend to become congealed and conservative in their positions. Federal Judge Wyzanski once put it this way: "One of the dangers of extraordinary experience is that those who have it may fall into the grooves created by their own expertness. They refuse to believe that hurdles which they have learned from experience are insurmountable can in fact be overcome by fresh, independent minds."[113] In addition, the extent of disagreement among the experts is still substantial in many fields. Finally, remember that agency expertise doesn't necessarily go hand in hand with wise policy-making; that "expertness is not wisdom and that the relative ordering of values in a society — the ultimate problem of choosing between alternative courses of action — is something we do *after* the expert has completed his task of collecting data, describing, and, to a limited extent, predicting."[114] (Emphasis added.)

113. United States v. United Shoe Mach. Corp., 110 F. Supp. 295, 346 (D. Mass. 1953).
114. Schwartz, "Legal Restriction of Competition in the Regulated Industries: An Abdication of Judicial Responsibility," 67 Harv. L. Rev. 436, 472 (1954).

4. SOME INTERRELATIONS AMONG THE LAW'S AGENCIES

In the course of dealing with the major categories of the agencies of law, I have already pointed to some interrelations among them, as in the case of executive pressure on legislatures and legislative supervision over the agencies. What I want to do here is sketch a broader — though still not complete — picture of interrelationships. I hope to explain why it can be said that instead of the theoretical ideal of a "separation" of judicial, legislative, and executive power we have in fact an "integration" of power — not only a mixture of functions within each of the three major institutions, but also mutual interactions among them, of control and counter-control.

a. Chief Executive and Executive-Administrative Agencies

Before considering examples of truly *inter*agency relations, let me first dispose of what looks, in part at least, like an *intra*agency relation. I refer to the relation between the chief executive and the executive and administrative agencies.

I referred earlier to the fact that an administrative agency has more independence from the president than does the executive department within the president's cabinet. This has given rise to two major criticisms. One is that semi-independence makes more difficult the effective coordination of policies and programs by the chief executive (who, moreover, has been popularly elected, whereas the agency members have not). The second criticism is that relative lack of executive control makes more possible an often-noted phenomenon: an agency tendency to lose its initial regulatory zeal, and to identify the public interest with the interest of the regulated industry.

The second criticism is more vulnerable to rebuttal than the first. Thus, the regular departments may have as much tendency toward industry-orientation as the administrative agencies. Says a veteran administrative law scholar: "Anyone

who follows the activities of the Department of Agriculture,
for example, comes to feel (though this too is no doubt an
exaggeration) that the Department is a glorified farmers'
lobby." And it is doubtful "that an executive agency will be
much different from an independent agency in periods when
public opinion or statutory policy [or, he might have added,
executive policy] is slack, indeterminate, or lacking in
conviction."[115] Notice that the last sentence includes a
reference to indeterminate statutory policy. This has been a
particular point of comment by students of the administrative agency. There is much room for improvement, it is
argued, in the legislature's formulation of standards: it could,
by clearer policy guidance than is afforded by statutory
phrases like "the public interest," counteract the tendency to
industry-orientation, and help resolve uncertainties for the
public and courts as well as for the agencies.[116]

Semi-independence has another interesting aspect worth
noting: its impact on the executive power of removal of
officers. The Supreme Court has held that the president
could freely remove a subordinate executive employee (a
postmaster) from office without the congressional consent
which Congress had specified as necessary,[117] but that the
president could not remove a quasi-judicial officer (Federal
Trade Commissioner; War Claims Commissioner) on the
ground of disapproval of his policies or wanting a man of his
own selection, where Congress had specified not these but
other grounds (inefficiency, neglect of duty or malfeasance)
as a basis for removal,[118] or where Congress had been silent
on removal.[119] These cases, however, do not seem to prevent
a president from achieving removal of such a commissioner
by a different path. If he were to file charges of inefficiency
and neglect of duty and, after hearing, remove him, a court's

115. Jaffe, Book Review, 65 Yale L.J. 1068, 1071, 1074 (1956).
116. Id. at 1072-1074; Friendly, The Federal Administrative Agencies: The
Need for a Better Definition of Standards (1962).
117. Myers v. United States, 272 U.S. 52 (1926).
118. Rathbun v. United States, 295 U.S. 602 (1935).
119. Wiener v. United States, 357 U.S. 349 (1958).

deference to executive fact-finding in such a situation would probably lead it to affirm, even if the proof were slight.

More important as an executive control over administrative agencies is the funneling through a presidential bureau (Office of Management and Budget) of agency requests to Congress for substantive legislation and for funds. The chief executive, further, can influence the attitudes of executive and agency personnel through policies announced in speeches, press conference statements, and the like. He can also, within statutory limits, organize and reorganize agencies and delegate powers to them. On this matter of subdelegation, it is of course true that an occasional statute may require particular decisions to be made only by the chief executive, or only by the head of an agency. But in the absence of such provision, it is usually assumed that the authority to delegate to subordinates does exist; and in 1950 Congress officially recognized the president's authority, within certain broad limits, by the Presidential Subdelegation Act.[120]

I turn now to relations of a more clearly *inter*agency nature.

b. Legislature and Executive

You know that the chief executive exerts influence over the legislature through his power over patronage and the allocation of funds and projects, the doing of other favors asked by legislators for themselves or their constituents, and exerting indirect pressure through the kind of direct appeals to the voter that were mentioned above.

You know, too, that the legislature exerts a counter-control.[120a] The Senate is in a position to check presidential appointments by majority vote, under the constitutional clause that such appointments of federal "officers" be "by and with the advice and consent of the Senate" (though the appointment of "inferior officers" may be vested by Con-

120. On subdelegation, see Davis, supra note 112, at 215-217; Gellhorn and Byse, Administrative Law — Cases and Comments 106-108 (5th ed. 1970).

120a. On control through impeachment, see Berger, Impeachment (1973).

gress "in the President alone, in the courts of law, or in the heads of departments"). Further, even though Executive Orders can be significant exercises of power of both an executive and legislative nature, they cannot go beyond certain bounds expressly or impliedly set by the legislature. The legislature may of course expressly confer considerable power on the executive — as, for instance, when it passes a statute authorizing certain authority over drugs by the Health, Education and Welfare Department and authorizes promulgation of legislative-type regulations by the department. And there may be times when the executive can act without such authorization from Congress if he is acting in an area where executive and legislative authority is deemed to be "concurrent." But if a court concludes that the executive action is inconsistent with the express or implied will of the legislature, the executive action cannot stand. President Truman discovered this truth when the Supreme Court invalidated his 1952 attempt to avert a steel strike by seizing the steel mills during the Korean War.[121]

As this was being written — at the start of President Nixon's second term — another conflict-producing instance of executive overreaching was looming. This was over the alleged executive usurpation of congressional power of the purse by the refusal to spend large portions of actual appropriations for particular purposes, e.g., pollution control or rural electrification. The constitutional question would be answered more clearly were Congress's appropriation explicit and unqualified as to its desire to have the money spent in spite of, rather than subject to, the president's possibly conflicting duties under anti-inflation or other statutes.[121a]

Another interesting aspect of legislative-executive relations is the question of limits on legislative power to obtain information from the executive. Congress has a potent power of investigation, but the executive branch sometimes counters with a power of nondisclosure stemming from the doctrine of "executive privilege." The 1966 Freedom of

121. Youngstown Sheet and Tube Co. v. Sawyer, 343 U.S. 579 (1952).
121a. See Note, 82 Yale L.J. 1636 (1973).

Information Act requiring disclosure of government records to "any person," with stated exceptions, is silent about executive privilege (though some of the exemptions seem to be part of the executive privilege), and it is doubtful that any change in that doctrine was intended by the act.[122] President Eisenhower sketched the doctrine broadly when he wrote to a congressional committee that "throughout our history the President has withheld information whenever he found that what was sought was confidential or its disclosure would be incompatible with the public interest or jeopardize the safety of the nation;"[123] and the Department of Justice has claimed that a similar privilege exists in the heads of departments.[124] The privilege is seldom invoked, however, The Department of Defense reported that in a three-year period it complied with 300,000 inquiries from Congress and refused to comply in only 13 instances.[125]

The Supreme Court has seldom handled this conflict of legislative-executive power. Its 1971 decision in the famous "Pentagon Papers" case did not involve such a conflict. (It held that the government had not met its burden of proof to show justification for an injunction against newspaper publication of a confidential Pentagon history of Vietnam War policy; and it left open the question of criminal liability of those doing the publishing and those who unauthorizedly take such documents and supply them for publication.)[126] But the Court did recently limit the executive privilege defense made by President Nixon in a Watergate scandal case.[126a]

122. See Davis, supra note 112, at § §3A.3, 3A.20.

123. Hearings on S. 921 (Freedom of Information and Secrecy in Government) Before the Subcomm. on Constitutional Rights, Senate Comm. on the Judiciary, 85th Cong., 2d Sess. 271 (1958).

124. See id. at 63-146.

125. Id. at 385-387.

126. New York Times Co. v. United States, 403 U.S. 713 (1971). See Henkin, "The Right to Know and the Duty to Withhold: The Case of the Pentagon Papers," 120 U. Pa. L. Rev. 271 (1972); "Developments in the Law: The National Security Interest and Civil Liberties," 84 Harv. L. Rev. 1130, 1189-1244 (1972).

126a. He could not legally resist disclosure of his tapes and documents for use

The question whether a court may compel disclosures under some circumstances, in spite of a claim of executive privilege, did receive some discussion by the Supreme Court in a 1952 suit under the Federal Tort Claims Act by a widow of a civilian killed in the crash of a military aircraft testing some secret electronic equipment.[127] Discussing the plaintiff's request to see the Air Force Accident Investigation Report and statements given in the investigation by three surviving crew members, the Court made some things clear about the privilege: First, it was open to the courts to determine the proper limits of the privilege doctrine in its application to particular facts. Second, this didn't mean that the court should routinely examine for itself the allegedly privileged information. Rather, "In each case, the showing of necessity [for the information] which is made will determine how far the court should probe in satisfying itself that the occasion for invoking the privilege is appropriate." Third, "even the most compelling necessity cannot overcome the claim of privilege if the court is ultimately satisfied that military secrets are at stake." Fourth, in this case, "where necessity is dubious, a formal claim of privilege . . . will have to prevail. Here, necessity was greatly minimized by an available alternative, which might have given [plaintiffs] the evidence to make out their case without forcing a showdown on the claim of privilege" — i.e., the alternative of accepting the government's offer to let the three survivors testify on nonclassified information.

Returning now to the impact of the executive privilege on *legislative* power: The preceding case has a bearing on the limits of legislative investigative power, too. But I want also to call your attention to another aspect of the problem that has blossomed only recently, namely, whether actual disclosure by members of Congress, directly or through their

in a pending criminal case, by a generalized claim of executive privilege (as distinct from a specific claim of protecting national secrets). United States v. Nixon, 94 S. Ct. 3090 (1974). See also Nixon v. Sirica, 487 F. 2d 700 (D.C. Cir. 1973).

127. United States v. Reynolds, 345 U.S. 1 (1952).

aides, of secret executive documents, may subject them or their aides to any liability, or at least to grand jury questioning about the securing and disseminating of the documents. A 1972 decision of the Supreme Court[128] dealt with (1) events at Alaska Senator Mike Gravel's 1971 impromptu meeting of his Senate Subcommittee on Buildings and Grounds (i.e., his extensive reading from the confidential "Pentagon Papers" on the Vietnam War, and his making all 47 volumes part of the public record); and (2) his aide's negotiations with Beacon Press for publication of the documents in book form. The Court ruled that the Constitution's "speech or debate" clause (declaring with respect to members of Congress that "for any speech or debate in either House, they shall not be questioned in any other place") extends only to "legislative acts," and hence would protect the Senator and his aide from grand jury questioning about events at the subcommittee meeting, but would not protect them from questioning concerning arrangements for private publication of the papers. Nor was there, in the latter type of inquiry, any general "legislative immunity" from testifying, stemming from a nonconstitutional source. The Court cautioned that the speech or debate clause "does not privilege either Senator or aide to violate an otherwise valid criminal law in preparing for or implementing legislative acts."

On the same day, it decided that the speech or debate clause did not immunize a senator from criminal liability for accepting a bribe in exchange for a promise relating to a legislative act, i.e., a vote or decision.[129] The Court made clear that the bribery offense was complete whether or not the promised legislative act actually occurred; nor, in view of the "speech or debate" clause, should inquiry be made into such occurrence. And where the bribe was for bringing improper influence to bear on the Justice Department, as in an earlier case, validity of the prosecution was still clearer, since the situation did not involve a legislative act at all. The

128. Gravel v. United States, 409 U.S. 606 (1972).
129. United States v. Brewster, 408 U.S. 501 (1972).

clause, said the Court, "does not prohibit inquiry into activities which are casually or incidentally related to legislative affairs, but not a part of the legislative process itself."

c. Legislature and Administrative Agencies

At an earlier point, i.e., in discussing the functions of the legislature, I tried to analyze the ways in which legislatures discharge an "oversight" function with respect to administrative agencies, so I needn't go into that relationship again. I should add here, however, that there is more than "oversight" in the interaction between legislature and agency. Agencies may develop a close relation of mutual assistance with particular legislative committees or members. This includes — in spite of the funneling of agency legislative requests through the Office of Management and Budget — direct legislative-agency contacts over content and drafting of proposed legislation.

But what I want to dwell on, at this point, is the vital role of the legislature before there is any administrative agency to "oversee." That is, it is the legislature that brings the administrative agency into being, by a statute describing (among other things) its composition, functions, and powers. It is the legislature that determines whether the agency is to hold hearings and exercise the judicial power to adjudicate disputes, whether it is to have the power to issue rules and regulations with the force of law, make investigations and inspections, issue subpoenas, and bring enforcement suits in court.

Among the questions thus raised, I wish briefly to discuss four.

(1) When an agency is vested with judicial power, can it be objected that the legislature has transgressed the constitutional separation of powers by giving an agency what the constitution contemplates for courts? Generally, the answer nowadays is no. To sustain this objection, said the Supreme Court in 1940, "would be to turn back the clock on at least a

half century of administrative law."[130] The reasons that administrative law has developed in this direction are probably (a) the courts are aware of the impossible burden that would be placed on the courts themselves if the agencies could not help in shouldering the adjudicative burden (recall the statistics in my earlier discussion of the functioning of administrative agencies). (b) the courts are aware that the typical agency adjudication is not the final word — it is subject to court review. Still, there are a few maverick decisions in state courts finding that agency adjudication violates the separation of powers principle under the state constitution.[131]

(2) Even if exercise of a judicial function by a noncourt is permissible, doesn't it become impermissible when the legislature allows this function to be *joined* in the same body with prosecutorial and other executive as well as legislative functions? Hasn't the integrity of the adjudicative process been impaired? A 1972 empirical study suggests, on the basis of a limited sample, a negative answer.[132] Nor have courts ruled against the joinder, at least not in the case of the typical large federal agency with an *internal separation* of functions. One aspect of the hearing officer's independence is that under the federal Administrative Procedure Act they are appointed by the agency from civil service registers. They are subject to civil service requirements, are generally assigned to cases in rotation, and "may not perform duties inconsistent with their duties and responsibilities as hearing examiners." Moreover, the act provides that no hearing officer may "be

130. Sunshine Anthracite Coal Co. v. Adkins, 310 U.S. 381 (1940). See also NLRB v. Jones and Laughlin Steel Corp., 301 U.S. 1 (1937); Union Bridge Co. v. United States, 204 U.S. 364 (1907); Brown, "Administrative Commissions and the Judicial Power," 19 Minn. L. Rev. 261 (1935).

131. A New Mexico court so held in 1957 with respect to the Workmen's Compensation Commission (State v. Mechem, 63 N.M. 250, 316 P.2d 1069 (1957)), and a New Hampshire court so held with respect to a proposed administrative agency system for adjudicating auto accident cases (In re Opinion of the Justices, 87 N.H. 492, 179 A. 344 (1933)).

132. See Posner, "The Behavior of Administrative Agencies," 1 J. Legal Studies 305, 323-344 (1972).

responsible to or subject to the supervision and direction of
any officer, employee or agent engaged in the performance of
investigative or prosecuting functions for any agency"; and,
generally, those participating in investigation or prosecution
of an administratively adjudicated case are not to "participate or advise on the decision" of that case or a factually
related case.[133]

True, the act makes these latter provisions specifically
inapplicable to the heads of agencies; but a leading textbook
points out that agency heads "are rarely concerned with the
details of cases at preliminary stages in a way that could
accurately be characterized as investigative or prosecutive,"
and "federal courts have been scantily impressed by lawyers'
outcries against the combination of responsibilities to be
found in large administrative bodies."[134] As a federal court
of appeals observed in 1962, "It is well settled that a
combination of investigative and judicial functions within an
agency does not violate due process."[135] A contrary
conclusion has occasionally been reached, especially when
the agency is a small one.[136]

(3) Even though constitutionality of joinder of functions
be conceded, many have urged the desirability of safeguarding the integrity of adjudication and strengthening the
process of policy-making by *separating* these two functions — i.e., removing the adjudicative functions from quasi-
judicial agencies and transferring them to the regular courts,
or to new specialized courts like a trade regulation court, a
tax court, or a labor court.

133. For the most pertinent provisions of the act, see 5 U.S.C. § §554(d),
556, 559, 3105. Particular statutes may effect a still more drastic internal
separation of adjudication from policy-making. Thus the 1947 Taft-Hartley Act
saw to it that the adjudicative and prosecutorial staffs handling labor-relations
cases didn't have the same boss. The General Counsel of the National Labor
Relations Board has final authority over investigatory and prosecutorial policies.
He is not controlled by the board, which has final authority over adjudication.

134. Gellhorn and Byse, supra note 120, at 805.

135. Pangburn v. CAB, 311 F.2d 349, 356 (1st Cir. 1962). See cases cited at
that page, and Davis, supra note 112, at §13.02.

136. Gellhorn and Byse, supra note 120, at 804.

Why have such proposals so far been unsuccessful? To begin with, a significant amount of separation of functions already exists, as described above. Further, as opponents of complete separation point out, it is often difficult to distinguish adjudication from policy-making — e.g., the process of licensing or granting of subsidies involves elements of both. More positively, they assert that there are *advantages* in amalgamation of the two functions in one body; that experience in one function helps in discharging the other. When Louis Hector, a proponent of separation, had argued that planning an air route is an executive function, but that selecting which carrier should operate it is a judicial function for a court, Professor Carl Auerbach replied: "The CAB . . . planned its international air routes pretty much as Mr. Hector would have wished. But in the subsequent proceedings involving the selection of carriers, evidence was introduced to cause it to modify its plans in important respects. The selection of the carrier affects the route to be chosen, and vice versa."[137]

Thus the argument is: (a) an agency stripped of its adjudicative functions would be lacking in an important source of information for its executive and legislative functions; (b) the proposed administrative court would lack the knowledge that comes from exercise of executive and legislative functions (including the concomitant day-to-day contact with the specialized staff and the problems of the industry). It would therefore be making less-informed policy, for it is a mistake to assume that adjudication does not involve policy judgments. This is a point you will see more clearly from the discussion in Chapter 4. While I have summarized the arguments which have thus far been persuasive, I should add that from time to time a responsible

137. Auerbach, "Some Thoughts on the Hector Memorandum," 1960 Wis. L. Rev. 183, 186. See also Auerbach, "Should Administrative Agencies Perform Adjudicatory Functions?" 1959 Wis. L. Rev. 95; Cary, "Why I Oppose the Divorce of the Judicial Function From Federal Regulatory Agencies," 51 A.B.A.J. 33 (1965).

official announces his views the other way — one of the most recent being Commissioner Philip Elman, who ended an active two-term career on the FTC in 1970. Newton Minow so spoke in 1963 on leaving the FCC, and Louis Hector on leaving the CAB in 1959.[138]

(4) Insofar as the legislature confers *legislative* power on the agency, i.e., power to make rules and regulations with the force of law, can this be attacked as another violation of the separation of powers principle; has not the legislature abdicated its own constitutional responsibility for exercising the legislative power? Again, speaking generally, the answer is no. True, there have been plenty of cases in which the courts have asserted that the legislature cannot make a "delegation" (or an "undue delegation") of its legislative power. But in the entire history of the Supreme Court to the present, there were only two cases in which that Court thought Congress had made such an invalid delegation to another branch of government — both of them involving aspects of the National Industrial Recovery Act of 1933.[139] Whatever be the special factors that may explain those decisions which found the statute lacking in sufficient "standards" to guide the delegate's discretion, the Supreme Court has since upheld numerous statutes no less lacking in standards. The trend in the federal cases is to look less at statutory standards than at the fairness of the agency procedures and results — with the trend in state cases somewhat behind.[140] Explaining the trend is probably the increased judicial awareness that for complex and changing regulatory problems, a legislature

138. The Hector memorandum was published as "Problems of the CAB and the Independent Regulatory Commissions," in 69 Yale L.J. 931 (1960). Minow's position, originally in the form of a May 31, 1963 letter to President Kennedy appears in "Suggestions for Improvements of the Administrative Process," 15 Admin. L. Rev. 146 (1963). Elman's position appears in his "A Modest Proposal for Radical Reform," 56 A.B.A.J. 1045 (1970). William L. Cary, former SEC chairman, after leaving the SEC took specific issue with both Minow and Hector in his article cited in the preceding footnote, and in his later book, Politics and the Regulatory Agencies (1967).

139. Panama Refining Co. v. Ryan, 293 U.S. 388 (1935); Schecter Poultry Corp. v. United States, 295 U.S. 495 (1935).

140. See Davis, supra note 112, c. 2.

simply cannot lay down precise, detailed standards in advance.

d. Court and Executive-Administrative Agencies

Under this heading it might have been appropriate to discuss some of the things discussed above. For in talking about the legislature in relation to the agencies, I talked also about court reactions — i.e., court reactions to legislative vesting of judicial power in the agency, and legislative joinder of it with executive powers in the same agency; and court reactions to legislative delegation of legislative power to the agency.

But my chief concerns under the present topic are three other questions: First, what are the kinds of questions that courts may properly consider in reviewing the action of administrative agencies? Second, what is the scope of the court's review? Third, what are some ways in which courts pay deference to the agency?

(1) There are some limits on the kinds of questions a reviewing court can consider. Not all questions qualify as "judicial." There is a "political question" doctrine, for instance, under which a court may conclude that a particular issue is not "judicial" but "political," to be resolved by the other branches of government. Some lower courts applied this doctrine to the issue of legality of presidential action in the Vietnam War.[141] On that issue the Supreme Court denied certiorari review (a discretionary review applicable to most cases coming to that court), with occasional individual dissents from the denial.[142] The Supreme Court made clear, a long time ago, that the question whether a state has a "republican form of government" as required by the Consti-

---

141. Velvel v. Nixon, 415 F.2d 236 (10th Cir.), cert. denied, 396 U.S. 1042 (1970); Luftig v. McNamara, 373 F.2d 664 (D.C. Cir.), cert. denied, 387 U.S. 945 (1967). A contrary view was taken, however, in Massachusetts v. Laird, 451 F.2d 26 (1st Cir. 1971); Berk v. Laird, 429 F.2d 302 (2d Cir. 1970); Orlando v. Laird, 443 F.2d 1039(2d Cir.), cert denied, 404 U.S. 869 (1971).

142. See, e.g., the dissents in the denials of certiorari in: Da Costa v. Laird, 405 U.S. 979 (1972); Mora v. McNamara, 389 U.S. 934 (1967); Mitchell v. United States, 386 U.S. 972 (1967).

tution is a political question.[143] The scope of the doctrine
has been diminishing in recent years. But where the president's action involving other countries is concerned, the
hands-off attitude expressed by the "political question"
doctrine is reinforced by a traditional deference to his broad
constitutional power in foreign affairs.[144]

Another reason for saying a particular question is not a
"judicial" one appropriate for a court's resolution is that it
looks like the kind of executive or administrative question
that has in the past been handled only by executive or
administrative agencies. Thus, if a statute authorizes licensing
by an agency, and authorizes a *de novo* judicial review — i.e.,
not limited to questions of law and to determining whether
the agency fact-findings were supported by substantial
evidence, but rather covering the entire exercise of *administrative discretion* on issuance or revocation of the license,
including an independent determination of fact and
law — you *may* find a court saying the statute invalidly
lodges a "nonjudicial" question in the court. Or you may
find the court saving the constitutionality of the statute by
interpreting it narrowly — in spite of its broad language — to
allow only the normal, limited judicial review.[145] De novo
judicial review of agency action is rarely authorized — even
where a strong element of discretionary administrative policy
is *not* involved. But there are special situations where a court
might hold de novo review (in the sense of an independent
determination of fact and law, though not necessarily on the

143. Luther v. Borden, 48 U.S. (7 How.) 1 (1849).
144. See, e.g., Chicago and Southern Airlines v. Waterman S.S. Corp., 333
U.S. 103 (1948).
Another aspect of judicial deference to the executive in the foreign affairs area
is the so-called "act of state" doctrine. This doctrine bars inquiry by courts into
the legality of acts of foreign governments done within their own territories,
partly because (and some justices think solely because) such adjudication may
embarrass the executive conduct of foreign policy. But a Supreme Court majority
presently believes that the doctrine applies even in a case where the executive has
expressly advised the Court that American foreign policy interests would not be
advanced by applying the doctrine. See First Natl. City Bank v. Banco Nacional
De Cuba, 406 U.S. 759 (1972).
145. See Davis, supra note 112, at §29.09.

basis of a new evidentiary trial in court) to be constitutionally required.[146]

(2) What then are the judicial questions that a court can properly handle in its review of executive and administrative action, and what is the nature of that review? One such question is whether the evidence at a hearing by an executive or administrative agency adequately supports the fact findings of the agency. In answering this question, a court does not weigh the evidence in the way it would if it were the initial fact finder, to see whether a preponderance of the evidence supports the fact findings in question. It asks, rather, whether there is "substantial evidence" to support the findings. This question means: could a reasonable mind believe such evidence to be enough to support the findings even though the court (presumably another reasonable mind) might not, if it were the original fact finder, have believed it to be enough? The court is thus paying some deference to the agency; it is not substituting its own independent judgment.

When you shift from a strictly fact question to a question of "law" or a "mixed question of fact or law," the cases on the scope of court review of agency determinations are in great confusion. The problem is easy enough if the agency procedure or decision is alleged to violate a constitutional standard or some clear statutory mandate whose application by the court requires no deference to the agency, because its expertise, or its face-to-face confrontation with witnesses, is not involved in the matter. On these questions of law, the court substitutes its own independent judgment.

But suppose the case involves interpretation of the statutory language to determine whether or not the language applies to the facts of the case. For example, is a newsstand operator who has, according to agency findings, certain economic relationships with the newspaper publisher, an "employee" within the meaning of that term as used in the National Labor Relations Act? This kind of question has

146. See Davis, supra note 112, at §29.08; Jaffe, Judicial Control of Administrative Action, c. 16 (1965); Strong, "The Persistent Doctrine of Constitutional Fact," 46 N.C.L. Rev. 223 (1968).

sometimes been called a question of law, sometimes a "mixed question of fact and law." In this type of case you will find some Supreme Court cases deferring to the administrative judgment in the way the Court does toward fact findings; in other cases the Court has substituted its own independent judgment on the question. When it does the former, (a) the Court may use its independent judgment on *some* aspects of the problem (e.g., on what was the overall purpose of the statute, what was the common law meaning of the disputed statutory word, etc.);[147] (b) it is likely to be found asserting the oft-heard proposition that an administrative agency's interpretation of its own statute is entitled to receive great weight by the reviewing court — especially where the interpretation has been long-continued and had been, in effect, "ratified" by subsequent legislative appropriations for continued enforcement of the statute and/or legislative reenactments of it without any change in the interpreted language.[148]

Predicting when the Supreme Court will take the deferential attitude and when the other, in these cases of applying statutory language to the facts, is extremely difficult. The Court has thus far done a poor job of rationalizing its decisions in this area.[149]

(3) It may be helpful to round up some other ways in which courts pay deference to agencies — i.e., other than in review of fact findings and other than in the kind of review they *sometimes* give to agency applications of statutory language to the facts.

Suppose a company claims that a regulation issued by the Food and Drug Administration is unconstitutional. This is regarded as a question of law, like the question of constitutionality of a statute. Nonetheless, just as courts say there is generally a "presumption" of constitutionality of a statute, they say the same about an administrative regulation.[150]

---

147. See NLRB v. Hearst Publications, Inc., 322 U.S. 111 (1944).
148. See Davis, supra note 112, at 126-133.
149. Id. c 30.
150. Pacific States Box and Basket Co. v. White, 296 U.S. 176 (1935).

This is a deference to the agency; it puts the burden of persuasion on the side of the party attacking the agency's regulation.

Suppose the National Labor Relations Board sent a company a notice that the Board would hold a hearing on a specified date to determine whether the company had engaged in an unfair labor practice under the act. The company, claiming that the business of the plant involved intrastate rather than interstate commerce and therefore did not come under the act, went into federal court for an injunction to restrain the board from holding the hearing. The Supreme Court has said that a "long-settled rule of judicial administration" should be applied to this situation, the rule of "exhaustion of administrative remedies." The board having initiated an administrative proceeding, it was the company's duty to exhaust this remedy before going to the court.[151] The exhaustion rule has been riddled with exceptions by some courts — typically where wholly non-factual determinations are involved — but the basic rule does illustrate a court deference to the agency. The court wishes to gain the benefit of agency expertise before it concerns itself with the problem.

Analogous to the exhaustion rule is that of "primary jurisdiction." Here, unlike the situation in an exhaustion case, no administrative proceeding has been or is about to be commenced. The case has been brought in court and at least one of the issues is an issue that an administrative agency has special competence and adequate authority to handle (and no statute has given exclusive authority to either court or agency), so the court says the agency should have priority on the issue. The court either dismisses the suit or retains the case on its docket to await the agency action. This was the situation, for instance, when the government sued in federal district court to restrain alleged violations of the antitrust laws by the Far East Conference of steamship companies, and the Supreme Court ultimately held that the case should have

151. Myers v. Bethlehem Shipbuilding Corp., 303 U.S. 41 (1938).

been dismissed because primary jurisdiction rested with the Federal Maritime Board.[152]

One other illustration of court deference to the agency is the law applicable to "mandamus." Mandamus is a court remedy, one of whose uses is to command an official to perform a public duty. The remedy is hedged about with qualifications designed to avoid undue interference with the functioning of officials. Thus, courts are found saying that the remedy is available to command the exercise of only "ministerial," i.e., nondiscretionary duties, or to compel an officer who has failed to perform a discretionary duty to do so, but not to compel him to exercise his discretion in a particular way. True, exceptions have been recognized in cases where an official's exercise of discretion has been "arbitrary," and indeed alternative remedies like injunction may avoid the limits a court puts on the mandamus remedy, but the classical mandamus doctrine does reflect a concern by courts for the prerogatives of a sister agency of government.[153]

e. Court and Legislature

The sharpest confrontation between court and legislature occurs when a court strikes down a statute as unconstitutional. This phenomenon won't be treated at this point, because it is considered at some length in Chapter 5. So too, I am postponing until Chapter 3 two other aspects of court-legislature relations: the process of court interpretation of statutes, and the phenomenon of a court resolving a common law problem (i.e., a nonstatutory problem) in the light of a statutory policy in a related field. At this point, I want to deal with a number of miscellaneous other problems posed by the coexistence of courts and legislatures.

(1) Consider, first, some salient differences in the functioning of these two institutions.

What a court can do is rather strictly limited by what the parties bring to it. In general, the issues considered by the

---

152. Far East Conference v. United States, 342 U.S. 570 (1952).
153. On mandamus generally, see Davis, supra note 112, at § §23.06, and 24.03.

court are only those raised by the parties, and the facts considered are only those in the "record" of oral and documentary evidence presented by the parties. The court's judgment represents *not* its view of the optimum solution for all people who find themselves facing the same kind of social problem presented by the case, but only whether the particular record justifies the granting or denial of the particular relief requested by the particular plaintiff. There are some qualifications to this generalization. There have been occasions when courts considered issues not raised by the parties and granted a form of relief not requested. And persons other than the parties are being listened to when an appellate court grants permission to, say, the American Civil Liberties Union or the Association of American Railroads to file a written argument as "amicus curiae" (friend of the court).[154] From that source, moreover (or, indeed, from the parties' written arguments or from the court's own investigation or general knowledge), certain facts not in the record may properly be "judicially noticed" by the court. The doctrine of judicial notice traditionally has allowed a court to give weight to facts that are outside the record but so reliable that no proof is needed. The doctrine has been rather loosely applied in recent years, modifications are being suggested, and its boundaries are presently unclear.[155]

One other feature of a court's functioning should be added: At the same time that it is attempting to do justice in the particular case, it is attempting to integrate the case into the body of preexisting principle. This continuing, reasoned elaboration of principle was stressed by Henry M. Hart as a distinctive virtue of the judicial process in legal development.[156]

In the respects discussed above, a legislature is more freewheeling than a court. Though it pays some attention to

154. See Comment, "The Amicus Curiae," 55 Nw. L. Rev. 469 (1961); Auerbach, Garrison, Hurst, and Mermin, The Legal Process 228-231 (1961).

155. See Davis, supra note 112, c. 15; McCormick, "Judicial Notice," 5 Vand. L. Rev. 296 (1952).

156. Hart's comments are in Paulsen, ed., Legal Institutions Today and Tomorrow 46-48 (1959).

how its new laws fit in with existing statutes, it is not focusing on the weaving of a consistent body of principle. Further, the facts and issues and solutions that the legislature considers don't depend on what the parties to a particular dispute put before it. A legislative committee may receive input from anyone interested in its investigation or in the bill the committee is considering. Nor is the committee limited by that input; it may supplement it by its own staff studies or other material bearing on the relevant facts as well as on arguments and possible solutions to the problems being considered. Compared to the court's limited options, the legislature's range of solutions is broad: It may choose from a variety of different forms of statutes, with different kinds of sanctions, perhaps with provision for an administrative agency to provide continuous attention to the problems giving rise to the statute. One thing the legislature can *not* do consistently with the Constitution is to enact a "bill of attainder" — one which singles out persons or groups for punishment without trial.[157]

In general, the legislature is concerned with rules for people generally or for large groups of people, rather than with a dispute between two antagonists; and is formulating rules for the future rather than being concerned with the rights of two parties with respect to some past happenings. There is a maxim of statutory interpretation to the effect that a statute is "presumed" to have been intended to operate prospectively only, unless it deals with a matter of procedure rather than substance. However, this is only a rebuttable presumption, and some substantive statutes have been construed as operating retroactively. As so construed, the statute may be upheld where the court is convinced that the legislature had good reason to make it retroactive and the backward impact is not unreasonably harsh.[158]

157. See United States v. Brown, 381 U.S. 437 (1965); Annot., 4 L. Ed. 2d 2155 (1959).
158 See, e.g., Hochman, "The Supreme Court and the Constitutionality of Retroactive Legislation," 73 Harv. L. Rev. 692 (1960); Auerbach et al., supra note 154, at 173.

To this qualification on the distinction between legislatures and courts there should be added another: a court decision need not always address itself to past facts. A comparatively recent development in judicial practice is this: where there is announced a new rule, that either overrules an earlier decision or applies to a situation never before adjudicated, the court may avoid a possibly harsh retroactive impact by making the new rule apply only to future cases, or to future cases and the case being decided.[159]

Under the orthodox approach, the new rule would apply not only to similar future cases and the case being decided but also to anyone whose situation arising before the decision was similar to the situation in the decided case. He would, generally speaking, have the benefit or burden of the decision when his situation was brought to court — assuming that the "statute of limitations," which puts a limit on the time within which a suit can be brought, hadn't yet expired. If his case had already been decided the other way prior to the case announcing the new rule, traditionally he would not be affected by the new rule, because of the principle of "res judicata" (the matter has been adjudicated). However, in spite of this salutary policy against the constant relitigation of cases, some exceptions have developed in this "new law" situation, especially in criminal cases.[160]

Finally, there is a sense in which statutory law has more of a *planned* quality about it — even discounting the fact that pressures from those who stand to gain or lose from the proposed legislation make the planning process something less than balanced and disinterested. That is, statutory law is not so dependent on a *chance* element which afflicts the system of nonstatutory law — the fact that a court will not deal with a problem until a genuine controversy between two

---

159. Schaefer, "The Control of 'Sunbursts': Techniques of Prospective Overruling," 41 N.Y.U.L. Rev. 631 (1967); Levy, "Realist Jurisprudence and Prospective Overruling," 109 U. Pa. L. Rev. 1 (1960); Auerbach et al., supra note 154, at 175-178. The problem is discussed again in Chapter 4 (pages 263-267).
160. See Auerbach et al., supra note 154, at 174-175.

parties has happened to occur and been placed by them before the court.

(2) This chance element in the case law system requires some elaboration. One wonders how a legal system can develop in a socially desirable way when its rules are made *ad hoc* for particular parties who happen to have come into the kind of conflict that brought them to court. Karl Llewellyn once explained the social efficacy of the case law system by saying that litigation arises out of conflict, and conflict arises in fields of social activity where growth is taking place — where the relative strength of interest groups is changing. To which Lon Fuller responded: where social change is rapid, case law with its crowded calendars can't keep up; the pecuniary interest of an individual may be so slight as to make litigation or appeal impracticable (citing the abuses that grew up without judicial curb in the field of weekly premium "industrial life insurance"); and the chance element may have an unhealthy effect on the direction of legal growth.[161]

In explanation of the last point: Llewellyn himself had recognized that often a whole field of law may be (as paraphrased by Fuller) "influenced permanently by the particular turn taken by the first case arising in the field. This case may have carried a certain factual and ethical complexion which was actually the determinative element in its decision. The court in deciding it, however, may lay down a categorical rule which subsequently becomes divorced from the particular circumstances of its first utterance, and controls perhaps hundreds of cases which from an ethical or factual viewpoint are quite different from the first and 'critical' case." And "organized interest-groups . . . may see to it that these cases 'come up in the right way.' "[162]

To this importance of the "first case," Fuller added the importance of the *order* in which the later cases come up. There might be an "accidental absence of a decision which

161. Fuller, "American Legal Realism," 82 U. Pa. L. Rev. 429, 438-442 (1934).
162. Id. at 440.

might serve as a doctrinal bridge between existing rules and needed new law." He cited as an example the case of Shuey v. United States,[163] in which the Supreme Court decided that a published offer of a reward could be effectively revoked by an announcement given equal publicity, even though the revocation was not then known by the plaintiff, who therafter expended his efforts to do the things for which the reward was offered. Prior to this decision, the general rule was that a revocation of an offer was not effective until communicated. Hence, while Pollock, a leading British writer on contracts, found the decision reasonable, he thought it a "strong piece of judicial legislation." Fuller commented: Suppose that between the earlier cases and the Shuey case, a case had come up "in which a letter of revocation had been promptly delivered at the place of business of the offeree and had been allowed to remain unopened on his desk. Without much question a court would have held that such a revocation was 'communicated' so soon as the offeree had had a fair opportunity to become familiar with it. And had such a case existed before the Shuey case is it likely that anyone would have regarded that decision as a 'strong piece of judicial legislation'? Pollock's attitude was influenced by the purely fortuitous circumstances that there did not exist a case which could operate to carry his mind, without shock, from the older cases to the decision in the Shuey case."[164]

(3) The differences already mentioned in the functioning of courts and legislatures have some bearing on the recurrent question of whether a reform in the law should be by way of common law or by statute.

In recent years the issue has been posed sharply by cases in a number of states dealing with the issue of whether a particular immunity from tort liability should be abolished. Largely because of the widespread availability of insurance to potential defendants, we live in an era of expanding pressures for the proposition that injured people should be compensated for their injuries. So, long-standing tort immunities

163. 92 U.S. 73 (1875).
164. Fuller, supra note 161, at 441.

have been under attack, in state after state: immunity of the municipal and state governments, of hospitals and other charitable corporations, of parent to child and spouse to spouse.[165] One of the problems raised was whether the court should overrule its precedents establishing the immunity or whether it should leave it up to the legislature to make the reform. Most of the courts facing the issue have decided to take the plunge themselves — even, in some instances, where a legislative bill to make the change had died in committee or had been voted down by the legislature. A legislature which failed to act, or which acted negatively, was viewed by these courts as wanting to leave it up to the courts to retain or modify their own judge-made doctrines, rather than as wanting the courts to retain those doctrines.[166]

The choice that a court makes between judicial reform and possible legislative reform requires an assessment of the competing virtues of courts and legislatures for the job. As I have already suggested, the legislature typically has an advantage in broader access to relevant facts, broader representation of interests, broader range of solutions. This was why Justice Brandeis dissented in a well-known case that recognized for the first time a kind of property right in the news. The International News Service had been copying, and distributing as its own, news items that had appeared in early editions of newspapers affiliated with the Associated Press or in publicly posted AP news bulletins. The Supreme Court majority supported AP's claims and enjoined the INS practices. Justice Brandeis's dissent recognized that the common law has a "capacity for growth," but thought that in this case, court "recognition of a new private right may work serious injury to the general public unless the boundaries of the right are definitely established and wisely

165. See Prosser, Law of Torts 984-987 (governments), 992-996 (charities), 859-867 (parent-child and husband-wife) (4th ed. 1971).

166. See, e.g., Holytz v. City of Milwaukee, 17 Wis. 2d 26, 36-39, 42-43, 115 N.W.2d 618, 623-625, 626-627 (1962), and cases cited therein. See also Battala v. State, 20 N.Y.2d 237, 176 N.E.2d 729 (1961); Collopy v. Newark Eye and Ear Infirmary, 27 N.J. 29, 141 A.2d 276 (1958).

guarded." The legislature might wish to bar injunctions while allowing damages, perhaps in fixed amount; it might allow remedies only if the AP had assumed the obligation of supplying news at reasonable rates and without discrimination to all newspapers applying; it might wish to establish an administrative agency. "Courts are ill-equipped to make the investigations which should precede a determination of the limitation which should be set upon any property right in news, or of the circumstances under which news gathered by a private agency should be deemed affected with the public interest. Courts would be powerless to prescribe the detailed regulations essential to full enjoyment of the rights conferred, or to introduce the machinery required for enforcement of such regulations . . ."[167]

But note some limitations on the preference for legislative action. The situation is one in which the legislature, after all, *has not* acted. And this may not be the result of a deliberative choice, mindful of the public interest. Just as the blatant inaction of malaportioned state legislatures finally led the Supreme Court to change its mind and treat a constitutional attack on malaportionment as a justiciable controversy, some kinds of legislative inaction may induce courts to make common law reforms that might not otherwise have been made. Legislative action, for instance, may be stymied by the fact that the interest to be benefited by the reform — as in the case of the injured victim of a tort — is underrepresented before the legislature. It may be an unorganized interest, opposed by an organized interest that stands to lose from the reform. Or the relevant facts may be well enough known to (or available to) courts, so that legislative superiority in fact-gathering is immaterial. Or no complex, regulatory solution may be needed — merely a right of action in court.

Such factors are pertinent to the court's intelligent choice — along with other facts about the characteristics and

167. International News Service v. Associated Press, 248 U.S. 215, 262-267 (1918).

operations of state legislators, which are sometimes cited in order to question whether legislators are better representatives of the public interest than members of the typical state supreme court are.[168]

Thus, a reasonable approach to the issue of court versus legislature in law reform seems to be not to favor one or the other for all law reforms, but to choose one or the other depending on its appropriateness for the particular reform being considered.[169]

Assuming the court has chosen judicial reform, this doesn't mean the legislature is barred from acting on the subject thereafter. In the tort cases I have mentioned, for instance, there were times when a legislature struck back by modifying the judicial reform. Thus when the Supreme Court of Wisconsin overruled its precedents supporting municipal immunity from tort liability, the legislature passed a statute making municipalities liable in tort but establishing certain exceptions and fixing a $25,000 maximum liability.[170]

So the legislature can have the last word when it comes to modifying a common law doctrine. It also has the last word when it modifies a judicial interpretation of the meaning of a statute. This was true, for instance, when the Supreme Court's ruling that the Sherman antitrust law applied to insurance transactions across state lines was followed by the McCarran Act renouncing federal antitrust controls and consenting to state regulation of the insurance industry.[171] Where the Court has the last word is in a ruling that a statute is unconstitutional. To change that ruling, if the Court can't be persuaded to change its mind, the Constitution itself

168. See Peck, "The Role of Courts and Legislatures in the Reform of Tort Law," 48 Minn. L. Rev. 265, 270-285 (1963).

169. Id. at 296-312.

170. See Holytz v. City of Milwaukee, 17 Wis. 2d 26, 115 N.W.2d 618 (1962), and Wis. Laws 1963, c. 198 (Wis. Stat. §895.43 (1969)). See also the legislative responses in Minnesota, Illinois, New Jersey, and California, described in Peck, supra note 168 at 287-289.

171. See United States v. South-Eastern Underwriters Assn., 322 U.S. 533 (1944), and 59 Stat. 33 (1945), 15 U.S.C. §§1011-1015 (1958). See also Prudential Ins. Co. v. Benjamin, 328 U.S. 408 (1946).

would have to be amended. This happened, for example, when the Supreme Court's invalidation of the federal income tax law[172] was followed by the Sixteenth Amendment, and invalidation of the federal provision for 18-year-olds' voting in state elections[173] was followed by the Twenty-sixth Amendment.

However, even on constitutional issues there may be some indirect and preventive weapons available to the legislature. One is control over court jurisdiction. Thus, you will recall that Article III of the Constitution, after specifying the Supreme Court's original jurisdiction, says that in other cases the Supreme Court shall have appellate jurisdiction "with such exceptions and under such regulations as the Congress shall make." This congressional control over Supreme Court appellate jurisdiction was invoked by Senator Jenner in a bill he introduced after some Supreme Court decisions in 1956 and 1957. The decisions, which he considered too liberal, dealt with the power of congressional investigating committees, federal and state programs aimed at subversive activities, and state requirements for admission to the bar. His bill would have deprived the Supreme Court thereafter of appellate jurisdiction in these classes of cases. The precedent that he thought supported the bill was the post-Civil War case of Ex parte McCardle.[174] Here Congress, in order to prevent Supreme Court determination of the constitutionality of certain Reconstruction legislation, had passed a law withdrawing from the Court's appellate jurisdiction certain kinds of habeas corpus cases — of which McCardle's case was one. The case had already been argued before the Supreme Court and was awaiting decision at the time the law was adopted. Still, the Supreme Court unanimously decided that the law had validly deprived it of the authority to decide the case.

However, the decision doesn't necessarily mean that there are no limits upon this weapon of Congress. In the first place,

172. Pollock v. Farmers' Loan and Trust Co., 157 U.S. 429 (1895); rehearing, 158 U.S. 601 (1895).
173. Oregon v. Mitchell, 400 U.S. 112 (1970).
174. 74 U.S. (7 Wall.) 506 (1868).

the Court in the McCardle case had not sanctioned a major impairment of its power to deal with the issue in the case. This is because other statutes permitted the Supreme Court to consider habeas corpus petitions in the exercise of its *original* jurisdiction, and in the following year it held that it had jurisdiction to grant habeas corpus in such an original suit, raising the same issue of constitutionality of the Reconstruction legislation.[175] Secondly, remember that Article III vests in the Supreme Court, and in such inferior federal courts as Congress may establish, the federal judicial power — a power which extends to "all cases in law and equity, arising under" the Constitution, laws, and treaties; and remember further that the very concept of an effective Supreme Court under our constitutional plan seems to imply a court power to keep the Congress as well as the executive and the states within their prescribed powers. These considerations plausibly lead to a narrow reading of the power given to Congress over the Court's appellate jurisdiction. As Professor Henry M. Hart has put it, the exceptions that Congress may make to the Court's appellate jurisdiction must not be such as would "destroy the essential role of the Supreme Court in the constitutional plan."[176] The Constitution, in other words, is not to be read as authorizing its own destruction.

Besides Congressional regulation of Supreme Court appellate jurisdiction, there is another weapon that Congress might try to use — but again, I think, not a potent one. I refer to congressional control over the size of the Supreme Court (the Constitution being silent on the number of justices). The Court originally had six justices, and at various times had seven and ten, but has had nine since 1869. President Roosevelt's famous "court-packing" plan of 1937 (call it

175. Ex parte Yerger, 75 U.S. (8 Wall.) 85 (1869). There was no decision rendered on the constitutional issue, because Yerger had been released from the challenged military custody, thus making the case "moot," i.e., presenting a dead issue.

176. Hart, "The Power of Congress to Limit the Jurisdiction of Federal Courts," 66 Harv. L. Rev. 1362, 1365 (1953). See also Berger, Congress v. The Supreme Court 285-296 (1969).

"court enlargement" if you would have favored the plan)
differed from the earlier legislation changing the size of the
court because it was more clearly aimed at overcoming
existing attitudes of the Court on constitutional issues. The
reasons initially given were largely in terms of the volume of
work, but these reasons were soon demolished by a letter
from Chief Justice Hughes and Justices Van de Vanter and
Brandeis to the chairman of the Senate Judiciary Committee.
The real reasons seemed to most lawyers — even some New
Dealers — to make the proposed legislation violative of the
spirit if not the letter of the Constitution. It seemed contrary
to the spirit of constitutional provisions safeguarding judicial
independence (life tenure; no diminution of pay while in
office). This undoubtedly contributed to the defeat of the
bill.[177]

5. TECHNIQUES: A SUMMARY OUTLINE

In the preceding sections on the functions and functioning
of the various agencies of the law, I have already referred, in
an incomplete way, to the distinctive techniques by which
their respective functions are carried out. Here is a summary
roundup of these techniques.[178]

(a) *Techniques associated with the legislature are:*
(1) Setting standards of conduct by statute, which may be
accompanied by fixing of one or more sanctions for
violation — though sometimes the standards are announced without penalty, and sometimes they are
requirements in a government contract, or standards of
eligibility for subsidy or other government benefit.
(2) Providing machinery and rules pursuant to which such
standards and sanctions can be set.

177. Basic materials in the debate on the plan will be found in Hearings on S.
1392 Before the Senate Comm. On the Judiciary, 75th Cong., 1st Sess. (1937); S.
Rep. No. 711, 75th Cong., 1st Sess. (1937).
178. See generally Summers, "The Technique Element in Law," 59 Calif. L.
Rev. 733 (1971).

(3) Investigating to determine the need for new or amending legislation.

(4) Taxing and spending, and otherwise providing for distribution of benefits — which may be widely distributed like public health, education, highways, etc. or more narrowly as in the case of welfare payments and subsidies to particular industries.

(5) Providing machinery and rules pursuant to which people may make — subject to certain controls — their own private arrangements for association, self-regulation, and dispute-settling (such as rules with respect to making wills, forming corporations and unions, and entering into contractual arrangements on commercial and noncommercial matters, including agreements to arbitrate disputes).

(b) *Techniques associated with executive and administrative agencies are:*

(1) Setting standards of conduct and eligibility as in (a)(1) above — though sanctions or penalties are not normally prescribed by the agencies. (The normal pattern is for the legislature to prescribe the sanctions, with the agency going to court to have them imposed. But there are some instances, where the sanction is noncriminal, of legislative authorization for agency prescription and even for agency imposition.)

(2) Carrying on investigations, inspections, and negotiations, and making informal decisions — all aimed principally at administering statutory or agency standards, obtaining compliance with standards, and obtaining information relevant to establishment and modification of standards.

(3) Using more formal efforts to enforce compliance with standards of conduct and eligibility, through (in some of these situations, after administrative hearing) administrative cease-and-desist orders, granting and revocation of licenses, granting and revocation of subsidies and other financial benefits, publicizing derelictions, seizing offending articles like adulterated or misbranded food

and drugs, and engaging in various criminal enforcement activities — including surveillance, arrest, search and seizure, administering prison regulations, and probation and parole supervision.

(4) Providing procedural rules, interpretations, statements of agency organization and the like, that will assist people in dealing with the agency and meeting its requirements.

(c) *Techniques associated with courts are:*

(1) The ordering of punishment (i.e., imprisonment and/ or fine) and semipunishment (such as the award of "punitive damages" in addition to compensatory damages in a noncriminal suit, or civil monetary penalties, or forfeitures of goods).

(2) Ordering actual performance of a named obligation (e.g., the obligation to convey a piece of real estate you had agreed to convey and now refuse to convey) or restraining the performance of a named activity (e.g., your continued selling of certain unregistered securities in violation of a statute, or an official's continued enforcement of a statute).

(3) Ordering payment of compensation for a legal injury. This is typically the well-known remedy of "damages" to one suffering some legal injury to his personal or property rights. The compensation may take different forms, such as the compelled return of an item of property, the value of plaintiff's expenditures in labor, goods, or services that he made in reliance on defendant's promise, or an amount that would put plaintiff in as good a position as he would have been in if defendant hadn't committed the wrong against him.

(4) In arriving at its decision, the trial court uses an adversary hearing procedure — which is not used by the legislature nor, for some of their activities, by the agencies. However, there are also some atypical activities of courts that may involve no adversary hearings, such as naturalizing aliens, supervising the bankruptcy referee, establishing court rules of procedure, establish-

ing and supervising administration of requirements concerning membership in the bar of the court, and handling uncontested proceedings such as often occur, e.g., in the field of probate and divorce.

CHAPTER 2

The Illustrative Case
(Initial Aspects)

Having tried to give you, however sketchily, an overview of the legal system as a whole, I propose now to treat some aspects of it in greater detail. I shall do this by presenting a specific court case, and supplementing some features of it with background notes, in this and succeeding chapters.

The case was brought in a federal district court of South Carolina in 1962. The two women plaintiffs each filed the same "complaint." Reproduced below is the text of one of the complaints and the defendant's "motion to dismiss." The district court's order and opinion granting the motion to dismiss are also reproduced, together with the Fourth Circuit Court of Appeals opinion supporting reversal of the district court, and a small portion of the lawyers' briefs on appeal.

A. HOW IT ALL HAPPENED

1. *THE COMPLAINT*

Patricia A. Nappier, Plaintiff	)
vs.	)
	)
Jefferson Standard Life Insurance Company	) COMPLAINT
and Jefferson Standard Broadcasting Co.,	)
a subsidiary of Jefferson Standard Life	)
Insurance Co., Defendants	)

The plaintiff complaining of the defendants herein alleges:

1. That the plaintiff is a resident of the County of Spartanburg, State of South Carolina.

2. That the defendant, Jefferson Standard Life Insurance Company is a foreign corporation organized and existing under and by virtue of the laws of one of the States of the United States other than the State of South Carolina, is licensed to do and was at the times hereinafter alleged doing

business in the State of South Carolina; that the defendant
Jefferson Standard Broadcasting Company is a corporation
duly chartered under the laws of the State of North Carolina,
is a subsidiary of Jefferson Standard Life Insurance Company, and, the defendants operate television station WBTW at
Florence, South Carolina. That, on information and belief,
the defendant, Jefferson Standard Life Insurance Company
owns 1326 shares of stock of Jefferson Standard Broadcasting Company, there being only 4 other outstanding shares,
and that the defendant, Jefferson Standard Broadcasting
Company is under the direct control and supervision of the
Jefferson Standard Life Insurance Company, that both
corporations have common officers and directors and Jefferson Standard Life Insurance Company formulates and estab-
lishes the policies for the operation of Jefferson Standard
Broadcasting Company and television station WBTW. This
action is within the jurisdiction of this Court as there is a
diversity of citizenship between the plaintiff and the defendants and the amount in controversy exceeds Ten Thousand
($10,000) Dollars, exclusive of costs and interest.

3. That the plaintiff at the times hereinafter alleged and
for several years prior thereto was employed by the Dental
Division of the South Carolina Department of Health and
she, together with another young lady with whom she
constantly travelled throughout the state and particularly
throughout the area served by WBTW, put on dental health
demonstrations in the public schools of this state. That the
plaintiff and her co-worker were the only individuals in the
state engaged in this type of work, which consisted primarily
of putting on puppet demonstrations using a puppet which
was commonly referred to as "Little Jack," and that because
of their work this plaintiff and her co-worker were known
throughout the state as "The Little Jack Girls." To be used in
their work, the South Carolina Department of Health
furnished plaintiff and her co-worker a station wagon on
which was conspicuously inscribed on both sides "Little
Jack, Dental Division, South Carolina State Department of
Health."

4. That on November 27, 1961, this plaintiff together with her co-worker was in Kingstree, South Carolina, for the purpose of putting on their Little Jack Show in the public schools of Williamsburg County.

5. That this plaintiff who is a young, unmarried lady, together with her co-worker, had retired for the night on November 27, 1961, in a quiet, secluded motel at Kingstree, when during the early morning hours on November 28, 1961, a man broke into the quarters which plaintiff and her co-worker were occupying and raped each of them; that her attacker stole the said station wagon which was parked near the quarters she was occupying and fled.

6. That some time during the daylight hours on November 28, 1961, the subject station wagon was found abandoned in or near the City of Florence, and the defendants through their agents or servants, while acting within the scope and course of their employment, took pictures of the abandoned station wagon and televised the same on the news broadcast on Station WBTW at 6:30 P.M., and later that same day on the 11 P.M. telecast. That at both telecasts the words "Little Jack, Dental Division State Board of Health" were clearly visible on each side of the vehicle, both sides having been shown on the telecast pictures; the news announcer for the defendants identified the station wagon as that being used by the two young women who had been ravished at Kingstree, and further, the license number of the station wagon was shown in at least one of these pictures; all of which was done notwithstanding the fact that the defendants knew or reasonably should have known that the publication of these pictures of the station wagon would identify the rape victims.

7. That Sec. 16-81, Code of Laws of South Carolina, 1962, prohibits the publishing of the name of any female upon whom the crime of rape or assault with intent to ravish has been committed or alleged to have been committed in any type or form of publication.

8. That notwithstanding the above statute and without the permission or consent of the court or this plaintiff, the defendants willfully and deliberately published the pictures of the station wagon which plaintiff used in her work which clearly and positively identified this plaintiff as one of the

young ladies upon whom this horrible crime was perpetrated.

9. That many and various individuals saw either or both of these telecasts as the television station operated by these defendants has a vast and broad coverage throughout a large portion of South Carolina; that by reason of the exhibition and showing of plaintiff's vehicle it became common talk of people in South Carolina that plaintiff was one of the young ladies who was subjected to the rapist and that because of the showing of said pictures many of her friends and people generally know about the horrible episode that she experienced and by which she will be identified during her entire lifetime.

10. That the publication by the defendants was done willfully, wantonly and in utter disregard of the statute laws of this state and without regard or concern of the right of privacy of this plaintiff.

11. That as a result and in consequence of the foregoing publications, this plaintiff has been demoralized, embarrassed, has suffered great mental pain, humiliation, mortification, has become highly nervous and has been unable to perform her regular employment, all to her damage in the sum of One Hundred Seventy Five Thousand ($175,000) Dollars, actual and punitive damages.

WHEREFORE, plaintiff demands judgment against the defendants in the sum of One Hundred Seventy Five Thousand ($175,000) Dollars, actual and punitive damages, together with the costs of this action and further demands a jury trial in the cause above set forth.

2. THE MOTION TO DISMISS

Patricia A. Nappier, Plaintiff	)
vs.	)
	)
Jefferson Standard Life Insurance Company	) MOTION TO
and Jefferson Standard Broadcasting Co.,	) DISMISS
a subsidiary of Jefferson Standard Life	)
Insurance Co., Defendants	)

The defendant, Jefferson Standard Broadcasting Company, moves the Court as follows:

1. For a dismissal of the within action upon the ground that the complaint fails to state a claim against this defendant upon which relief can be granted.

> *McEachin, Townsend & Zeigler,*
> Attorneys for Defendant,
> Jefferson Standard Broadcast-
> ing Company.

Florence, S.C.
June 4, 1962

[Note: Each defendant upon due notice made the above motion in both cases.]

3. *DISTRICT COURT OPINION*

The text of the federal district court's opinion (reproduced below) is taken from the series of case reports known as *Federal Supplement*, which is confined to cases in the federal district courts. If you turn now to look at the reproduced opinion, what I am about to say will be clearer to you. The private publisher of these reports (West Publishing Co.) has added, after the identifying caption of the case and before the opinion itself, a short summary of the decision, plus six numbered sentences digesting six aspects of the opinion and fitted under four topics (Torts, Names, Statutes, and Tele-communications). The six numbers also appear in brackets before the paragraphs of the opinion from which the six numbered sentences are derived.

The four topics are listed together with a "key number" for each; for instance, the "Statutes" topic is listed with the number 190. The explanation of the numbering is this: If you look under the "Statutes" topic of West's *American Digest System*, you will find a breakdown of subtopics, of which one is "general rules of construction." Under that, a further subtopic is "meaning of language"; and of the 16 subtopics under that (covering key numbers 188 to 203), number 190 is listed as "existence of ambiguity." So West's editors decided that one sentiment in the opinion (which they summarized as "Court must apply the plain wording of an unambiguous statute regardless of how severe the consequences may be") should be fitted under their *Digest* topic "Statutes," keynote number 190. A future researcher interested in examining all court opinions that talk about the existence or nonexistence of ambiguity will find this sentiment from the Nappier case plus its citation listed among hundreds of others under "Statutes," keynote number 190 in the *American Digest System.*

Because the case was decided in 1963 in the United States District Court for the Eastern District of South Carolina, and the opinion text begins on page 174 of volume 213 of the *Federal Supplement*, the citation is: Nappier v. Jefferson Standard Life Insurance Co., 213 F. Supp. 174 (E.D.S.C. 1963). (While the decision deals with complaints by two separate plaintiffs, and each complaint lists two different defendants, it is common to use only the first plaintiff and defendant in the name of the case.)

Patricia A. NAPPIER, Plaintiff,

v.

JEFFERSON STANDARD LIFE INSURANCE COMPANY
and Jefferson Standard Broadcasting Company,
a subsidiary of Jefferson Standard Life
Insurance Company, Defendants.

S. Maxine GUNTER, Plaintiff,

v.

JEFFERSON STANDARD LIFE INSURANCE COMPANY
and Jefferson Standard Broadcasting Company,
a subsidiary of Jefferson Standard Life
Insurance Company, Defendants.

Civ. A. No. AC/911, AC/910

United States District Court
E.D. South Carolina,
Florence Division.
Jan. 23, 1963.

Actions against owners of television station for violation of state statute prohibiting publication of name of any woman who has been victim of an assault with intent to ravish or victim of rape, and for violation of right of privacy. The District Court, Wyche, J., held that defendants who were owners of television station which showed on newscasts the picture of state motor vehicle which had inscribed on the side thereof in part the name under which plaintiffs produced a show for school children and identified the station wagon as the one being used by two young women who had been ravished, did not violate South Carolina statute.

Actions dismissed.

1. Torts ➙ 8
Statute prohibiting the publication of the name of any woman or child upon whom crime of rape or assault with intent to ravish has been committed is penal and must be strictly construed in a civil as well as a criminal case, and one seeking relief thereunder must bring his case squarely within the statute affording the penalty or relief. Code S.C. 1962, §16-81.

2. Names ➙ 2
A person's "name" consists of one or more Christian or given names and one surname.
See publication Words and Phrases for other judicial constructions and definitions.

3. Statutes ➙ 190
Court must apply the plain wording of an unambiguous statute regardless of how severe the consequences may be.

4. Torts ➙ 8
South Carolina statute prohibiting publication of name of any woman or child upon whom crime of rape or an assault with intent to ravish has been committed does not prohibit

publication of "stage names" or "assumed names" of the victims of an incident of rape or assault. Code S.C. 1962, § 16-81.

5. Telecommunications → 439
Defendants, who were owners of television station which showed on newscasts the picture of state motor vehicle which had inscribed on side thereof in part the name under which plaintiffs produced a show for school children and identified station wagon as one being used by two young women who had been ravished, did not violate South Carolina statute, prohibiting publication of name of any woman who has been victim of rape or an assault with intent to ravish. Code S.C. 1962, § 16-81.

6. Telecommunications → 439
Owners of television station, which showed on newscasts a picture of state vehicle which was used by plaintiffs in traveling about the state and which had inscribed on the side thereof in part the name under which plaintiffs produced a show for school children and stated that station wagon was being used by two young women who had been ravished, did not sufficiently identify plaintiffs to give rise to cause of action for violation of their right of privacy.

Yancey A. McLeod, McLeod & Singletary, Harry M. Lightsey, Jr., Columbia, S.C., for plaintiffs.
P. H. McEachin, McEachin, Townsend & Zeigler, Florence, S.C., for defendants Jefferson Standard Life Insurance Co. and Jefferson Standard Broadcasting Co.

WYCHE, District Judge.
The above cases are before me upon motion of the defendants to dismiss upon the ground that the complaints do not allege a claim upon which relief can be granted.
The plaintiffs were in 1961, employed by the State of South Carolina as puppeteers, producing a show known as "Little Jack" which demonstrated health facts to the school children of the State. The plaintiffs were known throughout the State as "The Little Jack Girls" and traveled about the

State in a station-wagon on the side of which was conspicuously inscribed "Little Jack, Dental Division, South Carolina
State Department of Health." The defendants were and are
owners and operators of Television Station WBTW in
Florence, South Carolina. In November, 1961, the plaintiffs
were the victims of an assault while on a trip to Kingstree,
South Carolina, their attacker stealing the station-wagon
described above to make his escape. On the following day the
station-wagon was found abandoned in Florence, South
Carolina. That night on both its 6:30 P.M. and 11:00 P.M.
newscasts, the defendants broadcast pictures of the station-
wagon on which the words "Little Jack, Dental Division,
State Board of Health" together with the license number of
the vehicle, were visible to the viewers of the television
program. The announcer on these newscasts identified the
station-wagon as the one being used by the two girls who had
been raped in Kingstree.

Plaintiffs thereafter commenced these actions seeking
damages for their mental anguish and suffering which had
resulted from their alleged identification as the rape victims.
These actions seek the recovery of damages because of the
humiliation, mental pain, embarrassment and the subsequent
inability of the plaintiffs to continue their work as the result
of this television broadcast.

These actions are based upon the theory that the defendants have committed a tort through the violation of a South
Carolina Statute (§16-81, Code of Laws of South Carolina,
1962), and violated the right of privacy of the plaintiffs. The
defendants contend that the allegations of the complaints are
not sufficient to state a cause of action under Section 16-81
and the common law of privacy in South Carolina, or under
either of them, and that the complaints should be dismissed.

Section 16-81, Code of Laws of South Carolina, 1962,
provides: "Misdemeanor to publish name of person raped,
etc. Whoever publishes or causes to be published the name of
any woman, maid or woman child upon whom the crime of
rape or an assault with intent to ravish has been committed
or alleged to have been committed in this State in any

newspaper, magazine or other publication shall be deemed guilty of a misdemeanor and, upon conviction thereof, shall be punished by a fine of not more than one thousand dollars or imprisonment of not more than three years. But the provisions of this section shall not apply to publications made by order of court."

[1] This statute is penal and must therefore be strictly construed in a civil as well as a criminal case. One who seeks relief thereunder must bring his case squarely within the provisions of the statute affording the penalty or relief. State v. Lewis, et al., 141 S.C. 207, 139 S.E. 386; Darlington Theatres, Inc. v. Coker, Sheriff, 190 S.C. 282, 2 S.E.2d 782; State ex rel. Moody v. Stem, et al., 213 S.C. 465, 50 S.E.2d 175; Independence Ins. Co. v. Independent Life and Acc. Ins. Co., 218 S.C. 22, 61 S.E.2d 399; State ex rel. v. Nat. Linen Service Corp., 225 S.C. 232, 81 S.E.2d 342.

Publication of *the name* "of any woman, maid or woman child upon whom the crime of rape or an assault with intent to ravish has been committed" constitutes a violation of this statute.

[2] The word "name" as set forth in the statute is not ambiguous, does not bear two or more constructions, and is not of such doubtful or obscure meaning that reasonable minds may disagree as to its meaning. A person's "name" consists of one or more Christian or given names and one surname or family name. Therefore, when the word "name" as set forth in the statute is taken in its plain, ordinary and usual sense, it means that which is the given and family name of a woman.

[3] The statute is effective for the purpose which is plainly expressed therein, namely, to prevent publication of *the name* of a victim of rape or assault as referred to therein. The scope of the statute, without construction of the word "name" to mean identification also, is more limited than it would be if the word "name" as set forth therein were construed and enlarged to mean identification. However, it is not my function to define the scope of an unambiguous word or statute, but to apply the plain wording of a statute as it is

written, since the statute speaks for itself. I must adopt the plain meaning of a statute, however severe the consequences. Jay v. Boyd, 351 U.S. 345, 76 S. Ct. 919, 100 L. Ed. 1242.

[4] The plaintiffs allege in their complaints that they were known as "The Little Jack Girls," and contend that they have been named by the alleged publications of the defendants. Section 16-81 does not prohibit the publication of "stage names" or "assumed names" of the victims of an incident of rape or assault, it only prohibits publication of *the name*, which in plain, ordinary and usual terms means, as to these plaintiffs the name of "Maxine Gunter and Patricia Nappier."

[5] There is no allegation in the complaints that the "stage" or "assumed" names "The Little Jack Girls" were published. The plaintiffs simply allege that a station-wagon on which the words "Little Jack, Dental Division, State Board of Health" was shown, with the statement that the station-wagon was identified as being used by the two young women who had been ravished. The plaintiffs do not allege in their complaints that they have the "assumed" name of "Little Jack," which words they allege appeared on the side of the station-wagon.

It is my opinion that the defendants have not violated the South Carolina Statute, Section 16-81, Code of Laws of South Carolina, 1962.

[6] It is also my opinion that the defendants have not identified the plaintiffs sufficiently in the allegations of the complaint to allege a cause of action for damages for the violation of their right of privacy.

It is, therefore, ordered, that the motion to dismiss in each of the above entitled cases be and the same is hereby granted.

4. *COURT OF APPEALS OPINION*

The court of appeals majority and dissenting opinions are reproduced below exactly as they appear in the *Federal Reporter* system beginning at 322 F.2d 502 (4th Cir. 1963). The Fourth Circuit embraces, in addition to South Carolina, the states of Maryland, West Virginia, Virginia, and North

Carolina. The summary and key-number paragraphs added by the publisher in the *Federal Reporter* are here omitted, as is the court's statement of facts.

ALBERT V. BRYAN, Circuit Judge.

... The motion argued that the actual name of neither girl — as is true — was mentioned in the pictures or narrative, that the report was a matter of public interest and record, and so no cause of action for breach of privacy could be rested either upon the statute or on the common law. We disagree. "Name", we hold in the context of this case, is to be read in the statute as the equivalent of "identity". Since the broadcast, as pleaded, sufficiently identified the victims other than by name, it transgressed the statute and trespassed on the plaintiffs' privilege of privacy.

The meaning of the term "name" cannot be given the narrow import ascribed it by Standard without impairing the purpose of the statute. Aside from the personal protection of the woman involved, the object of this law, concededly, is to encourage a free report of the crime by the victim. Cf. State v. Evjue, 253 Wis. 146, 33 N.W.2d 305, 13 A.L.R.2d 1201 (1948). Fear of publicity might deter her from notifying the police. Thus the public interest is advanced by the statute: the crime is investigated promptly and the injured person is shielded.

These aims could not be fully achieved if only disclosure of one's proper name was forbidden. Publication of a description of the woman by identifying her through circumstances would in effect name her. After all, a name is but a designation, and a description is frequently a more positive identification than a name. State ex rel Lane v. Corneli, 347 Mo. 932, 149 S.W.2d 815 (1941). We recognize faces, or know persons by reputation, when we do not know them by name. Cf. Peck v. Tribune Co. 214 U.S. 185, 29 S. Ct. 554, 53 L. Ed. 960 (1909). An episode can be more revealing than a family name, a sobriquet than a surname.

In South Carolina the penal aspect of the statute does not require an interpretation so rigid as to strip its wording of its plain connotation. Carolina Amusement Co. v. Martin, 236

S.C. 558, 115 S.E.2d 273 (1960), cert. denied, 367 U.S. 904, 81 S. Ct. 1914, 6 L. Ed. 2d 1248 (1961); State v. Firemen's Ins. Co., 164 S.C. 313, 162 S.E. 334 (1931). This is certainly sound construction when, as here, the statute is only employed to provide civil redress. McKenzie v. Peoples Baking Co., 205 S.C. 149, 31 S.E.2d 154 (1944).

The Legislature could, of course, have used "identity" instead of "name", or put both in the statute, as do the laws of other states. E.g. Wisconsin Statutes of 1945, § 348.412, as quoted in the Evjue case, supra, 253 Wis. 146, 33 N.W.2d 305; Florida Statutes, § 794.03; Georgia Code, § 26-2105. But "name" alone in the environment of the policy evidenced by the South Carolina statute is sufficient to comprehend "identity". That a description serves the purpose of a name is amply demonstrated in defamation cases. A libelee is nonetheless libeled though his name be not mentioned. Peck v. Tribune Co., supra, 214 U.S. 185, 29 S. Ct. 554, 53 L. Ed. 960 (1909); Nash v. Sharper, 229 S.C. 451, 93 S.E.2d 457, 459 (1956); Prosser, Torts 583 (1955).

No support for Standard's position is found in decisions upon a statute prohibiting the unauthorized use of a personal name, portrait or picture in advertising. E.g.: Gardella v. Log Cabin Products Co., 89 F.2d 891 (2 Cir., 1937); Levey v. Warner Bros. Pictures, Inc., 57 F. Supp. 40 (S.D.N.Y. 1944). For advertising, only the name, pseudonym or picture of the person — usually because of his prominence — is significant. Any other description is of no value. Consequently, the object of the law is not impinged unless the publication embodies the name, portrait or picture. That is not so in the statute now in review.

To repeat, we think the allegations of the complaints adequately demonstrate that the television in effect divulged the names of the two women. Thus each states a cause of action for intrusion upon privacy. South Carolina recognizes the right of privacy and affords a cause of action for an infringement. In Meetze v. Associated Press, 230 S.C. 330, 95 S.E.2d 606, 608, 609 (1956), the Court said:

"... The following has been suggested as a fairly comprehensive definition of what constitutes an actionable invasion of the right of privacy: 'The unwarranted appropriation or exploitation of one's personality, the publicizing of one's private affairs with which the public has no legitimate concern, or the wrongful intrusion into one's private activities, in such manner as to outrage or cause mental suffering, shame, or humiliation to a person of ordinary sensibilities.' . . .

" 'The right of privacy is one which was not definitely recognized by the law until comparatively recent times. But we find ourselves in agreement with a number of authorities to the effect that the violation of such a right is under certain circumstances a tort which would entitle the injured person to recover damages.' "

While the plaintiffs have premised their suits, first, upon the breach of the statute and, second, upon the common law, there is no necessity to determine whether an action may be pitched solely on the statute, for it is clear the plaintiffs may sue under the common law as fortified by the statute.

Standard counters that the incident was a matter of public concern and record and so is exempted from the rule of privacy. Jenkins v. Dell Publishing Co., 251 F.2d 447 (3 Cir.), cert. denied, 357 U.S. 921, 78 S. Ct. 1362, 2 L. Ed. 2d 1365 (1958); Frith v. Associated Press, 176 F. Supp. 671, 674 (E.D.S.C. 1959); Meetze v. Associated Press, supra, 230 S.C. 330, 95 S.E.2d 606, 609 (1956); Prosser, Torts 643-44 (1955). The ready replication is that the statute states an exception to the exemption. No matter the news value, South Carolina has unequivocally declared the identity of the injured person shall not be made known in press or broadcast. Cf. State v. Evjue, supra, 253 Wis. 146, 33 N.W.2d 305. No constitutional infringement has been suggested. Indeed, Standard conceded in oral argument that if the broadcast did in fact and in law "name" the plaintiffs, then they had a right of action.

Dismissal of the complaints was error and the order must

be set aside, the actions remanded for trial. Whether or not the defendants did in fact "name" the plaintiffs will then be an issue to be settled by the court or jury. On this point we intimate no view.

Reversed and remanded.

BARKSDALE, District Judge (dissenting).

With due deference to the views of the majority so ably expressed in Judge Bryan's opinion, I find myself unable to agree with the majority opinion, and therefore I dissent.

Although no information as to the legislative history of the South Carolina statute here involved (Section 16-81, Code of Laws of South Carolina 1962) appears in the record, I am willing to concede that the apparent objects of the Act were the "personal protection of the woman involved," and "to encourage a free report of the crime by the victim". But I cannot agree that in a statutory inhibition of publication of the "name of the victim", "name" is equivalent to "identity": "identity" is a much broader term than "name". If the South Carolina Legislature had intended by its statute to proscribe the publication of information from which "identity" could be determined, it could quite readily have said so, as does the Wisconsin statute.

The common law right of privacy exists in South Carolina, and an unwarranted invasion of this right is tortious and actionable, but it is not an absolute right, and where the alleged invasion of privacy is the publication of matter of public concern and record, it is not tortious nor actionable. Meetze v. Associated Press, 230 S.C. 330, 95 S.E.2d 606.

The majority take the view that "the plaintiffs may sue under the common law as fortified by the statute". It seems clear to me that plaintiffs have no cause of action at common law, because the published matter came within the well recognized exceptions to the right of privacy, and that even a liberal construction does not justify the court in equating "name" with "identity".

I would affirm the judgment of the District Court.

5. *A GLIMPSE AT THE LAWYERS' BRIEFS; APPELLATE ADVOCACY*

I think you should have some idea of the form in which lawyers' written arguments are cast. While it would take too much space to reprint any substantial portion of the briefs, I am reproducing below the index pages of the appellees' brief, followed by some short excerpts from the argumentation on a particular point.

INDEX

TABLE OF CASES

[Omitted here are 38 additional cases listed alphabetically in
the brief.]

STATUTES

TEXT AND TREATISES

[Below is a portion of the argumentation from the appellees' brief, Point One, Part E.]

E. NEW YORK RIGHT OF PRIVACY STATUTE AND RELATED CASES

The state of New York has a right of privacy statute, the pertinent provisions of which are as follows:

"New York Civil Rights Law (Consol. Laws c. 6) Article 5 — Right of Privacy.

"Section 50: A person, firm or corporation that uses for advertising purposes, or for the purposes of trade, the name, portrait or picture of any living person without having first obtained the written consent of such person, or if a minor, of his or her parent or guardian, is guilty of a misdemeanor.

"Section 51: Any person whose name, portrait or picture is used within this state for advertising purposes or for the purposes of trade without the written consent first obtained as above provided may maintain an equitable action in the Supreme Court of this state against the person, firm or corporation so using his name, portrait or picture, to prevent and restrain the use thereof; and may also sue and recover damages for any injuries sustained by reason of such use and if the defendant shall have knowingly used such person's name, portrait or picture in such a manner as is forbidden or declared to be unlawful by the last section, the jury, in its discretion, may award exemplary damages. . . ."

The New York state courts, including the New York Supreme Court and the Federal courts in New York and other states, have had occasion to interpret, construe and apply this statute in a number of cases in the past. Inasmuch as this statute prohibits publication of a *name*, among other matters, and the statute is a right of privacy statute for the purposes therein expressed, the defendants submit that many of the decisions dealing with the word "name" as used in the New York statute are squarely in point with one of the vital issues involved in the cases at bar.

One of the earliest cases dealing with the word "name" in the New York statute is Pfaudler vs. Pfaudler Co., 114 Misc. 477, 186 N.Y.S. 725, affirmed without opinion at 197 App. Div. 921, 188 N.Y.S. 725, which case is directly in point with the cases at bar insofar as determining whether the defendants have violated Section 16-81 by publishing "the name" of the plaintiffs. The New York court said in the Pfaudler case:

"The cause of action alleged in the complaint rests upon the question whether or not the use of the plaintiff's surname by the defendants constitutes a violation of Civil Rights Law, Sections 50, 51, which prohibit a corporation from using *the name* (emphasis supplied) for advertising purposes or for purposes of trade." . . .

"The sole question is whether or not the Civil Rights Law prohibits the defendant from using the plaintiff's surname. The word 'name' as used in the statute, must mean a person's full name. It was evidently the purpose of the Legislature to prevent the use of the full name of a person, by which alone he could be identified. This identification is possible in the case of a portrait or picture, the use of which the statute also prohibits. It is not possible where only the surname of a person is employed. The word 'Pfaudler' does not identify the plaintiff as the person whose surname has been used, except to those persons who may know the origin of the company, and even then it is impossible to say whether the word refers to the plaintiff or to his brother Caspar, both of whom were at one time connected with the defendant's predecessor."

. . . Based on the authority of the Pfaudler case, it is submitted that a violation of Section 16-81 would not occur until the full name of a victim of rape or assault incident as contemplated by the statute, is published, and therefore, by no means has any such publication of the names of the plaintiffs in these cases occurred.

In 1954 in a proceeding entitled People on complaint of Maggio vs. Charles Scribner's Sons, et al, 205 Misc. 818, 130 N.Y.S. 2d 514, an action was brought by the state against a publisher and motion picture corporation under the afore-mentioned Section 50 on complaint that the character portrayed was that of the complainant and that he had been identified by the surname used in the publication. The book involved in this case was that entitled "From Here To Eternity," which had a wide and successful circulation. One of the characters portrayed is called "Angelo Maggio." The complainant, Joseph Anthony Maggio, was in the United States Army infantry regiment stationed in Hawaii during the period just before Pearl Harbor. The book and motion picture made therefrom tell a story about persons who were in the Army stationed in Hawaii during the period referred to. The court said that:

"To violate the statute, the name must be used in such a context as to unequivocally point to and identify the complainant. The use of the word 'name' in the statute, in association with the words 'portrait' or 'picture' clearly

indicates that this was intended. A portrait or picture leaves
no doubt as to the identity of the subject. Where a name is
used, it, like a portrait or picture, must upon meeting the eye
or ear, be unequivocally identified as that of the complainant. . ."

In the Maggio case the complaints were dismissed on the
ground that the complainant did not make out a case against
the defendants sufficient to constitute a violation of Section
50 of the Civil Rights Law. The court in that case strictly
interpreted and applied the New York statute with regard to
the word "name" as used therein. The court said that:
"Section 50, being penal in nature, must be strictly construed, (citing other New York cases) . . . and 'purely statutory offenses cannot be established by implication, . . .' " See
also Levy vs. Warner Bros. Pictures, 57 F. Supp. 40
(D.C.S.D.N.Y., 1944) which is a case very similar to the
Maggio case, involving Section 51 of the New York Statute. . . .

[The brief then invoked a 1936 federal district court case
in New York which had said the New York statute was
inapplicable to assumed names or stage names. (The plaintiff
Claire H. Davis had, under an assumed name of Cassandra,
become known as a psychic, palmist, etc., and her suit had
been against the makers of a movie containing a character
called Countess Casandra, a psychic presented in a derogatory
way.) The brief also argued that not even an assumed or stage
name had been used in the Nappier situation, since only
"Little Jack" rather than "Little Jack Girls" had appeared on
the televised picture of the station wagon.]

[Below is an excerpt from appellant's reply brief purporting to respond to the argument on the New York cases.]

III. The term "name" is not limited to the Christian and/or
family name of a person but extends to any common
designation by which he is known.

In seeking a restrictive interpretation of the word "name",
defendants rely upon several New York cases. Reflection will
show that these cases are not apposite. The State of New

York has never recognized the common-law right of privacy, Roberson v. Rochester Folding Box Company, 171 N.Y. 538, 64 N.E. 442, and the cases upon which plaintiffs rely are designed solely to prevent the exploitation of a person's "name, portrait or picture" for commercial purposes. New York Consolidated Laws, C. 6, Article 5. As such, it is obvious that they are more analogous in their implementation to the law of property than to the law of torts. The New York law is not intended to preclude undesired publicity, it is not designed to protect a person's right to be let alone. What is "naming" a person for the purpose of New York law and its intent to prohibit commercial rape of a person's property is a very different thing from what is "naming" a person under South Carolina law in such a manner as to deprive a person of privacy. . . .

———————

(a) Consider now, for a moment, the reply brief's answer to the New York cases. Would not a more effective answer to these cases have been possible? Could it not be said that the Pfaudler and Maggio cases decide merely this: The New York statutory "name" requirement is not satisfied by an advertiser's use of a surname only,[1] or by use of a name not identical in both Christian name and surname with the plaintiff's — because these uses would not produce the clear identification of the plaintiff that the statute was aimed at deterring. Hence these New York cases leave open the possibility that an advertiser's use of a description, other than an actual name, which does clearly identify the plaintiff (perhaps "The Little Tramp" in Charlie Chaplin's heyday, or "The Manassa Mauler" in Jack Dempsey's) would be covered by the New York statute.

In fact, there were some New York cases that seem to suggest precisely this. The federal court of appeals sitting in New York had said in 1937: "Having in mind the evident

———————

1. That *some* surnames can give a sufficient identification is shown by cases like that involving "Adrian," a famous dress designer. Adrian v. Unterman, 281 App. Div. 81, 118 N.Y.S.2d 121, aff'd, 306 N.Y. 770, 118 N.E.2d 477 (1952).

purpose of the statute, its application to a public or stage
name, as well as a private one, seems inevitable."[2] Hence the
court thought that Tess Gardella, a stage and radio performer
who had adopted the stage name "Aunt Jemima," would not
(because it was a stage name) be prevented from suing under
the New York statute. She had sued because of the use,
without her consent, of "Aunt Jemima" as the name of a
performer in the Quaker Oats massive radio advertising
campaign for Aunt Jemima pancake flour. (What made the
suit unsuccessful was the fact that Quaker Oats didn't need
the plaintiff's consent, since its rights to the use of the "Aunt
Jemima" name, on the product and for a performer, had
preceded plaintiff's use of the name.) This case was decided a
year later than, and by a higher court than, the Davis case
cited by the appellees' brief as precluding suits based on
assumed or stage names.

Another New York case that could have been cited, in
support of the proposition that clear identification through a
stage name or popular name is enough for a valid claim under
the statute, is one whose pertinence would rest on an *analogy*
to the stage name situation. The statute is equally operative
where a "portrait or picture" rather than a "name" is
involved. Hence if a case decides that the statute applies to a
clear identification through some means other than an actual
portrait or picture — such as impersonation of the plaintiff
through an actor in a movie — then why can't the case be
used as authority for saying that the statute applies to a clear
identification through some means other than an actual
name — such as a stage or popular name? The case I am
thinking of involved a wireless operator, John Binns, whose
distress signal when his ship collided with another in 1909
resulted in a dramatic sea rescue, making him famous as the
first man to use wireless in this way. The state court of
appeals thought the movie actor's impersonation could
qualify under the statute because the word "picture" was to
be construed as including "any representation" of the

2. Gardella v. Log Cabin Products Co., 89 F.2d 891 (2d Cir. 1937).

plaintiff.[3] Incidentally, there are limits to this approach. Can "representation" include a purely verbal portrayal in a novel — so as to support a plaintiff who claimed he had been the model for one of the major figures in John Hersey's *A Bell for Adano*, though neither his name nor his picture had been used? A New York court, with one dissenter, said no. It distinguished the Binns case by stressing that it had involved both the use of plaintiff's name and his representation through an actor.[4]

The arguments I have suggested in behalf of the plaintiff-appellants might have been used not only by them but also by the court of appeals majority which ruled in their favor. The actual argument by the court of appeals, you will recall, was rather curiously weak in the paragraph devoted to the New York cases. What it said was:

> No support for Standard's position is found in decisions upon a statute prohibiting the unauthorized use of a personal name, portrait or picture in advertising. E.g.: Gardella v. Log Cabin Products Co., 89 F.2d 891 (2 Cir. 1937); Levey v. Warner Bros. Pictures, Inc., 57 F. Supp. 40 (S.D.N.Y. 1944). For advertising, only the name, pseudonym or picture of the person — usually because of his prominence — is significant. Any other description is of no value. Consequently, the object of the law is not impinged unless the publication embodies the name, portrait or picture. That is not so in the statute now in review.

The court said this shortly after it had stressed the apparent South Carolina statutory policy to induce rape victims to report the crime by giving them broad protection against identification.

Thus the court's argument seems to amount to this: (1) the policy of the New York statute is different from South Carolina's "name of rape victim" statute: The New York legislature must have been confining itself to the kind of name which clearly identified the plaintiff. Any description

---

3. Binns v. Vitagraph Co., 210 N.Y. 51, 103 N.E. 1108 (1913).
4. Toscani v. Hersey, 271 App. Div. 445, 65 N.Y.S.2d 814 (1st Dept. 1946). For other decisions limiting the concept of "representation," see Molony v. Boy Comics Publ., Inc., 277 App. Div. 166, 98 N.Y.S.2d 119 (1st Dept 1950); Levey v. Warner Bros. Pictures, 57 F. Supp. 40 (S.D.N.Y. 1944).

in terms merely of "circumstances" or an "episode" wouldn't be appropriate or valuable for an advertiser; hence it would be outside the policy of the New York statute, but within the policy of the South Carolina statute aimed at inducing a woman to report the crime by assuring her against circumstantial, etc., forms of identification as well as against actual naming. (2) The policy of the two statutes being different, the New York cases are irrelevant.

I find the argument unnecessarily weak because the court need not have rested on this position. It could have supplemented the point with an "even if" argument: "Even if we are wrong in this view of a more limited policy under the New York statute, and hence the New York cases *are* relevant, *those cases are not unfavorable* to the plaintiff." Here the court could cite, for instance, the Gardella (Aunt Jemima) and Binns cases discussed above, as showing that publishing a popular name rather than an actual name could qualify for coverage under the statute. It could then have argued that the circumstances of publication (televised picture of "Little Jack" on the station wagon, coupled with the fact that the plaintiffs were widely known as the "Little Jack Girls") were the equivalent of publishing the popular name, "Little Jack Girls."

Alternatively, the court might have argued like this: (1) the cases under the New York statute (Gardella, etc.) are favorable as to the coverage of a popular name, and (2) they apply even more strongly (with "a fortiori" force, as lawyers like to put it) since they were decided under a statute whose policy in behalf of the plaintiff suggests a narrower coverage of "name" than under the South Carolina statute (here would follow the court's actual argument above on this).[5]

5.   The court of appeals' failure to capitalize on the favorable New York cases may have stemmed from an overly hasty assessment that they were unfavorable — since the two cases it referred to (Gardella and Levey, supra notes 2 and 4) had both ruled against the plaintiff. But as I have said above, there was an extraneous reason in the Gardella case why plaintiff Aunt Jemima didn't win. And in the Levey case, the reason why the ex-wife of George M. Cohan was unsuccessful in her attack on the portrayal of her in the movie biography of Cohan was that the movie actress did "not look nor act like plaintiff." The

The argumentative techniques I have pointed to — use of analogy, "even if," "a fortiori" — are quite common in lawyers' briefs. I think the "even if" gambit is the one most often encountered. It has the obvious advantage of "covering the waterfront" of possibilities, and hence playing it safe. One can't be sure which of some multiple assumptions or analyses may be accepted by the court, hence it is safer to argue the case on the basis of alternative assumptions or analyses. One limit on this approach is the possibility of weakening one's position in the eyes of the court by seeming to concede the possibility of error in one's first position. Still, unless the first position looks impregnable, lawyers have generally opted for presenting alternative positions.

(b) It may interest you to know that the plaintiffs, who lost in the trial court and won as appellants in the court of appeals, had in the latter court filed a 17-page printed brief, and a 5-page reply brief to the appellee broadcasting company's 45-page brief. The ultimate loser had filed a more elaborate (and more highly organized) brief — which merely points up the fact that the advocates' contribution does not necessarily determine the decision. Still, the advocates' contribution *can* be crucial. Federal Judge Medina observed early in his experience on the Second Circuit that he had to

admit that the cogency of a lawyer's argument, the skill and ingenuity with which he built up his propositions in logical sequence and the research he brought to bear upon his presentation of the case really did much more than merely clarify the issues and then leave the case for me to decide. After all, as I view the administration of American justice, it is a cooperative effort in which the best results are obtained by the interaction of the minds of the court and counsel, and it is silly to suppose that the judge loses any of his dignity or authority when he admits that the art of persuasion still flourishes.[6]

At the same time, as an experienced practitioner and

---

statutory words "portrait or picture" require, said the court, " a representation of a person at least approaching likeness." Levey v. Warner Bros. Pictures, 57 F. Supp. 40, 41-42 (S.D.N.Y. 1944).

6. Medina, "Some Reflections on the Judicial Function," 38 A.B.A.J. 107-108 (1952).

student of appellate advocacy has observed: ". . . after making due allowance for the frailties of mankind, it is really amazing how few good arguments are presented and heard, quite irrespective of the tribunal concerned. About a dozen years ago, I was told by a Justice of the Supreme Court of the United States that four out of every five arguments to which he is required to listen were 'not good' . . ."[7] While this was said of oral argument, similar observations have been made about briefs. Why so? An at least partial explanation is that a lawyer's busy schedule or the smallness of the amount at stake in the litigation may render not feasible the expenditure of time required for a first-rate job.

Here is an interesting critical comment on the nature of current written and oral appellate argument, voiced by Justice Schaefer of the Illinois Supreme Court:

Judges are interested of course in what has been said, and what has been decided, and the traditions and formal ritual of courtroom advocacy encourages lawyers to pitch their arguments on that ground. In most cases that may be enough. But in any case, it is desirable that the thrust go deeper, and in cases on the frontiers of the law a deeper thrust is imperative. Those cases are not decided just upon the ground that "it was so held" in such and such a case. They are decided upon a consideration of why it was so held and upon an appraisal of the results of that holding in actual operation plus the anticipated consequences of an expansion or curtailing of that holding. This is the level upon which [judicial] conference room advocacy operates. It is also the level upon which the most effective courtroom advocacy operates.[8]

Similar sentiments have been expressed by Chief Justice Currie of the Wisconsin Supreme Court[9] and Justice Rutledge of the United States Supreme Court,[10] among others.

It may seem to you that the court of appeals opinion did not follow the quoted advice about reconsidering the validity of a precedent and assessing the consequences of expanding

7. Wiener, Briefing and Arguing Federal Appeals 6 (1967).
8. Schaefer, "The Advocate in the Reviewing Courts," 1956 U. Ill. L. Forum, 203, 210.
9. Currie, "Some Aspects of Appellate Practice Before the Wisconsin Supreme Court," 1955 Wis. L. Rev. 554, 558.
10. Rutledge, "The Appellate Brief," 28 A.B.A.J. 251, 253 (1942).

or not expanding it to cover the new situation. But
remember: (1) the advice was directed at advocacy in the
courtroom and the judicial conference room, not at the form
in which judicial opinions should be written (judges are often
reticent about discussing in their opinions all the policy
reasons that may have influenced the decision); (2) the court
was not being confronted with precedents of its own that it
might want to reevaluate; it was a federal court applying state
law — which included no precedents on the specific problem
of statutory interpretation, and involved a statute whose
soundness the court had no authority to reconsider. The
court's emphasis on the *purpose* of the statute, in considering
whether the New York precedents were pertinent, did
conform to the spirit of the quoted advice.

A final observation: techniques of lawyer advocacy, in
both trial and appellate courts, have been a relatively
neglected part of law school curricula, along with other
practical skills like client interviewing and counseling, and
negotiating. Recent years, however, have witnessed the
beginnings of a substantial curricular movement in those
directions.

B. BACKGROUND NOTE:
PROCEDURAL ASPECTS

1. *FEDERAL RULES OF CIVIL PROCEDURE*

The procedural rules governing the preceding lawsuit were
not the South Carolina rules applying to courts of that state,
but the separate Federal Rules of Civil Procedure applying to
federal court suits throughout the country. Before adoption
of these rules in 1938, federal statutes required federal court
procedure in suits "at law" — which included damage suits
like this one — to conform to the procedures of the courts of
the state in which the federal court sat. Separate federal rules
did apply in actions *not* "at law" — e.g., in maritime cases
("admiralty") and in "equity" cases.

A further word about "equity." Under the old English system, there were "equity courts" separate from the common law courts. The latter courts were typically confined to the remedy of damages; the equity court could grant "specific" relief like ordering the defendant to convey a piece of land which (in violation of his contract) he had refused to convey to plaintiff, or ordering defendant to stop infringing plaintiff's patent, or stop trespassing on his land. And the jury trial right was recognized in most actions in common law courts, whereas the equity court decisions were by judges without juries. When Congress in 1934 authorized the Supreme Court to make separate procedural rules for the federal courts, it also authorized it to *unite* law and equity. This they did. There is no longer a "suit at common law" as distinguished from a "suit in equity." Under the rules there is one form of action, called a civil action, and the court can grant whatever type of relief is appropriate. However, whether there is a jury trial right depends on whether historically there would have been such a right in the kind of case involved. That generalization doesn't cover all possible complications, but in general it is true that if it is an action for damages there would be a right to a jury, and if for injunction or other specific relief there would be no such right.[11] You will recall that plaintiff's complaint in the present damage suit did demand a jury trial.

I said that Congress had authorized the Supreme Court to formulate the federal rules. I should also note that some have thought the legislature has no constitutional authority over court procedure at all — though there is little dissent from the proposition that courts have more competence to regulate in this field.[12] The Supreme Court, incidentally, did not create the rules by itself. It appointed an advisory committee of distinguished lawyers and professors, and adopted their recommendations together with some changes of its own at the end of 1937. They were submitted to Congress, as the enabling act required, and in the absence of

11. Wright, Handbook of the Law of Federal Courts §92 (2d ed. 1970).
12. See authorities cited, id. at 258 nn.2-3.

adverse legislation by Congress, they became effective in September 1938.

The rules effected many important changes besides the union of law and equity in a single form of action. Probably the most significant other ones were: (a) a theory of the parties' written pleadings which puts little stock in technicalities, and recognizes the sufficiency of a complaint that simply gives "a short and plain statement of the claim showing that the pleader is entitled to relief"; and (b) "discovery" procedures prior to trial — which serve to inform each party of important aspects of the other party's case, and which tend to simplify the issues. I'll have something to say about both of these changes later in this chapter.

About half the states have adopted the federal rules for use in state courts, and many other states have been substantially influenced.

2. SERVICE OF SUMMONS AND COMPLAINT

Under the Federal Rules of Civil Procedure, the date that the complaint is filed in court counts as the date of commencement of the action — though in some state courts, the date that "process" (i.e., a summons) is served on the defendant is the commencement date.

After filing of the complaint, the court clerk issues a summons and delivers it to the marshal, or other person specially appointed by the court, for service on the defendant, together with a copy of the complaint. An individual can be served by delivering the summons and complaint to him personally. This is the best way, but alternatives are permitted: leaving copies at his "dwelling house or usual place of abode" with "a person of suitable age and discretion residing therein"; or delivering them to an "agent authorized by appointment or by law to receive service of process." Moreover, for serving individuals or corporations, service is permissible in the manner that may be authorized by a particular federal statute, or by the law of the state for serving in state courts of general jurisdiction.

In the case of corporations there are some alternatives in addition to those in the preceding sentence. The present suit, remember, involves two corporations as defendants. Service can properly be made on a corporate officer, a managing or general agent, or any other corporate agent authorized by appointment or by law to receive service.

Sometimes there is a problem about whether a corporation is subject to suit in the state if it is a "foreign" corporation — i.e., organized in a different state or different country. (Here we know that the two defendant corporations were incorporated outside the state of South Carolina.) The problem arises from the Supreme Court view that to subject to a lawsuit in X State a foreign corporation which has insufficient "contacts" with X State would violate its constitutional "due process" right to fair treatment. In order to be subject to suit in the state, the corporation must have such minimum contacts with the state as would show it wished to avail itself of the privilege of conducting activities there. It would then incur corresponding obligations, so that maintenance of the suit against it would not offend "traditional notions of fair play and effective justice."[13]

There are many cases litigating the question of what constitutes the necessary minimal contacts, and the matter is still unclear, though the Supreme Court has sometimes found a very slight amount of business in the state as sufficient.[14] In the present case — referring back to the complaint — the alleged operation of a television station in South Carolina by one defendant corporation clearly constituted enough contact with the state. The defendant life insurance company's doing of business in the state was alleged in the complaint, and the motion to dismiss did not assert lack of jurisdiction over the defendant corporation on the ground that the business done in the state was insufficient to subject the defendant to suit in the state. The defendant's motion to dismiss asserted simply that the facts alleged were insufficient to make out a case for damage liability; i.e., the facts did not

13. See International Shoe Co. v. Washington, 326 U.S. 310, 319-320 (1945).
14. McGee v. International Life Ins. Co., 355 U.S. 220 (1957).

state "a claim against this defendant upon which relief can be granted."

3. FEDERAL COURT ORGANIZATION

In Chapter 1, in discussing the courts as agencies of the law, I described the organization of state courts. This is an appropriate point at which to describe the organization of federal courts — before going on to analyze their jurisdiction.

There are three layers in the federal court hierarchy: the trial courts of general jurisdiction known as the district courts, the eleven courts of appeal, and the Supreme Court. There are also a few specialized courts, e.g., Court of Claims, Customs Court, Court of Customs and Patent Appeals. (Two "courts" which were once not part of the judiciary at all were the Tax Court, which was actually an executive agency, and the Court of Military Appeals, which was part of the separate system of Military Government; but both were given a special status as "legislative courts" in 1969.[15])

About half the states have one federal district court each. In the others the greater volume of business has necessitated creation of additional districts within the state. Thus, in New York State there are eastern, western, northern, and southern districts. In Illinois there are eastern, northern, and southern districts. In Wisconsin, the two districts are eastern and western (headquartered in Milwaukee and Madison respectively). As volume of business has increased still further but localized within highly populous areas, Congress instead of

15. See 26 U.S.C. §§7441, 7443, as amended by 83 Stat. 730 (1969). Legislative courts are created by Congress under its Article I legislative powers. Judges of such courts do not enjoy the independence of judges on courts created under Article III. Article III judges hold tenure during good behavior (which generally means life tenure), and their compensation cannot be diminished while they are in office. The doctrine of legislative courts has had a long and confusing history. The Court of Claims, Court of Customs and Patent Appeals, and Customs Court were once legislative courts and apparently have been changed into constitutional courts. Before the 1969 changes in the status of the Tax Court and Court of Military Appeals into legislative courts, it was thought that the only remaining legislative courts were the district courts for Guam, the Virgin Islands, and the Canal Zone. See Wright, supra note 11 at 26-34.

creating larger numbers of districts has simply increased the number of judges within the same district. Thus the Southern District of New York, in which most of New York City is located, has about 25 judges; the Northern District of Illinois has a dozen or so; Wisconsin's Eastern District has 3, and the Western District has 1, with at least one more to be added soon. A federal district court case is heard by a single judge (with jury, where one has been rightfully demanded). There are instances, however, where a 3-judge panel sits, notably under statutes that require such a panel when the plaintiff is seeking to enjoin enforcement of a federal or state law because of its alleged violation of the Federal Constitution. In addition, in cases of special significance, all the judges of a particular district have been known to sit together on a case ("en banc").[16]

The eleven courts of appeal are assigned to ten numbered circuits or areas into which the country is divided, plus the separate circuit for the District of Columbia. One of the busiest is the Second Circuit, which includes the state of New York (as well as Connecticut and Vermont) and therefore handles much important commercial litigation. The District of Columbia Circuit handles more litigation involving government agencies than do the others. The District of Columbia Circuit covers the smallest area; the Ninth Circuit, the largest (Alaska, Arizona, California, Guam, Hawaii, Idaho, Montana, Nevada, Oregon, Washington). Another large area is in the Fifth Circuit, which covers (in addition to the Canal Zone) the whole lower tier of southern states (Alabama, Florida, Georgia, Louisiana, Mississippi, Texas). It is not surprising that these two massive circuits, the Fifth and Ninth, are the busiest of all, necessitating 15 and 13 judges respectively. Judges in the other circuits range from 3 for the First Circuit (Maine, Massachusetts, New Hampshire, Puerto Rico, Rhode

16. On organization and some general characteristics of the district courts, see 28 U.S.C. § §81-144; Surrency, "Federal District Court Judges and the History of Their Courts," 40 Federal Rules Decisions 139 (1966); Acheson, "Professional Responsibility and the Workload of the Federal District Courts," 52 Geo. L.J. 542 (1964).

Island) to 9 for the Second, Third, Sixth, and District of
Columbia Circuits. Any of these courts of appeal normally
sits in a panel of 3 judges — sometimes including (when the
spot cannot be filled by a regular circuit judge) a district
judge from within the circuit as in the Nappier case, or a
district or circuit judge from another circuit. In an occasional
case of particular importance, a court of appeals consisting of
more than 3 judges will sit "en banc." The unsuccessful
litigant in a district court can take an appeal, as a matter of
right, to the court of appeals.[17]

The Supreme Court of the United States has 9 members.
Its annual term begins in October and usually ends in June.
Each case is handled by the entire Court rather than by a
panel. A quorum is 6. In the Court year designated as
October Term, 1970, the Court disposed of 3318 cases,
though only between 10% and 15% were disposed of "on the
merits," i.e., by deciding the substance of the legal issues
presented. There were 122 full written opinions of the Court
and 200 very brief "per curiam" opinions. The bulk of the
dispositions were *denials* of review: 2836 denials or dismissals
of "petitions" which were largely "certiorari" petitions,
invoking the Court's discretionary jurisdiction. Of the cases
disposed of with full written opinions, the majority (69) were
civil actions from federal courts, most of them involving the
federal or a state or local government; 16 were civil actions
from state courts, most of them involving federal, state, or
local governments; 14 were federal criminal cases; 12 were
state criminal cases; 7 were federal habeas corpus and 2 were
state habeas corpus cases. Of these full opinions, only 19%
were unanimous.[18]

17. On organization and general characteristics of the courts of appeal, see 28
U.S.C. § §41-48; Shafroth, "Surveys of The United States Courts of Appeals," 42
Federal Rules Decisions 243 (1967); Carrington, "Crowded Dockets and the
Courts of Appeals: The Threat to the Function of Review and the National Law,"
82 Harv. L. Rev. 542 (1968); Lumbard, "Current Problems of the Federal Courts
of Appeals," 54 Cornell L. Rev. 29 (1968).
18. For complete statistics on the October 1970 Term, see "The Supreme
Court — 1970 Term," 85 Harv. L. Rev. 38, 344-353 (1971).

4. *FEDERAL COURT JURISDICTION*

On the matter of jurisdiction, I'll reverse the order and start from the Supreme Court.

a. Supreme Court Original Jurisdiction

The Supreme Court has, to begin with, an "original" jurisdiction — i.e., power to consider and decide certain cases that are *started* in the Supreme Court. These are, according to Article III of the Constitution, "Cases affecting Ambassadors, other public Ministers and Consuls, and those in which a State shall be Party . . ." The first of these two classes of cases has almost never come to the Court, whereas the second class comes occasionally. In the October 1970 Term there were 7 such cases, of which 5 were disposed of on the merits with 2 full opinions. These two opinions covered one case filed by the state of Utah concerning shorelands around Great Salt Lake, and four cases in which four different states were either plaintiffs or defendants in litigation about the 1970 federal voting rights law.[19] Not every case in which a state is a party will qualify for the Court's original jurisdiction, since the case must also fall within the classes of cases specified in Article III, Section 2, as being within the "judicial power of the United States" — such as cases between two or more states, between a state and citizens of another state, and cases to which the United States is a party. Moreover, the jurisdiction extends only to *civil* cases. Also, statutes have in some situations (e.g., suits between two states) treated the Supreme Court's original jurisdiction as *exclusive*, and in others (e.g., suit by the United States against a state) as *concurrent*, i.e., the suit may alternatively be brought in the lower federal courts. Finally, if a case invoking the Court's original jurisdiction requires fact-finding as the Great Salt Lake shorelands case did, the Supreme Court does not itself hold a trial, but rather appoints a master to take evidence and

---

19. See Utah v. United States, 403 U.S. 9 (1971); Oregon v. Mitchell, Texas v. Mitchell, United States v. Arizona, United States v. Idaho, 400 U.S. 112 (1971), and "The Supreme Court — 1970 Term," 85 Harv. L. Rev. 38, 346, 347 (1971).

make a report to the Court, on which briefs and arguments can then be presented to the Court.[20]

b. Supreme Court Appellate Jurisdiction

The Constitution doesn't spell out the Supreme Court's appellate jurisdiction, but instead leaves it to Congress, as we saw in the Chapter 1 discussion of the ways in which Congress could exert some control over the Court. To relieve the Court from an intolerable burden of cases, Congress has seen to it, particularly by a 1925 statute, that the bulk of cases that come before the Court don't have to be considered by it. They are within the Court's discretionary "certiorari" jurisdiction. Recall my earlier reference to the bulk of the October 1970 Term cases having been disposed of by *denial* of certiorari. The Court's Rule 19 shows it is more likely to grant the writ of certiorari under circumstances where (in very rough summary) the lower court has ruled contrary to decisions of the Supreme Court or other courts, or has decided an important question of federal law that should be settled by the Supreme Court, or has departed too much "from the accepted and usual course of judicial proceedings." However, a denial of certiorari, the Court has often said, is not to be read as saying anything one way or the other on the merits of the issues presented. The denial means, Justice Frankfurter once commented,

that fewer than four members of the Court deemed it desirable to review a decision of the lower court as a matter "of sound judicial discretion." A variety of considerations underlie denials of the writ, and as to the same petition different reasons may lead different Justices to the same result. This is especially true [with respect] to a State court. Narrowly technical reasons may lead to denials. Review may be sought too late; the judgment of the lower court may not be final; it may not be the judgment of a State court of last resort; the decision may be supportable as a matter of State law. . . . A decision may satisfy all these technical requirements and yet may commend itself for review to fewer than four members of the Court. Pertinent considerations of judicial policy here come into play. A case may raise an important

20. Generally on the Supreme Court's original jurisdiction, see Wright, supra note 11, c. 13.

question but the record may be cloudy. It may be desirable to have different aspects of an issue further illumined by the lower courts. Wise adjudication has its own time for ripening.[21]

What then of the small minority of cases which Congress has said the Supreme Court *must* review — the cases where there is an "appeal" as a matter of right, rather than merely an opportunity to petition the Court to exercise its discretionary review by certiorari? Congress has set up various classes of cases for such appeal. They are typically concerned with the issue of constitutionality of federal and state laws, but there are others, too.[22]

When a litigant takes an "appeal" to the Supreme Court, he files a "jurisdictional statement" which has to show why he thinks the Court has jurisdiction of the appeal. But it is important to note that under Supreme Court Rule 15 he must also show "why the questions presented are so substantial as to require plenary consideration, with briefs on the merits and oral argument, for their resolution." And under Rule 16 the appellee's motion to dismiss the appeal or affirm the lower judgment may be based "on any other grounds which the appellee wishes to present as reasons why the court should not set the case for argument." That is, the Court long ago decided that even where an appellant shows he comes within one of the jurisdictional statutes governing appeals so that he can appeal as a matter of right, the Court need not give *full* consideration to all appeals. It need not give it to an appeal which, from the jurisdictional papers (the

21. Maryland v. Baltimore Radio Show, 338 U.S. 912, 917-918 (1950) (opinion of Frankfurter, J.).

22. Congress has set up the following classes of cases for such appeal: (1) where a *federal law* has been held *unconstitutional* by any federal district court or court of appeals in a civil suit to which the United States or federal officer is a party; or a federal law or treaty has been held unconstitutional by the highest court of a state (28 U.S.C. § §1252, 1257 (1)); (2) where a *state law* has been held by a federal court of appeals to be *unconstitutional or* contrary to federal laws or treaties (28 U.S.C. §1254); (3) where a *state law* has been *upheld* by the highest court of a state against the claim of violation of Federal Constitution, laws, or treaties (28 U.S.C. § 1257(2)); (4) where a *three-judge district court* grants or denies an injunction in a civil action required to be heard by three judges (28 U.S.C. §1253). Such three-judge courts are required in suits to restrain

jurisdictional statement, appellee's motion to dismiss the appeal or affirm the judgment, and appellant's reply), it determines to be *clearly* without legal merit. In such case, instead of taking the normal course of issuing an "order noting probable jurisdiction" after which briefs with fuller treatment of the merits could be filed and oral argument would be heard, it disposes of the case summarily. It may affirm the judgment or dismiss the appeal without opinion, or state that dismissal is "for want of a substantial federal question." These dispositions, unlike the denial of certiorari, are officially judgments on the merits of the case. However, students of the Court have suggested that considerations similar to those affecting the granting or denial of certiorari (importance of the question; whether there are conflicts in the lower courts; pressure of the Court's workload) help account for the growing increase in such dismissals. In recent years a majority of appeals have been handled in summary fashion.[23]

c. Court of Appeals Jurisdiction

What of the jurisdiction of federal courts below the Supreme Court? The courts of appeals of course have jurisdiction over appeals from the district courts. As noted before, these are appeals as of right. And no "substantiality" doctrine like that just described has developed so as to limit an appellant's right of full review. A second important class of appeals is from federal administrative agencies. While there

---

enforcement of a state or federal statute on the ground of unconstitutionality (28 U.S.C. § §2281, 2282) as well as in suits to set aside Interstate Commerce Commission orders (28 U.S.C. §2325), (5) where a district court of one or three judges has entered judgment in civil action brought by the Federal government to enforce the *antitrust laws*, the *Interstate Commerce Act*, or *Title II of the Federal Communications Act* (15 U.S.C. §29; 49 U.S.C. §45, as amended by 62 Stat. 989; 47 U.S.C. §401 (d); (6) where a district court in a *criminal* case has entered one of certain kinds of judgment *adverse to the United States* (18 U.S.C. §3731).

Generally on the Supreme Court's appellate jurisdiction, see Wright, supra note 11, c. 12; Stern and Gressman, Supreme Court Practice § §2.5 to 2.7, 2.9 to 2.17, 3.2 to 3.4 (4th ed. 1969).

23. See Stern and Gressman, supra note 22 at 193-202; Wright, supra note 11, at 493-495.

are other modes of review of administrative agencies (e.g., injunction and declaratory judgment in the district court; special statutory review of ICC orders by a 3-judge district court), the standard statutory pattern is by petition for review by a court of appeals. Review is generally on the basis of the record before the administrative agency, and agency findings of fact will be accepted if based on substantial evidence in the light of the whole record. The latter review is regarded as *more* accepting of the findings than court of appeals review of district court fact-findings, which are accepted if not "clearly erroneous."[24]

d. District Court Jurisdiction

Remember that Article III of the Constitution vests the "judicial power of the United States" in the Supreme Court "and in such inferior courts as the Congress may from time to time ordain and establish." Congress in establishing the inferior federal courts was limited in its grant of jurisdiction by the scope of the judicial power as defined in Article III. The most significant part of this definition covered (1) what has come to be known as "federal question" cases (cases arising under the Constitution or federal laws or treaties); (2) what is known as "diversity of citizenship" cases (cases between citizens of different states); (3) cases to which the United States is a party.[25] These three categories account for the bulk of cases in the federal courts. Much the largest category is of the cases in which the United States is a party, if you count the *criminal* cases; otherwise the three categories are somewhat more evenly divided. Thus, statistics for the fiscal year ending June 1971[26] show that total *civil* cases

24. Davis, Administrative Law Text, §29.02 (3d ed. 1972). On the courts of appeals generally, see Wright, supra note 11, at 7-9, 452-470.

25. The other categories of the "judicial power of the United States" are: cases affecting ambassadors, other public ministers, and consuls; admiralty and maritime cases; cases between two or more states; between a state and citizens of another state; between citizens of the same state claiming lands under grants of different states; and between a state or its citizens and foreign countries, citizens, or subjects.

26. Director of the Administrative Office of United States Courts, Annual Report 262, 317 (1971).

commenced in the district courts were 93,396, of which 25,086 were cases in which the United States was a party (13,183 as plaintiff and 11,903 as defendant), 39,612 were private cases involving a federal question,[27] and 24,620 were diversity of citizenship cases (of which more than half were personal injury suits). Criminal cases commenced were 43,157.

Federal jurisdiction is a complicated legal specialty, and I can here only indulge in a few basic generalizations about each of the three major categories of civil jurisdiction.

(1) Cases to Which the United States Is a Party (herein of Sovereign Immunity)

Consider first the cases to which the United States is a party. A federal statute follows up the constitutional grant of federal judicial power in this type of case by, in general, granting federal jurisdiction in suits *commenced* by the United States or by an agency or officer expressly authorized to sue. No jurisdictional statute attempts to do this for suits *against* the United States, and indeed there is some Supreme Court authority that the latter type of suit is not covered by the constitutional clause on the federal judicial power. This seems to have stemmed from the fact that at the time of the Constitution, suits against the sovereign were unknown. The ancient "sovereign immunity" doctrine is that the sovereign cannot be sued without its consent. However, several statutes do give the consent of the United States to be sued in various situations, notably for certain contract and tort claims; and suits under *those* statutes would generally qualify for federal jurisdiction in the *federal question* category as suits "arising under" federal statutes.[28] Incidentally, it is possible that the sovereign immunity doctrine can be circumvented if the suit is for injunctive or declaratory relief, against the federal *officer* involved, and alleges the statute is unconstitu-

27. This is a rather misleading figure, since it is swollen by inclusion of about 12,000 prisoner petitions — which one might not expect to be classed as private civil suits. The 39,612 figure also includes about 9,000 "marine" cases, both contract and tort.
28. Wright, supra note 11, at 68-71.

tional, or that the officer's conduct violates plaintiff's constitutional rights or is wholly outside the bounds of statutory authority. I say "it is possible" because, while some Supreme Court authority suggests it, the cases appear to be in great confusion.[29]

(2) Federal Question Cases

The federal statute granting "federal question" jurisdiction is in much the same language as the constitutional clause which recognizes this kind of case as falling within the federal judicial power. That is, the statute refers to a civil case that "arises under" the Federal Constitution, laws, or treaties. This quoted phrase has provoked much litigation. Attempts have been made to have it cover disputes which only remotely and indirectly involve federal law. The courts have struggled with tests that are formulated in terms of federal law being an "ingredient" of the claim, or that federal law creates the right of action, or that the case involves the validity, meaning, or effect of the federal law, or that the claim is basic or essential to, or founded directly upon, the federal law. No one formula has carried the day. Professor Charles Wright concludes that existing cases are neither consistent nor entirely analytical in their approach; they imply, he thinks, that certain "pragmatic considerations" are important. Another thing worth noting is that "laws" in the jurisdictional statute is construed to include federal administrative regulations issued under a federal law.[30]

(3) Diversity of Citizenship Cases (herein of the Nappier Case Jurisdiction, and of Corporate Citizenship and Other Fictions)

The "diversity of citizenship" jurisdiction is what was invoked in our South Carolina Nappier case, set out at the beginning of this chapter. Why should there be this kind of federal jurisdiction at all, when there is no federal question,

---

29. Davis, supra note 24, c. 27.
30. For matters in this paragraph, see Wright, supra note 11, at 54-59.

the federal government is not a party, and the federal court
will be struggling with questions of state law? The major
justification offered is the fear that the state court would be
prejudiced against the out-of-state litigant. It is not at all
clear whether, in an increasingly mobile society, this fear is
justified. But the argument runs that whether or not the fear
is justified, it exists — especially on the part of would-be
investors in out-of-state enterprises such as a corporation
planning expansion into another state. One of the other
considerations motivating the defenders of diversity jurisdiction today is the allegedly higher quality of justice obtainable
in the federal courts.[31]

Those who offer proposals to substantially reduce the
diversity jurisdiction try mainly to exclude from it those
claims against which the risk of prejudice is deemed minimal.
These might be claims arising out of substantial local
involvement of the out-of-state party, as by the operation of
a "local establishment." A 1958 federal law went part of the
way toward this objective by saying a corporation shall be
deemed a citizen of any state in which it has been
incorporated (which hitherto had, roughly speaking, been
true), *and* of the state in which it has its principal place of
business. Thus if a corporation organized in Delaware with
principal place of business in New York is a party, diversity
of citizenship is lacking if any party on the other side is a
citizen of either Delaware or New York.

The reasons for wanting to reduce diversity jurisdiction are
mainly: (a) the congestion in the federal courts; (b) the desire
to avoid the difficulties of the federal courts' having to apply
state substantive law in these suits (a problem discussed in
subsection 5 below, on relations between federal and state
courts). The American Law Institute study of diversity
jurisdiction has resulted in recommendations that would
probably reduce the volume of diversity cases by half; but
the proposals are still a matter of sharp debate.[32]

31. See Wright, supra note 11, at 78.
32. Id. at 75-76.

An important matter of interpretation of the meaning of diversity arises in cases with multiple plaintiffs and/or multiple defendants. The statute granting diversity jurisdiction has been construed by the Supreme Court in such cases to mean that "complete diversity" is required. Each plaintiff must be a citizen of a different state from the state of which each defendant is a citizen. (The constitutional clause on diversity jurisdiction doesn't require this, so Congress could for a particular kind of situation change the rule, as it has done.)[33]

Look back now at the Nappier case complaint in the first part of this chapter. Notice that while the plaintiff alleges she is a South Carolina resident, one defendant is alleged to be incorporated in a state "other than the State of South Carolina," and the other in North Carolina. And while both defendants are alleged to be doing business in South Carolina, there is no indication that South Carolina is the principal place of business of either defendant — which, if it were true as to any party, would, under the 1958 law, destroy diversity as to that party and require dropping that party. This might result in dismissal of the suit if the dropped party is deemed indispensable to the suit.

From what I have said, it might appear that the complaint has properly alleged the elements of diversity jurisdiction. In fact it hasn't, though the defendants' motion to dismiss didn't make an issue of this. The complaint was defective, in varying degrees of importance, in at least these respects: (a) plaintiff describes herself as a South Carolina "resident." This was insufficient because citizenship, in diversity jurisdiction, involves not mere residence but rather the legal concept of "domicil." This refers to residing in a state, plus the intention of making that state one's home (or the lack of fixed intention to go elsewhere). The pleading defect here might be disregarded by the court where it is clear that residence in the domicil sense was intended, as indeed could be inferred from all the facts of this complaint. (b) The specific state under

33. Generally, on the subject of the preceding four paragraphs, see id. c. 4.

whose laws the defendant life insurance company was
organized should have been named, rather than merely
alleging that the state was other than South Carolina. (c) It
was not enough to allege that both defendants did business in
South Carolina and then to remain silent on the principal
place of business. Ever since the 1958 law, the complaint in a
diversity case would have to specifically allege that a
corporate defendant's principal place of business was in a
state other than the plaintiff's state. Finally, you should be
aware that there is considerable freedom to *amend* the
jurisdictional allegations of the complaint.[34]

A final word about corporations as citizens. How did they
ever get to be considered as "citizens" of a state in the first
place? Originally, it was held that the artificial entity known
as a corporation was *not* a citizen for purposes of the
diversity jurisdiction. But by mid-nineteenth-century the
Supreme Court was saying in Marshall v. B. & O. Railroad[35]
that though a corporation was not itself a citizen, and hence
the citizenship of its stockholders was what counted, fairness
required that *all stockholders* of a corporation be *conclusively presumed* to be citizens of the state where the
corporation was incorporated. (This has since been accepted
law, until modified by the above-mentioned 1958 law
declaring that a corporation "shall be deemed a citizen of any
State by which it has been incorporated and of the State
where it has its principal place of business."[36]) What the
Court was doing was indulging in a "legal fiction" — since it
would rarely be true that all stockholders of a publicly held
corporation were citizens of the state of incorporation. It was
doing the same thing that courts did when they held that a
buyer in good faith of real estate as to which a previous deed
or mortgage has, unknown to him, been recorded, has
"constructive notice" of the recording. They could have
spoken more realistically and said: for various practical

34. On this paragraph, see id. at 86-87, 290-291, 609-610.
35. 57 U.S. (16 How.) 314 (1853).
36. 28 U.S.C. §1332(c).

reasons a recorded mortgage as to which the buyer has no actual notice must be treated by the law as effective in the same way as one that he did know about; i.e., where the mortgage was recorded, notice is no longer a requirement.

And the Supreme Court might have reasoned more realistically, too, in dealing with the corporate citizenship problem. True, it was not free to discard the "citizen" category in the way the courts could have discarded their own "notice" category; the "citizen" category was specified by statute, pursuant to the Constitution. But they might have dealt more candidly with their changed interpretation of it instead of clinging to the old interpretation[37] as supplemented by the assumption of palpably untrue facts. In the above-mentioned Marshall case, instead of using a more realistic rationale[38] — either for *changing* the doctrine that a corporation wasn't a citizen for any purpose, or changing the doctrine that all stockholders had to have a state citizenship different from that of the plaintiff (in the Marshall case, a Virginia plaintiff) — the court found that all of the far-flung stockholders of the B. & O. Railroad, incorporated in Maryland, indeed "are citizens of that State" (i.e., are

37. By the "old interpretation" I refer to the opinion by Chief Justice Marshall in Bank of United States v. Devaux, 9 U.S. (5 Cranch) 61 (1809), declaring that the corporate artificial entity was "certainly not a citizen"; citizenship of the members would be controlling. Actually, just nine years prior to the mid-nineteenth-century view announced in Marshall v. B & O. (supra note 35) as described in the text, a short-lived decision had held that a corporation was "entitled, for the purpose of suing and being sued, to be deemed a citizen" of the chartering state. Louisville C. & C. R. Co. v. Letson, 43 U.S. (2 How.) 497 (1844).

38. The court might have said something like this: The developing role of corporations in the country make it a practical and equitable necessity to *change* our interpretation of "citizen." We will give a different and looser construction to "citizen" so as to bring a corporation within it for limited, diversity litigation purposes, as distinct from such other purposes as voting. Alternatively, and for the same reasons, the Court might have continued to assume, as it did, that a corporation was *not* a citizen, so that stockholder citizenship was controlling, and then gone on to say (1) the state of incorporation can be viewed as making *all* stockholders limited "citizens" of the state for limited group enterprise purposes including litigation, *or* (2) that it was time to *change* the requirement that *all* stockholders of the corporation being sued had to have a state citizenship different from that of each plaintiff.

conclusively "presumed" to be so).[39] The language of such a statement, like the language of the courts that said the ignorant buyer of the real estate did have notice of the recorded mortgage, made the statement seem contrary to fact.

Why do courts indulge in this fictional way of talking? M. R. Cohen's explanation is that "in moments of innovation, we cling all the more to old linguistic forms. The latter minister to the general feeling of security, especially where the prevailing myth or makebelieve is that the judge merely declares the law and cannot change or extend it. . . . From the point of view of social policy, fictions are, like eloquence, important in giving emotional drive to propositions that we wish to see accepted. They can be used . . . to soften the shock of innovation."[40]

Seeing the way in which fictions function outside the law helps illuminate their legal role. One of the most apt analogies to legal fictions is furnished by this passage from Roscoe Pound's article, "Law in Books and Law in Action":[41]

When Tom Sawyer and Huck Finn had determined to rescue Jim by digging under the cabin where he was confined, it seemed to the uninformed lay mind of Huck Finn that some old picks the boys had found were the proper implements to use. But Tom knew better. From reading he knew what was the right course in such cases, and he called for case-knives. "It don't make no difference," said Tom, "how foolish it is, it's the *right way* — and it's the regular way. And there ain't no other way that I ever heard of, and I've read all the books that gives any information about these things. They always dig out with a case-knife." So, in deference to the books and the proprieties, the boys set to work with case-knives. But after they had dug till nearly midnight and they were tired and their hands were blistered, and they had made little progress, a light came to Tom's legal mind. He dropped his knife and, turning to Huck, said firmly, "Gimme a case-knife." Let Huck tell the rest:

39. Marshall v. B. & O. R.R., 57 U.S. (16 How.) 314, 329 (1853).
40. 6 Ency. Soc. Sci. 228 (1931). See generally Fuller, Legal Fictions (1967).
41. 44 Am. L. Rev. 12 (1910).

"He had his own by him, but I handed him mine. He flung it down and says, 'Gimme a *case-knife*.'

"I didn't know just what to do — but then I thought. I scratched around amongst the old tools and got a pickaxe and give it to him, and he took it and went to work and never said a word.

"He was always just that particular. *Full of principle*."

Tom had made over again one of the earliest discoveries of the law. When tradition prescribed case-knives for those tasks for which pickaxes were better adapted, it seemed better to our forefathers, after a little vain struggle with case-knives, to adhere to principle — but use the pickaxe. They granted that law ought not to change. Changes in law were full of danger. But, on the other hand, it was highly inconvenient to use case-knives. And so the law has always managed to get a pickaxe in its hands, though it steadfastly demanded a case-knife, and to wield it in the virtuous belief that it was using the approved instrument.

(4) The Over $10,000 Jurisdictional Amount

While the Constitution itself is silent on the matter, *both* the jurisdictional statute for diversity cases and that for federal question cases specify that the amount in controversy be over $10,000, exclusive of costs and interests, before federal jurisdiction can be invoked. Congress has increased the amount a number of times. The $10,000 figure was fixed in 1958; the previous amount, in existence since 1911, was $3000.

This requirement has less significance in federal question cases because there are so many special jurisdictional statutes (on particular federal questions) that eliminate the requirement.[42] Some prominent examples of these statutes cover: cases arising under any federal law regulating commerce;[43] cases in which the United States is plaintiff, and *some* cases in which it is a defendant;[44] certain civil rights actions for damages or injunction — actions that are usually brought against state officials for conduct alleged to deprive the plaintiff of rights under the Constitution or federal statutes;[45] actions to recover fines, penalties or forfeitures

42. See Wright, supra note 11, at 108-110.
43. 28 U.S.C. §1337.
44. 28 U.S.C. §§1345, 1346, and 1361, among others.
45. 28 U.S.C. §1343.

incurred under federal law.[46] In all these situations and in a number of others, the jurisdictional statute mentions no jurisdictional amount. Perhaps the most significant gap in these special jurisdictional statutes is the failure to cover many suits against the federal government or its agencies or officers, claiming invalidity of governmental action. However, without getting into any detailed analysis, I think it fair to say that the jurisdictional amount requirement poses much less of a problem in such suits if the plaintiff is claiming violation of personal, constitutional rights.[47]

In the Nappier case complaint, you will note that the plaintiff alleges in paragraph number 11 that she has suffered damage in the sum of $175,000.

5. RELATIONS BETWEEN STATE AND FEDERAL COURTS

(a) Could the Nappier case have been brought in a state court of South Carolina? The answer is yes. A damage action for invasion of privacy would typically be brought in the state court of general jurisdiction. It is not one of those classes of action over which federal courts are by statute given exclusive jurisdiction (e.g., cases involving federal crimes, federal penalties, forfeitures or seizures, federal antitrust actions, bankruptcy proceedings, patent and copyright actions, certain maritime actions, and a few others). Thus, there was in this case a state court jurisdiction as well as a "concurrent" federal court jurisdiction based on diversity of citizenship. If there had been no such diversity, there would have been no federal jurisdiction, since the complaint had raised no issue that would qualify the case for "federal question" jurisdiction. Incidentally, if the Nappier plaintiff had sued in the state court, it could still wind up in the federal court — because the defendants would have the right

46. 28 U.S.C. §1355.
47. See the discussion by Judge Weinstein in Cortwright v. Resor, 325 F. Supp. 797 (E.D.N.Y. 1971), rev'd on other grounds, 447 F.2d 245 (2d Cir. 1971).

under "removal" statutes to remove the case to a federal court because the case qualified for federal court jurisdiction.[48]

(b) Suppose, now, that the Federal Communications Act, regulating commerce in broadcasting, had prohibited broadcasts violating a person's right of privacy, and had declared that the person aggrieved by such broadcast could sue for damages in a court of competent jurisdiction. It is clear that a federal district court would qualify, even in the absence of diversity, since the action would arise under a federal act regulating commerce. Would a state court of general jurisdiction also qualify? Would the mere fact that the right of action had been specified by a federal statute mean that only a federal court could have jurisdiction? The answer is that when Congress has created a right of action and has not intended to make federal jurisdiction exclusive (as it has in the case of federal crimes and other actions mentioned in the preceding paragraph), then the appropriate state court is authorized to take jurisdiction. Indeed it cannot refuse to take jurisdiction — assuming it would be the appropriate court for suits involving analogous rights created by state rather than federal statute. These principles have been applied many times to state court suits under the Federal Employers' Liability Act, and also under the Emergency Price Control Act of 1942 — in the first type of case, for damages to injured workers on interstate railroads, and in the second for treble-damage suits (even if considered "penal") by an overcharged tenant or consumer.[49] Congress had in both statutes specifically authorized a concurrent jurisdiction by state and federal courts.

Of course this isn't the only type of situation in which a state court may properly be dealing with questions of federal law. In *any* action in a state court that has authority to hear the case (including those in which the authority comes from state law), the court does not refrain from considering a

48. See Wright, supra note 11, c. 6.
49. See Testa v. Katt, 330 U.S. 386 (1947); Wright, supra note 11, at 171-174.

particular issue merely because it is one of federal law — such as whether a state statute violates the Federal Constitution. It decides the federal law issues along with any state law issues. And the decision on federal issues by the highest state court empowered to make the decision may be reviewable, by certiorari or appeal as previously described, in the Supreme Court.

(c) One of the most important aspects of relations between state and federal courts is this: when a plaintiff like the Nappier plaintiff has a damage claim under the law of the state and could sue in a state court, but chooses to invoke the diversity jurisdiction of the federal court, might this choice change the legal principles applicable to his claim? Might he choose the federal court simply because federal judge-made principles of privacy law are more favorable to him than the judge-made privacy law that would be applied by the state court? This line of strategy was once available to a plaintiff (or to a defendant who considered removal to a federal court). But, in general, this is no longer true. A brief story of the change is as follows: Section 34 of the Judiciary Act of 1789 — the so-called Rules of Decision Act, which in substantially similar language still exists[50] — declared that the "laws of the several states" shall apply in the federal courts unless the Federal Constitution, statutes, or treaties provided otherwise. In 1842 in the celebrated case of Swift v. Tyson[51] on an issue of commercial law, the Supreme Court held that "laws of the states" referred to statutes and not to the body of judicial decisions making up the common law. This came to mean that the federal courts were free to develop their own federal common law, in the fields of torts, contracts, and commercial relations not covered by state statutes.

But there was persistent objection that on a matter not governed by the Constitution or federal statutes (typically in a diversity of citizenship case), the applicable law for a given state should not depend on whether the case was in a federal

50. See 28 U.S.C. §1652.
51. 41 U.S. (16 Pet.) 1 (1842).

or state court of that state. Finally, almost a century later, the 1842 decision was overruled. The Supreme Court declared in the 1938 case of Erie R.R. v. Tompkins that the 1842 decision had misconstrued not only the Rules of Decision Act but the Constitution itself. Henceforth the rule was to be: "Except in matters governed by the Federal Constitution or by Acts of Congress, the law to be applied in any case is the law of the state. And whether the law of the state shall be declared by its Legislature in a statute or by its highest court in a decision is not a matter of federal concern. There is no federal general common law."[52] A qualification of the principle that, in the cases described, the outcome should not depend on whether the case was in state or federal court, is this: generally speaking, if the issue is regarded as one of "procedure" rather than substantive law, the federal court will apply its own rather than the state's procedural rules.[53]

The result of all this, as far as the Nappier case is concerned, is that the federal court sitting in a "diversity of citizenship" case in South Carolina, faced with a question of the substantive law of privacy, had to apply the judge-made privacy law of the state of South Carolina (as well as give the South Carolina criminal statute whatever relevance the court thought it had for this damage suit).

(d) An important federal statute on the subject of relations between federal and state courts is the one which prohibits certain kinds of federal court interference with state court proceedings. The present statute, which has in some form been on the books from almost the beginning, was revised in 1948 to read as follows: "A court of the United States *may not grant an injunction to stay proceedings in a State court* except as expressly authorized by Act of Congress, or where necessary in aid of its jurisdiction, or to protect or effectuate its judgments."[54] (Emphasis added.)

52. 304 U.S. 64, 78 (1938).
53. On the many complications that have arisen in applying the Erie doctrine, see Wright, supra note 11, c. 9.
54. 28 U.S.C. §2283.

There are some other special anti-injunction statutes — directed at restraint against certain state officers[55] — but this is the important general statute.

The "except" clauses have produced many judicial interpretations, which I can't go into here, but I do want to call attention to one problem of interpretation — the relation of the "except as expressly authorized by Act of Congress" clause to a type of case that has been coming up with considerable frequency in recent years. I refer to the cases under U.S.C. Title 42, Section 1983, which goes back to the Civil Rights Act of 1871. To summarize §1983 loosely: it declares that persons who, acting "under color of" law (e.g., state or municipal officers), subject another to deprivation of his rights under the Constitution or federal statutes, "shall be liable to the party injured in an action at law, suit in equity, or other proper proceeding for redress" — which, generally, means liable for damages and/or injunction. Suppose then that a man is indicted by a state grand jury under a "criminal syndicalism" statute (prohibiting certain activities directed at overthrow of the government), and he then sues in a federal district court under §1983, requesting an injunction to stay or restrain the state criminal proceeding on the ground that the prosecution and the statute violate his federal constitutional rights of free speech and press. Would such a federal court injunction against a state court proceeding be treated as "expressly authorized by Act of Congress" (i.e., by §1983) so as to be outside the ban of the statute mentioned in the preceding paragraph?

The Supreme Court ducked answering this question in a 1971 case like the one just described. The Court said there was no need in that case to answer it, because even if the ban on injunctions were inapplicable (on the debatable ground that §1983 had "expressly" authorized injunctions against state court proceedings), there were *other* reasons for saying

55. For example, there is the Johnson Act withdrawing federal court jurisdiction from suits to enjoin certain state public utility orders. Another statute prohibits federal court injunctions against the assessment, levy, or collection of certain state taxes. See Wright, supra note 11, at 194-196.

that the injunction should be denied. The Court referred to "the basic doctrine of equity jurisprudence that courts of equity should not act, and particularly should not act to restrain a criminal prosecution, when the moving party has an adequate remedy at law and will not suffer irreparable injury if denied equitable relief." This "is reinforced by an even more vital consideration, the notion of 'comity,' that is a proper respect for state functions . . . and a continuance of the belief that the National Government will fare best if the States and their institutions are left free to perform their separate functions in their separate ways."[56]

Exceptions could be recognized, the Court thought, for cases where the state prosecution is conducted in bad faith, for harassment purposes rather than good faith enforcement purposes; or the highly unusual case where a statute is "flagrantly and patently" unconstitutional "in every clause" and no matter how, or against whom, it is applied. The Court disapproved of language in earlier opinions that had seemed to treat less extreme situations as sufficient.

These principles were left undisturbed in a 1972 Supreme Court decision[57] squarely facing the question which had earlier been ducked. The Court held that the anti-injunction statute didn't stand in the way of a § 1983 injunction against a state court proceeding (i.e., such an injunction was "expressly authorized by Act of Congress") — though of course the other factors mentioned in the 1971 case would, in the typical case, stand in the way.

(e) The considerations of "comity," mentioned by the Court in the above-mentioned 1971 case as a traditional brake upon federal court interference with state courts, are often referred to in connection with an "abstention" doctrine. The purport of this doctrine is that even where the necessary conditions for federal court jurisdiction exist, it does not follow that the court must exercise its jurisdiction; it may under certain circumstances "abstain" from exercising it. Application of the doctrine is not limited to situations of

56. Younger v. Harris, 401 U.S. 37, 43-44 (1971).
57. Mitchum v. Foster, 407 U.S. 225 (1972).

federal court interference with an already pending state court proceeding.

Let us say no state court enforcement proceeding has yet been brought under a state law but one is about to be, on account of alleged violation by Mr. X of a regulation issued by a commission under a state law. Mr. X sues in federal court to restrain enforcement on the ground of federal unconstitutionality of the law, and the further ground that the law had not authorized the regulation in question. The federal court may be unwilling to decide the constitutional issue, because courts traditionally avoid decisions of such issues if possible, and here there might be no need to decide it because: (1) under one of two reasonably possible interpretations of the ambiguous statute, let us say, no constitutional issue would arise, and the state court hasn't yet resolved the ambiguity; (2) if the statute were construed not to authorize the regulation (an issue not yet resolved by the state court), then that too would dispose of the case without the necessity of deciding the statute's constitutionality. Both these questions deal with the *meaning* of the state statute — an issue of state law on which the state courts are the final authority. So the federal court may choose to abstain from decision, and either dismiss the case or retain it on the docket, while the plaintiff seeks state court adjudications of the unresolved questions of state law. There are complexities in the abstention doctrine, but the foregoing example gives you, I think, a general idea of what it is about.[58]

(f) The only other federal-state court relations problem I want to bring to your attention is that of habeas corpus. As in the case of so many other complex topics discussed earlier, I shall confine myself to sketching a few basic features of it. The Federal Constitution, Article I, Section 9 declares that the writ of habeas corpus "shall not be suspended, unless when in cases of rebellion or invasion the public safety may require it"; and federal statutes have implemented this provision. The writ of habeas corpus directs anyone who has

58. For general discussion, see Wright, supra note 11, at 196-208.

custody or control of a person to bring the detained person before a named judge or court to have the ground of the detention inquired into. It used to be held that the only permissible attack on the detention was in terms of the committing court's lack of jurisdiction. However, the concept of "jurisdiction" took on a very broad meaning in habeas corpus cases, so that if the prisoner's constitutional rights had been violated this was said to undermine the committing court's jurisdiction. The Supreme Court abandoned this fiction in 1942,[59] declaring that a jurisdictional defect is not the sole basis for the writ; that any violation of the defendant's constitutional rights made him eligible, when in custody, to seek relief through habeas corpus.

When a state prisoner claims that the state violated the Fourteenth Amendment of the Federal Constitution by depriving him of "due process of law" or of the "equal protection of the laws," why doesn't he seek habeas corpus in the state court rather than the federal court? The answer is that he does go there first. The federal courts apply the rule that *state remedies must first be exhausted*. However, the exhaustion requirement is interpreted liberally. It does not include the seeking of certiorari review, by the Supreme Court, of the state highest court's denial of relief; the requirement applies only to the state remedies that are still open to him at the time he seeks federal habeas corpus, and not those he might have pursued in the past (like an appeal to a higher state court from his conviction) that are not still open to him; but "a deliberate by-passing of state procedures" would permit a federal court to deny habeas corpus.[60]

The 1963 decision establishing these propositions also reflected another kind of liberality. In an ordinary state criminal case (i.e., not habeas corpus) coming for review to the Supreme Court on a federal constitutional issue, the Court generally denies review on the federal question if the

59. Waley v. Johnston, 316 U.S. 101 (1942).
60. Fay v. Noia, 372 U.S. 391 (1963).

state supreme court decision rests on an "independent, adequate *state* ground," such as defendant's failure to comply with a state procedural requirement, like taking his appeal to the state supreme court within three months. Yet in this habeas corpus case the principle was not applied. The state supreme court had thought that the defendant's failure to appeal from his state court conviction to the state supreme court barred him from getting any habeas corpus type of relief years later in the state court, in spite of the concededly involuntary nature of his confession. But the Supreme Court, in review of his federal habeas corpus case, thought his right to federal habeas corpus was not barred by the "independent state ground" doctrine.

Under the federal statute on habeas corpus, if the state court after a hearing has made a determination of a *fact* issue (e.g., against defendant's contention that he had been held incommunicado after arrest, and that he had been coerced into his confession) "evidenced by a written finding, written opinion, or other reliable and adequate written indicia," then this determination "shall be presumed to be correct." That is, the burden is on the defendant to establish the contrary unless one of eight specified circumstances exists (including such things as lack of support in the state court record for the factual determination; lack of a full fair and adequate hearing, or other denial of due process of law).[61]

The most recent report of the Administrative Office of United States Courts observes:

Most inmate filings are from State rather than Federal prisons. And they are habeas corpus petitions in which the petitioners attack their convictions, their sentences, or the legality of the confinement. From 1962 to 1970 these State habeas corpus cases were generally increasing by at least a thousand per year, reaching 9,063 in 1970. However, for fiscal year 1971, they dropped to 8,372 cases — a 7.6 percent decrease.

It is not clear why all of a sudden, we are seeing fewer State habeas pleas. Although we do not have statistical evidence to this effect, it is quite likely that the availability of more legal services to prisoners and the improvements being made in judicial and post-conviction procedure

61. 28 U.S.C. §2254.

in many States have begun to open other legal routes prisoners must exhaust before approaching a Federal court. Possibly also, based upon the fact of U.S. court experience that in 96.0 percent of the prisoner cases the matter prayed for is not granted, there is a spreading acceptance by prisoners of the futility of pressing unfounded or trivial claims.[62]

6. *THE NECESSARY "STANDING" OR "JUSTICIABILITY"*

The Nappier case presented no problem of standing or justiciability, but since I am trying to familiarize you with some fundamental procedural aspects of a lawsuit, I want to include these important questions with the others that may or may not be specifically involved in the case.

a. General

Under the Anglo-American adversary system, not everyone qualifies as an adversary entitled to set the court machinery in motion. Not every kind of alleged injury to an alleged interest will do. The court must be satisfied that the plaintiff has suffered the necessary kind of injury to the necessary kind of interest. The courts have required that the dispute be a live one, rather than one laid to rest by subsequent events (i.e., made "moot"); involve plaintiff's own injury, not someone else's; be concrete and immediate, rather than a "hypothetical" dispute or one presenting a "premature" question for a mere "advisory opinion"; be not feigned or collusive; and not involve a question that is "nonjusticiable" — for instance, the kind of "political" question discussed in Chapter 1. In some circumstances, some kinds of interests and injuries, such as a federal taxpayer's or a competitor's, have been held insufficient to give standing.

In discussing these requirements, the Supreme Court has often invoked a constitutional source for some or all of them, in Article III, Section 2, which extends the judicial power of

62. Director of Administrative Office of United States Courts, Annual Report 132 (1971).

the United States to specified categories of "cases" and "controversies." Thus a dispute that lacks the adversary character described by the above requirements may be characterized as not a case or controversy within the meaning of the Constitution. The states, by state constitutional provision or otherwise, have adopted a similar view of the judicial function.

Before presenting some of the situations to which the above-mentioned concepts refer, I want first to deal with certain things to which they do *not* refer.

As I have said, *advisory opinions*, in the sense of judicial answers to hypothetical or premature questions are frowned on — and I'll say more about this later. However, there is a special kind of advisory opinion which is viewed as legitimate in several states. This is authorized by the constitutions of those states, but only when the opinion is sought by specified public bodies rather than private litigants. It is "not available to private or corporate or group parties generally. It is restricted, usually to the two houses of the legislature and the executive." It is "designed for use during the process of legislation, or in the process of executive action."[63]

Second, the legitimacy of the *declaratory judgment* proceeding is not undermined by the above-mentioned requirements, though the proceeding lacks some aspects of the typical court controversy. Under an applicable declaratory judgment statute (and one exists for federal courts in addition to the statutes of practically all the states for state courts), the plaintiff has standing in court even though he doesn't claim the defendant has committed or is immediately about to commit a wrong, and even though the plaintiff doesn't seek relief in the form of damages or injunctive restraint against the defendant. What he seeks is "declaratory" relief — a court declaration of respective rights of plaintiff and defendant. It is particularly useful as a means of obtaining an authoritative interpretation of a statute, con-

63. Field, "The Advisory Opinion — An Analysis," 24 Ind. L.J. 203, 222 (1949).

tract, or will, to avoid the adverse effect of conduct that would be taken in reliance on a mistaken interpretation. The court declaration is of course an official judgment — which may be enforced in case the losing party refuses to abide by it. And there is still a requirement, for declaratory relief, that the case involve a present live controversy, with the threat of real though not necessarily immediate injury.[64]

We turn now to some cases illustrating the basic concepts referred to earlier.

b. Whether a "Legal" Right or Interest Is Necessary; Types of Interests Covered

Not so many years ago, leading Supreme Court cases on standing were talking about a prerequisite in terms of a "legal right" having been invaded; there had to be "injury" to a "legally protected right."[65] This didn't mean that the Court had to decide the merits of the case before deciding the standing issue. The Court didn't mean by "legal right" or "legal interest" that the litigant would ultimately win on the merits. Rather, by this phrase the Court may simply have been posing the question whether the litigant was alleging the kind of substantial interest which a court has been in the habit of listening to.[66] But the phrase did lend itself to the other meaning, and in 1970 the Supreme Court repudiated its use. Data-processing service organizations had sued to challenge the Comptroller of the Currency's permission to national banks to render data-processing services to bank customers and other banks. The court of appeals held that plaintiffs lacked standing because they had no legal right or interest in being free from this competition. But the Supreme Court said: "The 'legal interest' test goes to the merits. The question of standing is different." It then announced a newly formulated test (applicable at least to cases involving statu-

---

64. See generally James, Civil Procedure 26-31, 371-377 (1965).
65. See Tennessee Electric Power Co. v. TVA, 306 U.S. 118 (1937); Joint Anti-Fascist Refugee Committee v. McGrath, 341 U.S. 123 (1951).
66. See Justice Frankfurter's concurring opinion in the Joint Anti-Fascist case cited in preceding footnote.

tory or constitutional provisions): the plaintiff's allegations must show (1) that the challenged conduct has caused him "injury in fact," and (2) that "the interest sought to be protected by the complainant is arguably within the zone of interests to be protected or regulated by the statute or constitutional guarantee in question." Moreover, the relevant interests, said the Court, are not merely economic; they may be aesthetic, conservational, recreational, or spiritual.

Here the Court cited recent cases recognizing the standing of environmentalists to contest construction projects damaging to the environment, and the standing of consumers and consumer organizations, including TV listeners wishing to persuade the FCC that a TV station's license should not be renewed. Pertinent at this point is a 1972 Supreme Court case, Sierra Club v. Morton,[67] which throws just a bit of a cloud on environmentalist standing. In a 4 to 3 decision, the Court found no standing in the Sierra Club to restrain a Walt Disney project for commercial exploitation of Mineral King Valley, a national game refuge adjacent to Sequoia National Park. The reason seemed to be a deficiency in the complaint's allegations. The club had alleged its special interest in conservation, that it represented persons similarly interested, and that the defendants' project would have a vital and adverse effect on the club's interests in conserving the resources of the Sierra Nevada Mountains. This failed to meet the "injury in fact" test, said the Court. "The alleged injury will be felt directly only by those who use Mineral King and Sequoia National Park, and for whom the aesthetic and recreational values of the area will be lessened by the highway and ski resort. The Sierra Club failed to allege that it or its members would be affected in any of their activities or pastimes by the Disney development. Nowhere in the pleadings or affidavits did the Club state that its members use Mineral King for any purpose, much less that they use it in any way that would be significantly affected by the proposed action of the respondents." The Court made clear that its

67. 405 U.S. 727 (1972).

decision "does not, of course, bar the Sierra Club from seeking in the District Court to amend its complaint."

One other type of interest I want to mention is the taxpayer interest. It had long been the rule that a federal taxpayer alleging, e.g., unconstitutionality of a federal statute, lacked standing to enjoin expenditure of general funds from the Treasury for administration of the statute. Largely, this was because the taxpayer's interest in such moneys " — partly realized from taxation and partly from other sources — is shared with millions of others, is comparatively minute and undeterminable, and the effect upon future taxation of any payment out of the funds, so remote, fluctuating and uncertain . . ."[68] However, in the 1968 case of Flast v. Cohen,[69] the Supreme Court recognized a federal taxpayer's standing to attack the expenditure of federal funds under the Elementary and Secondary Education Act of 1965 as allegedly violating the church-state separation clause of the First Amendment. The taxpayer's standing as taxpayer will exist, said the Court: (1) where he is attacking constitutionality of exercises of congressional power under the taxing and spending clause of the Constitution (as distinguished from attacking constitutionality of an essentially regulatory statute that involves incidental expenditure of tax funds to administer it); and (2) when the constitutional clause he claims to be violated is one that specifically restricts expenditures of federal funds. The First Amendment was viewed as such a "specific" restriction, but it is still unclear whether any other constitutional restriction will qualify.

The standing of a state or municipal taxpayer in a state court is, in general, treated by the state courts with greater liberality; and sometimes the taxpayer's standing to sue is recognized even where the challenged governmental action does not involve an expenditure of public funds.[70]

68. Frothingham v. Mellon, 262 U.S. 447 (1923).
69. 392 U.S. 83 (1968).
70. See generally, Note, "Taxpayer's Suits: A Survey and Summary," 69 Yale L.J. 895 (1960).

c. Mootness

Illustrating a once "live" case that was made "moot" by the passage of time is a well-known case on a New Jersey Bible-reading law. Some New Jersey taxpayers appealed to the Supreme Court from a state court decision upholding validity of a New Jersey law requiring Old Testament verses to be read at the opening of each public school day. In addition to a ruling that, under the circumstances of the case, the necessary "standing" to sue as taxpayer or as parent didn't exist, the Court ruled that the claim of a parent had been made moot by the fact that the child in question had graduated before the case reached the Supreme Court.[71]

Illustrating the *rejection* of a mootness claim is the case involving the late Congressman Adam Clayton Powell. When he was reelected to the House as a member of the 90th Congress in 1966, the House by resolution excluded him from membership because of certain alleged misconduct reported by a House committee. While his suit for injunctive and declaratory relief (including a back salary claim) was awaiting review by the Supreme Court, the 90th Congress terminated, Powell was elected to the 91st Congress, and a House resolution permitted him to sit in that Congress, though fining him $25,000 and annulling the seniority he had gained prior to the 91st Congress. The Supreme Court held among other things that Powell's exclusion from the 90th Congress was unlawful, because the House could not impose, for admission, qualifications additional to the age, citizenship, and residence qualifications specified in the Constitution. But the Court also had to consider, at the outset, the mootness issue. The Court concluded that whatever other claims had been mooted, "Powell's claim for back salary remains viable even though he has been seated in the 91st Congress"; hence the question of his right to sit in the already terminated 90th Congress was not moot.[72]

---

71. Doremus v. Board of Education, 342 U.S. 429 (1952).
72. Powell v. McCormack, 395 U.S. 486 (1969).

On whether a criminal case is moot after the defendant has served his sentence and been released, the Supreme Court has vacillated, but it now admits "the obvious fact of life that most criminal convictions do in fact entail adverse collateral legal consequences. The mere 'possibility' that this will be the case is enough to preserve a criminal case from ending 'ignominiously in the limbo of mootness.' "[73]

d. Raising the Rights of Others

Consider now the requirement that the injury complained of be plaintiff's own injury rather than someone else's. A well-known illustration is Tileston v. Ullman,[74] the first in a trilogy of cases on validity of the Connecticut birth control law prohibiting the use, and the counseling or assisting in the use, of contraceptive drugs and instruments. The plaintiff was a physician, Dr. Tileston, whose constitutional attack upon the statute was rejected by the Supreme Court because he was asserting the rights not of himself but of his patients, whose lives would allegedly be endangered by childbearing. "His patients are not parties to this proceeding and there is no basis on which we can say that he has standing to secure an adjudication of his patients' constitutional right to life, which they do not assert in their own behalf . . ."

The second Connecticut birth control case was Poe v. Ullman.[75] Here the procedural deficiencies in Tileston seemed to have been rectified: There was a declaratory judgment complaint by a physician alleging that the statute violated *his* own liberty and property rights under the Fourteenth Amendment; and there were declaratory judgment complaints by a married couple and by a wife, who alleged certain dangers to the women's lives or health unless the physician were legally free to prescribe birth control information. Nonetheless a Supreme Court majority of five dismissed the appeal from the state court decision dismissing the complaints. This time the Court found another kind of

---

73. Sibron v. New York, 392 U.S. 40, 55 (1968).
74. 318 U.S. 44 (1943).
75. 367 U.S. 497 (1961).

deficiency in standing: the long record of nonenforcement of the Connecticut statute showed it had become a dead letter. There was no genuine and immediate threat of prosecution.

In 1965, in Griswold v. Connecticut, the Supreme Court finally recognized sufficient standing in the litigants to attack the Connecticut law.[76] Officials of a birth control clinic had been prosecuted as accessories to the crime of use, for the advice they had given to married persons in the use of contraceptives. In holding that the statute unconstitutionally invaded the right of privacy of married persons, the majority said: "We think that appellants have standing to raise the constitutional rights of the married people with whom they had a professional relationship." The strict attitude against invocation of the constitutional rights of others that was taken in the Tileston case was inapplicable here, said the Court. Here, instead of a declaratory judgment suit by a doctor invoking his patients' rights, we have an actual "criminal conviction for serving married couples in violation of an aiding-and-abetting statute. Certainly the accessory should have standing to assert that the offense which he is charged with assisting is not, or cannot constitutionally be, a crime."

The Court also cited a number of cases where parties had indeed been permitted to invoke the constitutional rights of others. One example is the 1953 case of Barrows v. Jackson.[77] In that case, residential property owners had entered into an agreement — a "covenant running with the land" — prohibiting sale or rental to nonwhites. One owner, Jackson, violated the covenant by selling to a black, and was sued for damages by the other owners. Thus the situation was somewhat different from two 1948 cases generally treated together as Shelley v. Kraemer,[78] in which the defendant was not the violating owner but the black buyer, who was sued by other owners for an injunction. In one case the injunction was to oust him from possession, and in the other to restrain

76. 381 U.S. 479 (1965).
77. 346 U.S. 249 (1953).
78. 334 U.S. 1 (1948).

him from taking possession. There the Supreme Court had held that the state court judgment ousting the black from possession, or restraining his taking possession, would violate his right to equal protection of the laws under the Fourteenth Amendment. But in the present case, the white defendant, Mrs. Jackson, who had sold the property to a black purchaser, could not claim that a damage judgment against her by the other property owners would violate *her* constitutional rights. (Nor would it violate the constitutional rights of the black buyer in possession of the property.) The Court did allow her to invoke the constitutional rights of others. It said a damage judgment against her would unconstitutionally discriminate against *future black buyers*, since owners, under threat of damage suits, would either refuse to sell to blacks or charge them higher prices. "Under the peculiar circumstances of this case," said the Court, "we believe the reasons which underlie our rule denying standing to raise another's rights, which is only a rule of practice, are outweighed by the need to protect the fundamental rights which would be denied by permitting the damages action to be maintained."

This last quotation raises two important questions. First, why the description of the rule as "only a rule of practice" rather than as grounded in the case or controversy clause of Article III? The description illustrates an ambivalence in the Court's attitude, which has permeated many of its opinions. For as the Barrows opinion itself observed, the practice or policy limitation is "not always clearly distinguished from the constitutional limitation."

Secondly, why couldn't the Court distinguish the Barrows type of situation by saying it didn't involve standing to sue, but simply standing of the defendant to raise an argument in a suit brought by plaintiffs with standing to bring it? Professor Kenneth Davis has long been arguing the validity of this distinction, though the Court hasn't yet clearly adopted it.[79] The Court in Barrows, says Davis, may have felt

---

79. In a recent case, the Court may have gone part way toward adopting it. See Sierra Club v. Morton, 405 U.S. 727, 737 n.12 (1972).

(without articulating) the difference between initiating a proceeding and calling to the Court's attention something that the Court could do on its own motion. That is, the Court could on its own hook, without the urging of any party, reject a determination that would involve unconstitutionality or other illegality, since it has the affirmative obligation to avoid such illegality.[80]

A final observation on the matter of raising another person's constitutional rights: Remember that, as the Griswold opinion recognized, there have been a number of exceptional cases besides Barrows that allowed this to be done. Prominent among the more recent ones are those in the area of First Amendment freedom of speech, where a litigant has sometimes been allowed successfully to assert that an allegedly vague and overbroad statute has an invalid chilling effect on the legitimate exercise of constitutionally protected rights — even though the litigant's own conduct was clearly covered and validly prohibited. This is a legal area of considerable flux and uncertainty.[81]

e. Collusiveness

Consider now an illustration of the requirement that a dispute be not "feigned" or "collusive." A landlord who wanted a chance to invalidate in court the rent controls established under the Emergency Price Control Act of 1942 got his tenant to sue him under the act for treble the amount of the rent overcharge. The tenant had been assured that the landlord would finance the suit, and his attorney was selected by the landlord's attorney and filed no brief. The Supreme Court held the case had to be dismissed, since there had been no " 'honest and actual antagonistic assertion of rights' to be adjudicated — a safeguard essential to the integrity of the judicial process, and one which we have held to be

80. Davis, Administrative Law Treatise s 22.07 (1958; Supp. 1970).
81. See, e.g., Note, "The First Amendment Overbreadth Doctrine," 83 Harv. L. Rev. 844 (1970); Note, "The Chilling Effect in Constitutional Law," 69 Colum. L. Rev. 808 (1969); Sedler, "Standing to Assert Constitutional Jus Tertii in the Supreme Court," 71 Yale L.J., 599 (1962); Wright, supra note 11, at 44-45.

indispensable to the adjudication of constitutional questions by this Court."[82]

A collusive suit such as this is not the same as a "test case." The latter need not lack the necessary element of adverseness. Though both parties may welcome the "test," there may still be a genuine, unfeigned controversy between them over their respective rights.

f. Hypothetical or Premature Issues

That the issues presented must not be "hypothetical" or "premature" so as to call for a merely "advisory" opinion is one of the most frequently stated aspects of the "standing" requirement. We encountered this aspect in Poe v. Ullman, the second Connecticut birth control case, in which the Supreme Court saw no immediate threat to plaintiff's rights because the state's policy had been not to enforce the statute. While the policy against advisory opinions is often applied in cases raising the issue of constitutionality of statutes (which also is typically the issue in the cases as to which several states, noted earlier, specifically allow a legislature or governor to seek an advisory opinion from the state supreme court on a constitutional issue), the "advisory opinion" language has been used in nonconstitutional cases, too.[83] The advisory opinion concept is also reflected in the language often used in cases involving court review of administrative agency action — language to the effect that the case must be "ripe" for adjudication.

However, just *when* a case is so premature or hypothetical or unripe that adjudication would amount to an "advisory opinion" is a question that the courts have not found easy. And though some clarity may be starting to emerge, the confusing and, apparently inconsistent, answers by the Supreme Court have been severely criticized by Professor Davis, in the area of standing to get review of administrative action.[84] One of the most recent examples of Supreme Court

---

82. United States v. Johnson, 319 U.S. 302 (1943).
83. See, e.g., United States v. Fruehauf, 365 U.S. 146 (1961).
84. Davis, Administrative Law Text, c. 21 (3d ed. 1972).

attitude in this field is the 1972 case involving the Army Intelligence data-gathering system for surveillance of such political activities as might be related to future domestic disorder — the sources for the data being mainly news media, publications of general circulation, and public meetings. Most if not all of the plaintiff individuals or their organizations had been the subject of army surveillance reports. Plaintiffs complained of the "chilling effect" of the system on their First Amendment rights of free expression and association. But they were held to have no standing to complain, in the absence of more specific present harm or threat of specific future harm. The premature claim was labeled a request for an "advisory opinion."[85]

g. Political Questions

The "political question" doctrine was briefly described in Chapter 1.[86] The doctrine still has vitality in cases involving foreign affairs (including, recently, the issue of legality of the Vietnam War), validity of the process by which a statute or constitutional amendment was adopted, or the Article IV, Section 4 guaranty of a republican form of government to every state. But the doctrine has been slipping. It slipped noticeably in the 1962 case of Baker v. Carr[87] when the Supreme Court decided that a claimed violation of the equal protection clause by a state legislative apportionment was not properly viewed as a political question. A series of cases were then decided on the merits, involving apportionment of congressional seats as well as those in state and local government bodies.

Thereafter, among other decided cases that might previously have been thought to present political questions, was the 1969 case of Congressman Adam Clayton Powell discussed earlier under the heading of mootness. You will recall that the Court dealt with the issue of whether the House had validly denied Powell his seat in the 90th Congress. Even

85. Laird v. Tatum, 408 U.S. 1 (1972).
86. See pages 97-98.
87. 369 U.S. 186 (1962).

Baker v. Carr had included in a listing of possible types of
political questions, a question presented in the context of a
"textually demonstrable constitutional commitment of the
issue to a coordinate political department";[88] and it would
have been easy to hold in the Powell case that such a
commitment existed in the Article I, Section 5 provision that
"Each House shall be the Judge of the . . . Qualifications of
its own Members." The Court interpreted this clause to be a
commitment to Congress of the duty to judge the qualifications *expressly* set forth in the Constitution (age, citizenship,
and residence). Since the denial of Powell's seat had been
based on other grounds — certain alleged misconduct — the
validity of the denial was deemed justiciable rather than
political.[89]

h. Standing vs. Justiciability

In the discussion up to now, both the terms "standing"
and "justiciability" have been used. In the past some
confusion has been created by courts' using the terms
interchangeably. Thus if the court felt a nonjusticiable
question were involved, it might say that a litigant therefore
had no "standing" to raise it. In the more recent cases, the
Supreme Court has been careful to distinguish the terms.
Thus in Baker v. Carr (supra) there were separate discussions

88. Id. at 217. The other types listed were those presented in the context of:
"A lack of judicially discoverable and manageable standards for resolving it; or the
impossibility of deciding without an initial policy determination of a kind clearly
for non-judicial discretion; or the impossibility of a court's undertaking
independent resolution without expressing lack of the respect due coordinate
branches of government; or an unusual need for unquestioning adherence to a
political decision already made; or the potentiality of embarrassment from
multifarious pronouncements by various departments on one question. Unless one
of these formulations is inextricable from the case . . . , there should be no
dismissal for non-justiciability on the ground of a political question's presence."
Ibid.

89. On political questions generally, see Bean, "The Supreme Court and the
Political Question: Affirmation or Abdication?" 71 W. Va. L. Rev. 97 (1969);
Scharpf, "Judicial Review and the Political Question: A Functional Analysis," 75
Yale L.J. 517 (1966); Wright, supra note 11, at 45-48; Hughes, "Civil
Disobedience and the Political Question Doctrine," 43 N.Y.U.L. Rev. 1 (1968).

under the respective headings of "standing" and "justiciability." As the Court explained in Flast v. Cohen (supra),
standing was *one aspect* of the broad concept of *justiciability.* "[N]o justiciable controversy is presented when the
parties seek adjudication of only a political question, when
the parties are asking for an advisory opinion, when the
question sought to be adjudicated has been mooted by
subsequent developments, and when there is no standing to
maintain the action." The quoted passage separates the
"standing" problem even from the "advisory opinion" and
mootness problems, though they have often been treated as
the same problem, and I have up to now so treated them. As
the Court observed in the same opinion, "Standing has been
called one of the 'most amorphous [concepts] in the entire
domain of public law.' Some of the complexities peculiar to
standing problems result because standing 'serves, on occasion, as a shorthand expression for all the various elements of
justiciability.' "

But in general, the Court continued, the

> fundamental aspect of standing is that it focuses on the party seeking to
> get his complaint before a federal court and not on the issues he wishes
> to have adjudicated. The "gist of the question of standing" is whether
> the party seeking relief has "alleged such a personal stake in the outcome
> of the controversy as to assure that concrete adverseness which
> sharpens the presentation of issues upon which the court so largely
> depends for illumination of difficult constitutional questions." . . . [I]n
> other words, when standing is placed in issue in a case, the question is
> whether the person whose standing is challenged is a proper party to
> request an adjudication of a particular issue and not whether the issue
> itself is justiciable. Thus a party may have standing in a particular case,
> but the federal court may nevertheless decline to pass on the merits of
> the case because, for example, it presents a political question.[90]

7. THE "MOTION TO DISMISS" AND OTHER PLEADINGS

Recall that the defendants in our Nappier case filed a
motion to dismiss. How does this pleading relate to other
pleadings in a civil lawsuit in federal court?

90. Flast v. Cohen, 392 U.S. 83, 95, 99-100 (1968).

Under the Federal Rules of Civil Procedure, the plaintiff's complaint is required to set forth (1) a short and plain statement of the grounds upon which the court's jurisdiction depends, (2) a short and plain statement of his claim showing that he is entitled to relief, and (3) a demand for judgment for the relief to which he deems himself entitled. The basic pleading of the defendant is an "answer." In the answer: (1) he must admit or deny each allegation ("averment") of the complaint, or state he is without knowledge or information sufficient to form a belief as to the truth of the averment (which has the effect of a denial). Averments not denied are deemed to be admitted. (2) He must state whatever constitutes an "avoidance or affirmative defense" to the complaint — for instance, a legal defense to the effect that the plaintiff's claim based on defendant's alleged negligence was barred because of the plaintiff's own ("contributory") negligence, or that it was barred because the statute of limitations had already run.

But some defenses, according to Rule 12(b), may "at the option of the pleader" be made by *motion*. Lack of jurisdiction is one of these defenses. Another — and this is the one invoked by the defendant's motion in the Nappier case — is "*the failure to state a claim upon which relief can be granted.*" Such a motion to dismiss is analogous to what in many state courts is called a "demurrer" (which, according to one wag, is not to be confused with the comparative form of an obsolete adjective formerly applied to young ladies). Instead of denying any facts in the complaint, the motion is in effect saying: even assuming, for purposes of this motion, that the facts alleged are true, your claim is legally insufficient; the law does not, on such facts, permit the granting of the requested relief against me. Thus you will note that in granting the motion to dismiss in the Nappier case the district judge did not question the truth of any of the facts stated in the complaint.

If the motion to dismiss had been denied, then the defendants would have had the right to file an answer denying any of the factual averments, or stating they were without knowledge or information sufficient to form a belief as to the truth of an averment. They might say the latter, for instance, about the averment in paragraph 3 of the complaint that the two girls were "known throughout the state" as The Little Jack Girls; or the averment in paragraph 9 that as a result of the broadcast "it became common talk of people in South Carolina" that plaintiff was one of the young ladies who had been raped, and that "people generally know about" the episode "by which she will be identified during her entire lifetime"; or the averment in paragraph 11 that plaintiff "has been demoralized, embarrassed, has suffered great mental pain, humiliation, mortification, has become highly nervous and has been unable to perform her regular employment." Plaintiff then would have the burden of establishing by his proof the averments that have been thus denied. While the averments that are not denied are deemed admitted, this is not true of averments as to amount of damage.

Some additional pleadings and additional motions are permitted in special situations.[91]

8. *THE TRIAL THAT MIGHT HAVE BEEN: JURY AND JUDGE*

Assuming for the moment that defendants had filed an answer and the case went to trial, would the plaintiffs have had a right to the jury trial they demanded in the final clause of their complaint? The answer is yes. The Seventh Amendment of the Constitution, applicable to the federal courts, requires a jury trial in "suits at common law, where the value in controversy shall exceed twenty dollars." (Practically all state constitutions have a similar guarantee for state courts.) Under Federal Rule of Civil Procedure 38, a party is deemed to have "waived" or given up his right to a jury trial by failure to make timely demand for it under the

91. On pleadings and motions generally, see Wright, supra note 11, at 273-292; James, Civil Procedure, cc. 2-5 (1965).

rules — though under Rule 39 the judge has discretion, in spite of such failure, to grant a motion for jury trial of any or all issues.

What qualifies as a suit "at common law" is determined, in general, by reference to the type of suit that could be heard in the law courts rather than the equity courts at the time the Seventh Amendment was adopted in 1791. An action for damages, such as the Nappier case was, would so qualify — even though the kind of injury claimed (invasion of privacy) may not have been redressable at that time.

This does not mean that the jury would have to be composed of twelve persons, the traditional number, or that they would have to be unanimous in their verdict. Federal Rule 48 allows the parties to "stipulate that the jury shall consist of any number less than twelve or that a verdict or a finding of a stated majority of the jurors shall be taken as the verdict or finding of the jury." More important, recent Supreme Court decisions have upheld even in state criminal cases the use of juries of less than twelve,[92] and less than unanimous verdicts,[93] so that there is little doubt of the validity of similar practices in civil cases.[94] The Judicial Conference of the United States voted in 1971 to reduce the size of civil juries in federal courts,[95] and the number of districts that have promulgated local rules reducing the size (e.g., to six) is spreading rapidly.[96]

You are also reminded at this point of the discussion in Chapter 1 of the moderating role that the jury can play, and of the University of Chicago studies on the comparative

92. Williams v. Florida, 399 U.S. 78 (1970), upheld the use of a six-man jury in a state noncapital case as not violating Fourteenth Amendment due process of law.

93. A five-sixths and a three-fourths unanimity verdict by a twelve-man jury in a state noncapital case was held not to violate Fourteenth Amendment due process of law in Johnson v. Louisiana and Apodaca v. Oregon, 406 U.S. 356, 404 (1972).

94. But see Gibbons, "The New Minijuries," 58 A.B.A.J. 594 (1972).

95. Reports of Proceedings of the Judicial Conference of the United States 41 (1971).

96. See Devitt, "Six-Member Civil Juries Gain Backing," 57 A.B.A.J. 1111 (1971).

attitudes of judge and jury in civil suits for personal injuries.

Finally, a word about the respective roles of judge and jury at the trial. The rule of thumb is that the judge decides questions of law and the jury decides questions of fact — a rule that is not always easy to apply, and the complexities of which we cannot go into here. In the Nappier case, prior to any impaneling of a jury, the judge disposed of a legal question, i.e., the legal sufficiency of the complaint. If there had been a jury trial, there would have been a number of legal matters handled by the judge. First of all (disregarding the judge's role as to various pretrial matters, such as a motion for "judgment on the pleadings" or the "discovery" procedures I shall be discussing in the next subsection), the judge at the federal trial of a jury case could be called on to rule on various motions designed to have *him* rather than the jury decide the case. There could be a "motion for directed verdict," under Rule 50, by either party at the close of the evidence offered by his opponent. This would be based on the idea that reasonable men could not differ as to the conclusions to be drawn from the evidence, hence there was no role for the jury to play. After the jury verdict, there could be a Rule 50 motion for a "judgment notwithstanding the verdict" — based on the idea that a reasonable jury could not have arrived at that verdict. Under Rule 59, there could also be a "motion for new trial," or the judge could order a new trial on his own initiative, for such reasons as these: the verdict is against the evidence; damages awarded are excessive or inadequate; newly discovered evidence; misconduct of jury, judge, or counsel; error in rulings on admissibility of evidence, or in the instructions to the jury.

The two last-mentioned errors point to the second and third major types of questions within the judge's province at the trial: rulings on admissibility of evidence, and the final instructions to the jurors prior to their retirement to deliberate on the verdict. In the Nappier case, the judge's instructions would have explained the circumstances in which damages for invasion of privacy could be recovered under the law of South Carolina, and would have asked the jury to apply the legal principles thus expounded to the facts it found from the evidence.

9. ADVERSARY NATURE OF THE PROCEDURE; LIMITS ON ADVERSARINESS

Our system of trial court procedure is often described as an "adversary system," meaning that the opposing parties to a dispute have the burden of bringing the dispute to court, of investigating it, and of presenting the facts in court through witnesses called by each side — with the judge acting as a relatively passive umpire and adjudicator. By contrast, in the systems of some other countries, the judge is in more active command. Lawyers inform the judge of their intended documentary proofs and the names of potential witnesses, and he makes his own investigation (directly or through another) and his own study before trial. He actively manages the trial. It is he who calls the witnesses (they are viewed as the *court's* witnesses; they will not have been previously interviewed by the lawyers) and questions them, though the lawyers can also question them. If necessary he calls impartial experts, drawn from a standing panel nominated by responsible agencies in each specialized field such as medicine or engineering.

What is the basis of the criticism leveled at the adversary system? One of the most distinguished critics, federal appellate Judge Jerome Frank, viewed the system as based on the "fight theory" rather than the "truth theory." Combat between two adversaries, he argued, was a poor way of getting at the truth. He pointed to inequalities between the combatant lawyers, and economic inequalities between opposing clients (leading to differing abilities to expend funds for investigation and for a lawyer). In addition he thought the emphasis on adversariness led to undesirable tactics: the lawyer's use of surprise, his unwillingness to concede harmful facts and willingness to discredit even truthful adverse witnesses, and his conscious or unconscious distortion of facts in the process of interviewing and coaching his witnesses.[97]

The indictment is strong but, I think, not fatal. In fact Judge Frank conceded that the existing system has qualities that we cannot afford to dispense with, and that a policy of reform within the adversary system was the best course.

(1) One favorable aspect of the system is that a *fuller presentation* of relevant facts and arguments on both sides of a point is more likely to occur when opposing lawyers, spurred by partisan interest, have been beating the bushes to dig up the relevant facts and arguments. Moreover, there is reason to think that the adjudication itself will be of a less partisan, *more objective* character when the combatants rather than the adjudicator have done this digging before trial, and when the proceedings at trial consist of opposing presentations managed by them, as distinct from a presentation managed primarily by the adjudicator himself.

The argument on this was well stated by a Report of the Joint Conference on Professional Responsibility of the Association of American Law Schools and the American Bar Association. Speaking first of the trial presentation managed by the adjudicator, the Report observed:

[A]t some early point, a familiar pattern will seem to emerge from the evidence; an accustomed label is waiting for the case and, without awaiting further proofs, this label is promptly assigned to it. It is a mistake to suppose that this premature cataloguing must necessarily result from impatience, prejudice or mental sloth. Often it proceeds from a very understandable desire to bring the hearing into some order and coherence, for without some tentative theory of the case there is no standard of relevance by which testimony may be measured. But what starts as a preliminary diagnosis designed to direct the inquiry tends quickly and imperceptibly, to become a fixed conclusion, as all that confirms the diagnosis makes a strong imprint on the mind, while all that runs counter to it is received with diverted attention.

An adversary presentation seems the only effective means for combatting this natural human tendency to judge too swiftly in terms of the familiar that which is not yet fully known. The arguments of

97. Frank, Courts on Trial 80-102 (1950).

counsel hold the case, as it were, in suspension, between two opposing interpretations of it. While the proper classification of the case is thus kept unresolved, there is time to explore all of its peculiarities and nuances.

This contrast was viewed as accentuated by the trial-managing adjudicator's pretrial investigation and study. The tribunal then

cannot truly be said to come to the hearing uncommitted, for it has itself appointed the channels along which the public inquiry is to run. If an unexpected turn in the testimony reveals a miscalculation in the design of these channels, there is no advocate to absorb the blame. The deciding tribunal is under a strong temptation to keep the hearing moving within the boundaries originally set for it. The result may be that the hearing loses its character as an open trial of the facts and issues, and becomes instead a ritual designed to provide public confirmation for what the tribunal considers it has already established in private. When this occurs, adjudication acquires the taint affecting all institutions that become subject to manipulation, presenting one aspect to the public, another to knowing participants, and discussion in 45 U. of Colo. L. Rev. 1 (1973).

Finally, the Report thought it significant that "the experienced judge or arbitrator desires and actively seeks to obtain an adversary presentation of the issues. Only when he has had the benefit of intelligent and vigorous advocacy on both sides can he feel fully confident of his decision."[98]

(2) True, there are disquieting aspects of the adversary system, but I think they do not outweigh the stated advantages, nor are they immune to reform. Inequalities do exist among advocates, but judges can to some extent correct the imbalance and are particularly apt to take a more active role when confronted with the inexperience of the fledgling lawyer. Indeed Professor Fleming James, a leading authority on civil procedure, points out that in spite of some judges' reluctance to exercise their powers, the common law tradi-

98. Report of the Joint Conference on Professional Responsibility (Lon L. Fuller and John D. Randall, Co-chairmen), 44 A.B.A.J. 1159 (1958). For an experimental study supporting this report's assumption that an adversary procedure is more likely to counteract bias in the decision-maker, see Thibaut, Walker, and Lind, "Adversary Presentation and Bias in Legal Decision-making," 86 Harv. L. Rev. 386 (1972), and discussion of the study in 45 U. Colo. L. Rev. 1 (1973).

tion and especially its modern development does give them authority to do more than an umpire's job: to go beyond a litigant's legal theory of his case or the specific relief requested, to put the court's own questions to witnesses examined by the parties, and even to call additional witnesses.[99] Statutes also commonly provide for the use of the court's neutral expert on particular issues such as insanity. Some states have successfully experimented with the use of a panel of such neutral experts for medical testimony in auto accident cases.

True, also, economic inequalities between the opposing parties can create serious imbalance in legal representation.[100] Thus, one party may be at a disadvantage because funds needed for thorough pretrial investigation of the case are not available. The time may come when, as Judge Jerome Frank once speculated,[101] there will be public financing of investigative as well as other functions of a public prosecutor of civil actions, who would exist as an alternative to the use of a private lawyer. That step — as well, of course, as the more radical step of complete socialization of the legal profession — is not exactly imminent in this country. The Supreme Court has recently decided that no criminal defendant who has not waived his right to counsel can be sentenced to any jail term without having been represented by counsel of his own or by free counsel if he can't afford his own;[102] but presumably only a minimal investigative expense would thereby be covered. This right of the indigent to counsel in a criminal case is a matter of constitutional right. The Supreme Court hasn't yet recognized such a right in civil cases, but "legal aid" services for civil cases are in fact available in larger cities — not enough to fill the need, though

99. James, Civil Procedure 3-8 (1965).
100. See Note, "Right to Aid in Addition to Counsel for Indigent Criminal Defendants," 47 Minn. L. Rev. 1054 (1963).
101. Frank, supra note 97, at 94-99.
102. Argersinger v. Hamlin, 407 U.S. 25 (1972), expanding the right to counsel recognized in the felony case of Gideon v. Wainwright, 372 U.S. 335 (1963).

on a broader scale than existed prior to the federal antipoverty program of recent years.

To the argument that the adversary system lends itself to tactics like the use of surprise and the concealment or distortion of the adverse aspects of one's case, there are two answers.

(a) The first is that the canons in the ABA Code of Professional Responsibility set some ethical limits on adversariness — limits which probably need more vigorous bar association enforcement, though violations are hard to ferret out. Thus, one disciplinary rule in the code prohibits a lawyer from engaging in "conduct involving dishonesty, fraud, deceit, or misrepresentation." Another declares he shall not "knowingly use perjured testimony or false evidence," or "participate in the creation or preservation of evidence when he knows or it is obvious that the evidence is false," or "counsel or assist his client in conduct that the lawyer knows to be illegal or fraudulent." Another requires him to disclose to the court "legal authority in the controlling jurisdiction known to him to be directly adverse to the position of his client and which is not disclosed by opposing counsel."[103]

In other words, a lawyer has duties not only to his client but also to the public and the legal system, including the court; he is an "officer of the court." Even the "attorney-client privilege," which requires the lawyer not to disclose his client's confidences, gives way when the disclosure would be of "the intention of his client to commit a crime and the information necessary to prevent the crime."[104]

(b) More important than the canons in dealing with surprise and concealment are the "discovery" procedures established by the Federal Rules of Civil Procedure for the federal courts and substantially adopted in most states. These

103. ABA Code of Professional Responsibility, Disciplinary Rules DR 1-102, DR 7-102, DR 7-106 (1970).

104. Id. DR 4-101(C). On legal ethics generally, see Patterson and Cheatham, The Profession of Law (1971); Countryman and Finman, The Lawyer in Modern Society (1966); Note, "Legal Ethics and Professionalism," 79 Yale L.J. 1179 (1970); "Symposium on Professional Responsibility," 4 Conn. L. Rev. 409 (1972); Drinker, Legal Ethics (1953).

procedures enable a party to discover, in advance of trial, facts that are known to, or evidence in possession of, the adverse party. Under the federal rules, either party may before trial do any of the following: (1) Take a sworn statement ("deposition") of any person upon *oral examination* or *written interrogatories* "for the purposes of discovery or for use as evidence in the action or for both purposes." (In the absence of a different agreement by the parties, the deposition is inadmissible as evidence at the trial unless the witness making it can't be produced in court or unless it is used to contradict or "impeach" the witness.) (2) Request from the other party an *admission* of the genuineness of "relevant documents" or "the truth of any relevant matters of fact set forth in the request." (3) Seek a court order allowing *inspection* of documents, persons, or things. In addition, "pretrial conferences" among the judge and the opposing lawyers may eliminate some issues and possibly result in a settlement of the case without trial.

C. BACKGROUND NOTE: THE LAW OF PRIVACY

I wish here to set the Nappier case ruling on privacy law against a broader background, so that various facets of the law of privacy can be distinguished, and the Nappier ruling can be better understood.

The idea of a tort action for invasion of privacy is a relative infant in the law, born in the fertile brains of Louis D. Brandeis and Samuel D. Warren. It was an idea whose time had come, when these Boston lawyers wrote their article "The Right to Privacy" in 1890[105] — though it may startle you to find them saying so long ago:

The intensity and complexity of life, attendant upon advancing civilization, have rendered necessary some retreat from the world, and man, under the refining influence of culture, has become more sensitive to publicity, so that solitude and privacy have become more essential to the individual; but modern enterprise and invention have, through

105. 4 Harv. L. Rev. 193 (1890).

invasions upon his privacy, subjected him to mental pain and distress, far greater than could be inflicted by mere bodily injury.[106]

Their argument for creation of a new category of tort liability was rejected in 1902 by a 4 to 3 vote of the highest New York court in a suit by an attractive young lady against a company which advertised its flour with a picture of the plaintiff, without her consent. But the New York legislature thereupon passed a statute authorizing both a criminal prosecution and a tort suit against use of the name, portrait, or picture of any person "for advertising purposes or for the purpose of trade" without the person's written consent. The Georgia Supreme Court accepted the Brandeis-Warren thesis in 1905 in a situation analogous to that in the New York case. By the 1930s the American Law Institute's *Restatement of Torts* had accepted it. Today only a few states reject it.[107]

Probably the most influential analysis of the privacy cases has been made by Prosser in his widely used *Torts* treatise. It has been argued against the analysis that it treats privacy as "a composite of the interests in reputation, emotional tranquillity and intangible property" rather than as an "independent value" protective of "human dignity."[108] Without entering into that debate, I shall set forth the Prosser classification, in which the Nappier case easily finds a niche.

Prosser analyzed the privacy cases as representing four kinds of invasions of four different interests:[109]

(1) The first group of cases are like the New York case: they involve the defendant's appropriating the plaintiff's identity, through his name or likeness, for defendant's benefit.

106. Id. at 196.
107. Doubts about desirability of the creation of the new tort are raised in Kalven, "Privacy in Tort Law — Were Warren and Brandeis Wrong?" 31 Law and Contemp. Prob. 326 (1966).
108. Bloustein, "Privacy as an Aspect of Human Dignity: An Answer to Dean Prosser," 39 N.Y.U.L. Rev. 962 (1964). Reprinted by permission of the New York University Law Review.
109. Prosser, Handbook of the Law of Torts 802-818 (4th ed. 1971).

(2) The second group of cases involve the defendant's engaging in publicity that puts the plaintiff in a false light — conduct that is objectionable though not necessarily defamatory. Many are like the cases in the first category in that they may involve unauthorized use of a name or photograph. Examples are cases of falsely and publicly attributing to the plaintiff the authorship of an opinion, book, or article, or unauthorizedly using his name on a petition or as a candidate for office.

(3) The third group of cases involve intrusion upon plaintiff's solitude or seclusion, examples being illegal entry or search, or eavesdropping.

(4) The fourth group of cases includes our Nappier case: they involve *public disclosure of certain "private" facts* — facts which may be true and hence would not support an action for defamation. They include cases in which the defendant put up a truthful notice in the street window of his garage that the plaintiff owed him money and wouldn't pay it; and in which a movie told the true story, and revealed the present identity, of a reformed prostitute who seven years before had been the defendant in a sensational murder trial.

Relevant to the Nappier case is the fact that as the common law of privacy developed, certain "privileges" developed, i.e., certain valid legal defenses to the alleged privacy violation. Among them were two privileges that tended to coalesce: the privilege of giving further publicity to a public figure or celebrity (including actors and entertainers), and publicizing news and other matters of public interest. Thus the latter privilege had (prior to the Nappier case) been recognized in a South Carolina case involving publicity to a twelve-year-old wife who had given birth to a child,[110] and a New Mexico case involving publicity to a girl who had been sexually assaulted by her older brother, aged sixteen, these facts being also part of a public court

110. Meetze v. Associated Press, 230 S.C. 330, 95 S.E.2d 606 (1956).

record.[111]   At common law, therefore, the defendants in Nappier may well have had a good defense, as the dissenting court of appeals judge indeed concluded.

As we've already seen, however, the appellate court majority thought the South Carolina criminal statute had the effect of removing the common law defense. We shall be discussing this reasoning in the next chapter. But at this point I should like to alert you to the *constitutional* aspect of the problem, which neither the district court nor the court of appeals discussed, and which we will again consider in Chapter 5.

That is, even if the statute makes a difference, statutes are subject to the Constitution. And there is a constitutional problem here because of the Supreme Court 1967 decision in Time, Inc. v. Hill,[112] which of course was not in existence at the time of the Nappier case. The case dealt with an illustrated 1955 *Life* magazine article about a Broadway play, *The Desperate Hours*, portraying the experience of the Hill family, who had been held prisoners in their home in 1952 by three escaped convicts. The article identified the family by name and treated the play as presenting the family's actual experience, but in fact some of the play's representations (indicating brutalities by the convicts) were false. The plaintiff Hill sued under the New York privacy statute previously described and won in the New York courts, but the Supreme Court reversed on constitutional grounds.

The Court established a proposition for privacy cases that was similar to one it had established in a famous New York Times case three years before[113] for defamation cases by public officials against their critics. It made clear that when there is an alleged invasion of privacy by reporting of matters of public interest, as in the Hill case, the First Amendment freedoms of speech and press come into play. That is, a court which granted damages for the alleged privacy invasion in the circumstances of the Hill case would be acting unconstitu-

tionally, *unless* the communication was *knowingly or recklessly false*. Thus even some false statements — those that are
made innocently or merely negligently — would be constitutionally privileged. The defendants' statements in our
Nappier case weren't false at all. So if the Hill case (involving
the second of the above-described four types of privacy tort
cases, namely the public putting of plaintiff in a false light)
also applies to the fourth type (public disclosure of certain
"private" facts), then the Nappier case might today be
decided for the defendant on constitutional grounds. The
Supreme Court did express a caution that the Hill case
presented no question about whether truthful publication of
"intimate and unwarranted revelations" would be constitutionally privileged.[114] But even if this caution means that
the quoted category will be treated differently, it is not yet
clear that the rape-victim identity facts reported by the
Nappier defendants as part of a newsworthy event would be
viewed as "unwarranted" intimate revelations.

Some other aspects of the constitutional problem of
privacy should be mentioned here to give you a more
rounded view of the matter. Constitutional freedoms of
speech and press are protected against *government* action.
The government activity in the Hill case that would have
violated these freedoms was a *court* award of damages to the
plaintiff. If a statute authorized the damages, then the *statute*
would be the government action that was unconstitutional.
When legislatures acted — as the courts were asked to do in
the Nappier and Hill cases — to *protect* privacy, the statutes
have been upheld when viewed as reasonable and not unduly
invading other rights. Thus the Supreme Court has upheld
laws protecting people against "loud and raucous" noises
from sound trucks on the streets,[115] and from the doorbell
ringing of commercial canvassers as distinguished from
religious solicitors.[116]

114. 385 U.S. 374, 383 n.7 (1967).
115. Kovacs v. Cooper, 336 U.S. 77 (1949).
116. Compare Martin v. Struthers, 319 U.S. 141 (1943), with Breard v. City
of Alexandria, 341 U.S. 622 (1951).

So too, where a law *invades* privacy instead of protecting it, the invasion may be upheld if regarded as not too unreasonable and as serving an important governmental interest. For instance, as discussed earlier, while birth control laws prohibiting use of contraceptives were an invalid invasion of marital privacy, and abortion prohibitions as applied to the first three months of pregnancy violated the woman's privacy right, the Court did hold that restrictions on abortion beyond the first three months were valid. It has also upheld a regulatory commission's permission to a street transportation company to invade the privacy of its passengers by having music, news broadcasts, and advertisements broadcast softly to passengers on the buses and streetcars — where no one-sided political propaganda was broadcast, and a public opinion poll had shown that a great majority of the public wanted the existing system of broadcasts.[117] And the Court has been willing to uphold an invasion of privacy through eavesdropping and wiretapping *if* the government agents have obtained a *judicial warrant* based on a showing of probability that a surveillance which is limited in scope and duration will reveal information on a specified subject and not extraneous information.[118] This judicial warrant requirement for electronic surveillance has been applied even to domestic security investigations.[119] Still to be authoritatively adjudicated is the issue posed by the threat to a person's private associations and beliefs from the growth, centralization, and computerization of government data banks on individuals. Professor Arthur Miller's recent study of that subject finds existing legal safeguards for privacy inadequate and urges congressional creation of a regulatory administrative agency.[120]

---

117. Public Utilities Commn. v. Pollak, 343 U.S. 451 (1952).
118. Katz v. United States, 389 U.S. 347 (1967). See also United States v. District Court, 407 U.S. 297 (1972).
119. United States v. District Court, 407 U.S. 297 (1972).
120. Miller, The Assault on Privacy, esp. cc. 5-7 (1971).

CHAPTER 3

Further Aspects of the Case: The Statute

A. COURT TREATMENT OF THE STATE
STATUTE; INTERPRETATION PROBLEMS
RAISED THEREBY

From Chapter 2 you will recall that the South Carolina statute made it a criminal misdemeanor to publish "in any newspaper, magazine or other publication," the "name" of the victim of a rape or attempted rape.

Remember also that the district court's reasoning was: (1) The statute had no application to the broadcast in this case because (a) there was no reason not to give the statute its plain or literal meaning, and when so construed it covered only publication of the actual names, not stage names, of the victims; (b) being a penal statute, it must be narrowly construed. (2) In any event, the complaint did not show that the defendants had identified the plaintiffs sufficiently to violate their common law right of privacy.

The court of appeals opinion took a different view: The statute applied to the broadcast, because there was good reason to give a nonliteral reading to the statute, so as to cover any identifications, whether or not by actual names; though penal, the statute didn't have to be narrowly construed; though not framed in terms of defenses to common law liability for privacy violation, the statute did show a legislative policy that was inconsistent with recognition of the common-law defense of publicizing newsworthy people and events, in this "name of rape victim" situation.

The Background Notes which follow shortly will deal with this latter problem of the statutory impact on a common law area to which the statute is not directly addressed, and also to the general theory of statutory interpretation. At this point, however, I wish to address myself mainly to the specific points of (1) literal vs. nonliteral reading of statutes, and (2) the narrow reading of penal statutes. I will do this by introducing you to a famous set of four cases, which went off in different directions on these points. They will serve as a good introduction, I think, to the going ways of treating these very common problems of statutory interpretation.

1. *EJUSDEM GENERIS*

Before beginning, I want to point out that two of the four cases are concerned with a maxim of interpretation that might also have been argued in the Nappier opinions but wasn't — the "ejusdem generis" maxim. According to this maxim (literally, "of the same genus or class"), when you have a series of specific enumerations followed by a catchall clause (e.g., "any other . . ."), the coverage of the catchall is to be construed in the light of the common charactcristics of the specific cnumcrations. That is, it should represent the same class or "genus" that they represent. Thus, when the South Carolina statute prohibited publishing the name of the rape victim "in any newspaper, magazine *or other publication*," the catchall I have italicized might be construed to cover only printed publications, i.e., to exclude a televised broadcast, since printing is the common characteristic of the specifically enumerated categories. This argument might be buttressed by the fact that the statute was enacted in 1902, when the legislature couldn't possibly have been thinking of television.

The answering argument would be that courts don't always apply the "ejusdem generis" approach to catchall clauses, any more than they always read a statute literally or always read a penal statute narrowly. The court would have to ask itself whether in the light of the statute's history and policy, its relation to other statutes, the reasonable expectations of those subject to it, etc., the scope of the catchall clause should be read restrictively. As to whether a word should be construed to cover an activity or process that was completely unknown to the enacting legislature that used the word, again the multiplicity of relevant factors may or may not lead a court to an affirmative answer. A "dangerous weapon" statute enacted in mid-nineteenth century, for instance, can be and has been interpreted to cover weapons thereafter invented. If the Nappier defendants had raised the argument that "publication" should exclude television broadcasts, it seems to me likely that this approach would have been rejected — though I am given pause by the fact that the district judge and one of the three appellate judges took an almost equally wooden approach to the word "name."

2. CASES REJECTING "PLAIN MEANING" (HEREIN ALSO OF "EXPRESS MENTION, IMPLIED EXCLUSION" AND THE RULE ON PENAL STATUTES)

I turn first, then, to two well-known Supreme Court cases which *rejected a proposed literal meaning*, and instead adopted, as did the Nappier court of appeals, a meaning derived from the statutory "purpose" or "policy" or "spirit."

The first case is the 1892 case of Holy Trinity Church v. United States.[1] An 1885 federal statute had prohibited prepaying the transportation, or in any way encouraging the importation, of aliens under contract "to perform labor or service of any kind in the United States . . ." There was a $1000 civil penalty for violation. The United States attorney sued the Holy Trinity Church in New York for the penalty because it had contracted with an English clergyman to come over to New York to be the church minister. The Supreme Court unanimously held that the statute didn't apply to this transaction. True, the plain and literal meaning of "labor or service of any kind" would cover the minister's services. But there were reasons for not applying a literal meaning here, said the Court. The title of the act plus the petitions and testimony before congressional committees, plus the reports of the House and Senate committee, showed that "the evil [the law] was designed to remedy" was the importation under contract of cheap manual labor. This together with the country's hospitable attitude toward religion led the Court to conclude, "We cannot think Congress intended to denounce

1. 143 U.S. 457 (1892).

with penalties a transaction like" this, involving services of a church minister.

Nor did the Court regard its departure from literal meaning as a novelty of the law. The Court said:

> It is a familiar rule that a thing may be within the letter of the statute and yet not within the statute because not within its spirit, nor within the intention of its makers. . . .[F] requently words . . . are . . . broad enough to include an act in question, and yet a consideration of the whole legislation, or of the circumstances surrounding its enactment, or of the absurd results which follow from giving such broad meaning to the words, makes it unreasonable to believe that the legislator intended to include the particular act.

One other aspect of the opinion ought to be mentioned. The Court conceded the fact that "as noticed by the Circuit Judge in his opinion, the fifth section which makes specific exceptions, among them professional actors, artists, lecturers, singers and domestic servants, strengthens the idea that every other kind of labor and service was intended to be reached by the first section." The Supreme Court was unmoved by this, but the circuit judge had stressed the "well-settled rule of statutory interpretation" that an exemption proviso carves out of the coverage provision "what would otherwise have been within it." Hence the exemption clause was "equivalent to a declaration that contracts to perform professional services except those of actors, artists, lecturers or singers are within the prohibition of the preceding sections."[2] The circuit judge might also have cited a related "well-settled rule" sometimes described as "express mention, implied exclusion." More elegantly known as "expressio unius, exclusio alterius," it embodies the thought that when the only things expressly specified by the legislature are A and B, then the intention is to exclude the disputed C. If you think about this a moment, I think you'll conclude that such an inference isn't always justified. Sometimes if you specify A and B, you don't mean *only* A and B; you may be using A

2. United States v. Church of the Holy Trinity, 36 F. 303, 305 (S.D.N.Y. 1888).

and B as illustrative examples. Still, it is true that a legislative specification, especially one within an exemption clause, is more likely to be intended to be exclusive (even if the legislature doesn't say "only"). But remember that even where a court concludes that the specification was intended to be exclusive, it might still believe that the legislature had *inadvertently omitted* an additional category, that applying the statute without it would lead to an absurd result, or that someone shouldn't be punished who acted on a reasonable belief to that effect. This was apparently the attitude of the Supreme Court toward the exemption categories in the Holy Trinity Church case.

The second of my two cases rejecting a literal construction is the 1931 case of McBoyle v. United States.[3] The National Motor Vehicle Theft Act of 1919 had prohibited interstate transportation of stolen motor vehicles known to be stolen, and had provided that "the term 'motor vehicle' shall include an automobile, automobile truck, automobile wagon, motorcycle, or any other self-propelled vehicle not designed for running on rails." The defendant McBoyle was convicted of having caused the stealing and interstate transportation of an airplane. The Tenth Circuit Court of Appeals affirmed by a 2 to 1 vote. But a unanimous Supreme Court, speaking through Justice Holmes, held that the conviction should be reversed, because the statute didn't cover airplanes.

He rejected a literal approach to "vehicle." He conceded that "no doubt etymologically it is possible to use the word to signify a conveyance working on land, water, or air, and sometimes legislation [specifically does so, and sometimes specifically does otherwise] ... But in everyday speech 'vehicle' calls up the picture of a thing moving on land." The "not designed for running on rails" language strengthens this "popular picture" of a vehicle running on land. "It is a vehicle that runs, not something not commonly called a vehicle, that flies." And this was fortified by contextual considerations (similar to those underlying the "ejusdem generis" maxim which had been invoked by the dissenting circuit court of appeals judge, though Holmes did not refer to

3. 283 U.S. 25 (1931).

the maxim as such): "It is impossible to read words that so carefully enumerate the different forms of motor vehicles and have no reference of any kind to aircraft, as including airplanes under a term that usage more and more precisely confines to a different class."

Moreover, "Airplanes were well known in 1919, when this statute was passed; but it is admitted that they were not mentioned in the reports or in the debates in Congress." The dissenting circuit court of appeals judge had treated the matter of legislative history more fully. He conceded that not all congressional proceedings can be given much weight in interpreting a statute; congressional debates have little weight compared to committee reports. But the debates can be used, the Supreme Court had previously held, to show the history of the period. And here, he said, "The discussions of the proposed measures are enlightening . . . from a historic stand-point in showing that the theft of automobiles was so prevalent over the land as to call for punitive restraint, but airplanes were never even mentioned." He also tied in this prevailing concern over automobile thefts and the rarity of airplane thefts — both of which he characterized as "familiar knowledge" — with the broad principle that had also been invoked in the Holy Trinity Church case: "The prevailing mischief sought to be corrected is an aid in the construction of a statute."

Finally the idea that penal statutes are to be strictly construed (i.e., narrowly construed to favor the defendant) — which was invoked by the Nappier district court, and by the dissenting circuit court of appeals judge in McBoyle — was also in Justice Holmes's opinion though the maxim was not cited as such: "Although it is not likely that a criminal will carefully consider the text of the law before he murders or steals, it is reasonable that a fair warning should be given to the world in language that the common world will understand, of what the law intends to do if a certain line is passed. To make the warning fair, so far as possible the line should be clear."

Before turning to my second pair of Supreme Court cases on the plain-meaning rule, let me say that there are cases in

which the Court's refusal to apply a plain-meaning approach
yields even more striking results than in McBoyle and Holy
Trinity. How do you react to a Court holding that "shall"
means "may," or "may" means "shall," or that "and" means
"or," or "or" means "and?"[4] Do you wonder whether the
Court isn't going too far? Remember that in these cases, too,
the Court was convinced that *in the particular circumstances*
it was more reasonable to conclude that the legislature
couldn't have intended the result to which a literal meaning
would lead. For instance, an important Supreme Court case,
Hecht Co. v. Bowles,[5] involved the interpretation of "shall"
in the injunction section of the Emergency Price Control Act
of 1942. The section said that upon the government's proof
of the defendant's violation of the act or any regulations
thereunder, the court "shall" issue an injunction. The case
involved a defendant department store that proved it had
made an unusually "good-faith" intensive effort to avoid
violations. The Court held that since the exercise of judicial
discretion was a hallmark of a court of equity's exercise of
the injunction power, and since there was nothing in the
legislative history to show that Congress was deliberately
making a drastic departure from this centuries-old tradition,
the Court could not give "shall" its literal, mandatory
meaning.

3. *CASES ADOPTING "PLAIN MEANING" (HEREIN ALSO OF INFERENCES FROM LEGISLATIVE ACTION AND INACTION)*

Coming to two well-known Supreme Court cases in which
a literal or plain-meaning approach was *adopted*: The first is
Caminetti v. United States,[6] involving the Mann Act. This act

4. On "shall" vs. "may," see Crawford, Statutory Construction §262 (1940);
Cairo and Fulton R. Co. v. Hecht, 95 U.S. 168, 170 (1877). On "and" vs. "or,"
see 50 Am. Jur. §282 (1944) and latest pocket supplement; DeSylva v.
Ballentine, 351 U.S. 570, 573-574 (1956); United States v. Fisk, 68 U.S. (3 Wall.)
445, 447 (1865).

5. 321 U.S. 321 (1944).

6. 242 U.S. 470 (1917).

made it a criminal offense knowingly to transport, or cause or aid the transportation of in interstate commerce, "any woman or girl for the purpose of prostitution or debauchery, or for any other immoral purpose. . . ." Caminetti's conviction under this law was for transporting a woman from Sacramento, California to Reno, Nevada, where she was to become, in the Court's words, his "concubine and mistress." A majority of the Supreme Court upheld his conviction.

Let me first summarize the view of the three dissenting justices. They opposed the view that "any other immoral purpose" must be given a plain, literal meaning so as to cover the admittedly immoral purpose of making a woman one's mistress. As you might have expected, they relied heavily on the principle of the Holy Trinity Church case, which they cited and quoted from. They said the "principle [of that case] is the simple one that the words of a statute will be extended or restricted to execute its purpose." And the sole purpose here, they said, was to punish those engaging in *commercialized* vice involving the crossing of state lines. This was clear from the House Committee Report and the statement of the bill's sponsor. The dissenters stressed that a congressional committee report was weighty evidence of legislative intent, much more so than the floor debates. They also cited an opinion of the attorney general, and the fact that § 8 of the act declared that the "Act shall be known and referred to as the 'White-slave Traffic Act.' " The latter point was supplemented by the argument that "It is a peremptory rule of construction that all parts of a statute must be taken into account in ascertaining its meaning, and it cannot be said that Sec. 8 has no object." Finally, the dissenters cited the principle that "a construction which leads to mischievous consequences" should be rejected if the statute is reasonably susceptible of another construction. And here, "Blackmailers of both sexes have arisen, using the terrors of the construction now sanctioned by this court as a help — indeed, the means — for their brigandage."

The Caminetti majority, on the other hand, relied heavily on the "plain-meaning rule," in the way the district judge in our Nappier case did. They saw the principle as making unnecessary any reference to committee reports, or maxims of construction, or any other aids that were extrinsic to the substance of the statute:

> [I] t has been so often affirmed as to become a recognized rule, when words are free from doubt they must be taken as the final expression of the legislative intent, and are not to be added to or subtracted from by considerations drawn from titles or designating names, or reports accompanying their introduction, or from any extraneous source. In other words, the language being plain, and not leading to absurd or wholly impracticable consequences, it is the sole evidence of the ultimate legislative intent.

"Plain" meaning tends not only to be the same as literal meaning but also the same as ordinary meaning (though remember that the literal or "etymological" meaning of "vehicle" in McBoyle was viewed differently from its meaning in "everyday speech"). The majority supplemented its general observations on the plain-meaning principle by saying this on ordinary meaning: "Statutory words are uniformly presumed, unless the contrary appears, to be used in their ordinary and usual sense, and with the meaning commonly attributed to them." To say that interstate transportation for the purpose of making someone a "concubine or mistress" is not for an "immoral" purpose "would shock the common understanding of what constitutes an immoral purpose when those terms are applied, as here, to sexual relations."

The majority recognized that the "ejusdem generis" principle would require that the conduct covered by "any other immoral purpose" be of the same general class as prostitution and debauchery. And they concluded that being a concubine or mistress *was* in that same class even though lacking the commercial element. The Supreme Court had already so held in construing a statute dealing with importation of alien women, and this construction, said the Caminetti majority, was presumably known to Congress when it enacted the similar language of the Mann Act. The reliance on construction of the other statute illustrates a principle which has been embodied in the "pari materia" maxim — to the effect that statutes involving the same subject matter should be construed together. The maxim, not surprisingly, doesn't always result in a court's adopting the natural conclusion that results from such a construing together.[7]

My second "plain-meaning" decision is the 1950 case of Alpers v. United States.[8] "The question in this case," said the Court, "is whether the shipment of obscene phonograph records in interstate commerce is prohibited by Sec. 245 of the Criminal Code, which makes illegal the interstate shipment of any 'obscene . . . book, pamphlet, picture, motion-picture film, paper, letter, writing, print, or other matter of indecent character'." The majority answered in the affirmative and upheld the conviction.

The three dissenting judges of course invoked the maxim about penal statutes, and the particular importance thereof in the field of freedom of expression.

Our system of justice is based on the principle that criminal statutes shall be couched in language sufficiently clear to apprise people of the precise conduct that is prohibited. Judicial interpretation deviates from this salutary principle when statutory language is expanded to include conduct that Congress might have barred, but did not, by the language it used. . . . The reluctance of courts to expand the coverage of criminal statutes is particularly important where, as here, the statute results in censorship.

The dissenters further invoked the "ejusdem generis" maxim, though not referring to it as such, when they complained that while the statute's specific list of indecent articles "applied only to articles that people could read or see," the majority "now adds to it articles capable of use to produce sounds that people can hear."

The majority's response to these positions was this: "We are aware that this is a criminal statute and must be strictly construed. This means that no offense may be created except

7. See Sutherland, Statutory Construction §§5201-5206 (3d ed., Horack, 1943; and latest pocket supplement).
8. 338 U.S. 680 (1950).

by the words of Congress used in their usual and ordinary sense." Quoting from an earlier Supreme Court opinion, they said, "while penal statutes are narrowly construed, this does not require rejection of that sense of the words which best harmonizes with the context and the end in view."

The "ejusdem generis" maxim also received short shrift: "We think that to apply the rule of *ejusdem generis* to the present case would be 'to defeat the obvious purpose of legislation.' The obvious purpose . . . was to prevent the channels of interstate commerce from being used to disseminate any matter that, in its essential nature, communicates obscene, lewd, lascivious or filthy ideas." The statute was intended to be a broad one, for it included other prohibitions, such as those against interstate shipment of contraceptives. "Statutes are construed in their entire context. This is a comprehensive statute, which should not be constricted by a mechanical rule of construction."

Nor was there anything in the legislative history to indicate a congressional intent to limit the catchall clause

to such indecent matter as is comprehended through the sense of sight. True, this statute was amended in 1920 to include "motion picture film." We are not persuaded that Congress, by adding motion-picture film to the specific provisions of the statute, evidenced an intent that obscene matter not specifically added was without the prohibition of the statute; nor do we think that Congress intended that only visual obscene matter was within the prohibition of the statute. The First World War gave considerable impetus to the making and distribution of motion-picture films. And in 1920 the public was considerably alarmed at the indecency of many of the films. It thus appears that with respect to this amendment, Congress was preoccupied with making doubly sure that motion-picture film was within the Act, and was concerned with nothing more or less.

The majority therefore applied the plain meaning of the catchall clause — though it was not applying a "plain meaning rule" in the sense of ignoring any evidences of legislative intent located outside the statutory words.

A further word on the majority's attitude toward the motion picture film amendment: its attitude was analogous to a rejection of an "express mention, implied exclusion" argument. That is, in cases where that maxim is rejected, you are likely to find the Court assuming that the legislature was merely giving examples, or — as the majority says in this *Alpers* case — was making "doubly sure" about the matters expressly mentioned.

The "doubly sure" line may also be taken in cases where a court wants to apply a law to conduct occurring prior to an amendment which explicitly covers that type of conduct. The inference from the amendment, that the conduct wasn't covered prior to the amendment, may be rejected by this reasoning: the legislature by its amendment wanted to "emphasize" or "clarify" or make "unmistakable" or "doubly sure" of the coverage. Consider for instance, Coplon v. United States, in which the District of Columbia Court of Appeals was dealing with the FBI's power to make an arrest without a warrant of a Department of Justice employee suspected of espionage. Another circuit court had already ruled that the statute governing FBI arrests didn't authorize arrests without a warrant for felonies in the presence of the officer. Congress had then amended the statute so as to expressly grant such an authority. The situation presented to the District of Columbia court had arisen prior to the amendment, but the court refused to conclude that the fact of the amendment itself showed a lack of arresting authority prior to its passage. The amendment had simply "made unmistakable what we think was true before revision...."[9]

But if you suspect that a court must have often, indeed usually, concluded that a legislative amendment — in the course of a bill's passage, or after its adoption — did reflect an intent to *change* the previously existing bill or statute, you are of course right.[10]

While on the subject of permissible interpretive inferences from what goes on in the legislature, I think you should know about this additional facet of the subject though I can't

9. Coplon v. United States, 191 F.2d 749, 755 (D.C. Cir. 1951). See also United States v. Lowden, 308 U.S. 225, 239 (1939); State v. Boliski, 156 Wis. 78, 145 N.W. 368 (1914).

10. See, e.g., United States v. Plesha, 352 U.S. 202, 208 (1957).

stop to elaborate on it: There are numerous cases on the issue
of whether the court can infer legislative approval of an
administrative or judicial interpretation of a statute from the
fact that (a) the legislature did nothing to change it; or (b)
during the process of passage of the statute, or after its
enactment, the effort to adopt a view contrary to the
interpretation in question died in a legislative committee or
was rejected by vote of one or both houses of the legislature.
Naturally, the vote of both houses against the opposing view
is much more likely to be taken as approval of the
interpretation in question than are the other kinds of
legislative action or inaction mentioned. But you will find
that there are cases going both ways in each of these
categories — simply because an inference of legislative
approval is sometimes outweighed by opposing considerations present in the particular case.

Now to develop a little further some aspects of the
interpretation problems common to the four cases I have
summarized and the Nappier case.

4. PROBLEMS IN THE "PLAIN MEANING" RULE

(a) First, a reminder of some ambiguities in the plain-
meaning rule. I've already referred to the point that a plain or
unambiguous meaning generally seems to coincide with a
"literal" meaning and with an "ordinary" meaning, but that
where there was a divergence between the latter two, the
Supreme Court in the stolen airplane case chose what it
conceived to be the ordinary meaning.

Another thing that may cause confusion is the relation of a
plain-meaning interpretation to a choice between *narrow or
broad* interpretation. I think we may tend to associate a
literal or ordinary meaning with the *broader* interpretation.
This association did indeed occur in the Holy Trinity Church
case (the rejected plain meaning of "labor or service of any
kind" would have *included* the minister's services), in
Caminetti (the plain meaning of "any other immoral pur-

pose" was adopted and held to *include* noncommercialized immorality), and in Alpers (the plain meaning of "other matter of indecent character" was adopted and held to *include* obscene phonograph records). Yet this association was not true in McBoyle — where the ordinary meaning of "vehicle" in the phrase "any other self-propelled vehicle not designed for running on rails" was adopted and held to *exclude* airplanes. Nor was it true in our Nappier case where the plain meaning of "name" as adopted by the district court and rejected by the court of appeals gave the *narrower* coverage.

Another erroneous association would be between the plain-meaning rule and the concept of "strict" construction. There is, no doubt, a sense in which a literal construction is a strict one. But in the field of statutory interpretation the term "strict" is generally used in the sense of *narrow*. Thus when we say a penal statute is to be construed strictly, we mean construed to give the narrower coverage that would favor the defendant, if such a construction is reasonably possible. So "strict" should not be used to characterize a literal construction via the plain-meaning rule, since (as we have already seen) such a construction sometimes yields the narrower, sometimes the broader interpretation.

(b) What can be said *in favor* of the plain-meaning rule? As good a statement as any was made by Justice Jackson, concurring in the 1951 case of Schwegmann Bros. v. Calvert Distillers Corp.[11] and protesting against the majority's unwillingness to rest the decision on the clear words of the statute, i.e., without reference to congressional debates and other items of legislative history:

Resort to legislative history is only justified where the face of the Act is inescapably ambiguous, and then I think we should not go beyond Committee reports, which presumably are well considered and carefully prepared. . . . The Rules of the House and Senate, with the sanction of the Constitution, require three readings of an Act in each House before final enactment. That is intended, I take it, to make sure that each

11. 341 U.S. 384, 395 (1951).

House knows what it is passing and passes what it wants, and that what is enacted was formally reduced to writing. . . . Moreover, it is only the words of the bill that have presidential approval, where that approval is given. It is not to be supposed that, in signing a bill, the President endorses the whole Congressional Record. . . .

Moreover, there are practical reasons why we should accept whenever possible the meaning which an enactment reveals on its face. Laws are intended for all of our people to live by; and the people go to law offices to learn what their rights under those laws are. Here is a controversy which affects every little merchant in many states. Aside from a few offices in the larger cities, the materials of a legislative history are not available to the lawyer who can afford neither the cost of acquisition, the cost of housing, nor the cost of repeatedly examining the whole congressional history. Moreover, if he could, he would not know any way of anticipating what would impress enough members of the Court to be controlling . . .

Another point can be added to the defense of the plain-meaning rule. It contains within itself a reasonable qualification. When the Caminetti majority stated the rule, they included the limitation that the plain-meaning must not be one "leading to absurd or wholly impracticable consequences."

(c) What can be said *against* the plain-meaning rule?

(1) To begin with, it deliberately cuts off from judicial consideration even the clearest evidence from extrinsic sources, such as legislative history, of what was the so-called legislative intent on the question in dispute. There may be cogent reasons for doing so, as is argued in the above-quoted opinion of Justice Jackson. But the evidentiary sacrifice involved is considerable.

(2) A more important difficulty stems from ambiguities within the rule. I have already tried to clarify some confusions about the meaning of the rule. But I'm now concerned with a deeper ambiguity. There is real uncertainty as to when the conditions exist for application of the rule: When are the statutory words *so clear* as to bar the court from looking beyond the words to the statute's underlying policy and legislative history? The uncertainty here has led one writer to refer to the "ambiguity of unambiguous statutes." That is, there are plenty of instances where, in

spite of a rather obvious ambiguity on the face of the statute, attested to in the opinions of a divided court, one group of judges within the divided court is unwilling to view it as the *degree* of ambiguity sufficient to make the plain-meaning rule inapplicable; hence they proclaim that the statute is unambiguous.

For example, in Packard Motor Co. v. NLRB[12] in 1947, the Supreme Court had to decide whether a plant foreman was an "employee" within the meaning of the National Labor Relations Act, so that a union of foremen would be entitled to rights of organization, collective bargaining, etc. under that act. The act declared that "The term 'employee' shall include any employee . . ." This looked in the direction of coverage. But "employer" was also defined: "The term 'employer' includes any person acting in the interest of an employer, directly or indirectly . . ." Read together, the definitions at least created an ambiguity. The three dissenting justices resolved the ambiguity by saying foremen were not covered as employees, and drew support from the absence — in the entire statute and its legislative history — of any reference to the problem of unionized supervisory personnel. They drew further support from the fact that certain other statutes in defining "employee" had specifically included subordinate officials. Yet the majority, speaking through Justice Jackson, read the statutory words as covering foremen, and solemnly intoned, "There is . . . no ambiguity in the Act to be clarified by resort to legislative history . . ."

(3) There is still another uncertainty as to when the conditions exist for application of the rule: When does the *exception* (quoted supra page 212 from the Caminetti opinion) come into play so as to make the rule inapplicable where it would result in "absurd or wholly impracticable consequences"? This is practically the same as asking: when does the rule of the Holy Trinity Church case come into play? For that case counseled rejection of a plain or literal meaning "when a consideration of the whole legislation or of

12. 330 U.S. 485 (1947).

the circumstances surrounding its enactment, or of the absurd results which follow from" that meaning "makes it unreasonable to believe that the legislator intended to include the particular act." This of course was also the approach of the court of appeals in the Nappier case when it looked at the purposes of the statute and thought that they would be frustrated by giving a literal reading to the word "name." In other words, in any case on the plain-meaning rule which is at all debatable, we are faced with a choice between it and its exception (or the Holy Trinity Church rule), and are given no precise way of choosing between opposite rules.

As a matter of fact, this point as to uncertainty over whether the rule or its opposite applies is even stronger than I have so far made it. For there is an opposite rule *additional* to the opposite rule just mentioned. What I have in mind is a rule which is even a more direct negation of the plain-meaning rule. It *denies* that a plain meaning on the face of the statute *ever* bars the interpreting court from looking beyond the face of the statute. Seven years before Justice Jackson refused in the Packard Motor case to look beyond the words of the National Labor Relations Act because the meaning of "employee" was plain, the Supreme Court had said in construing "employee" under the Motor Carrier Act:

Frequently, . . . even when the plain meaning did not produce absurd results but merely an unreasonable one "plainly at variance with the policy of the legislation as a whole," this Court has followed that purpose, rather than the literal words. When aid to construction of the meaning of words, as used in the statute, is available, there certainly can be no "rule of law" which forbids its use, however clear the words may appear on "superficial examination."[13]

And in the same year, 1940, the Court said:

It would be anomalous to close our minds to persuasive evidence of intention on the ground that reasonable men could not differ as to the meaning of the words. Legislative materials may be without probative value, or contradictory, or ambiguous, it is true, and in such cases will not be permitted to control the customary meaning of words or overcome rules of syntax or construction found by experience to be workable; they can scarcely be deemed to be incompetent or

13. United States v. American Trucking Assn., 310 U.S. 534, 543-544 (1940).

irrelevant. .... The meaning to be ascribed to an Act of Congress can only be derived from a considered weighing of every relevant aid to construction.[14]

When these two cases are juxtaposed with cases like Caminetti and Packard Motor, it is clear that the Supreme Court has precedents available for taking opposite positions on even the *existence* of a plain-meaning rule. This of course produces more flexibility both for the Court and for the advocates. But neither the Court nor the bar can view this situation as an example of the judicial process at its best.

5. *PROBLEMS IN THE RULE ON PENAL STATUTES*

What now of the rule on strict construction of penal statutes? Again there is something to be said *for* the policy underlying the rule: when something as drastic as a penal sanction is involved, it makes sense to say that of two reasonable alternative interpretations, the one favoring the defendant should be preferred in the absence of strong countervailing factors.

But again we are left in doubt about when the rule will be applied. One source of the doubt is the existence and scope of these countervailing factors and the lack of any precise formula for weighing all the competing factors. Another source of doubt is the ambiguity of "penal." Criminal statutes, the prosecution under which entails criminal procedure and can result in a penalty of imprisonment and/or fine, would clearly qualify. But there are civil sanctions, such as treble damages or property forfeitures or license revocations, that a particular court may or may not view as qualifying. Moreover, if one rule is that a penal statute is to be strictly construed, and another rule is that a remedial statute is to be broadly construed, how helpful can these rules be where a court concludes that a statute is partly remedial and partly penal?[15]

14. United States v. Dickerson, 310 U.S. 554, 562 (1940).
15. See, e.g., 3 Sutherland, Statutory Construction §5703 (3d ed., Horack, 1943).

There is still another ambivalence: the fact that a court has determined a statute to be penal for one purpose (such as whether the time period under a separate statute of limitations applying to "penal" actions should apply to this case) doesn't mean that the same court will necessarily view the same statute in another case as penal for another purpose, i.e., statutory construction.[16] Indeed, this kind of variability in the determination of whether a statute is penal is illustrated by the court of appeals opinion in the Nappier case. Here again are the court's words:

> In South Carolina the penal aspect of the statute does not require an interpretation so rigid as to strip its wording of its plain connotation. Carolina Amusement Co. v. Martin, 236 S.C. 558, 115 S.E.2d 273 (1960), cert. denied, 367 U.S. 904 . . . (1961); State v. Firemen's Ins. Co., 164 S.C. 313, 162 S.E. 334 (1931). This is certainly sound construction *when, as here, the statute is only employed to provide civil redress.* McKenzie v. Peoples Baking Co, 205 S.C. 149, 31 S.E.2d 154 (1944).[17] [Emphasis added.]

Thus, the court was suggesting that however rigid the interpretation might have to be in a criminal prosecution under the statute, it need not be that rigid in a civil suit for damages at common law, where the statute was involved in only an auxiliary way.

Notice also that the first sentence of the quotation, as well as the cases cited in support, illustrate anew that the rule contains qualifications and does not necessarily result in giving a penal statute the narrower of alternative interpretations. One of the cited cases puts it this way, quoting from a legal encyclopedia: " 'The rule that a penal statute must be strictly construed does not prevent the courts from calling to their aid all the other rules of construction and giving each its appropriate scope, and is not violated by giving the words of the statute a reasonable meaning according to the sense in which they were intended, and disregarding captious objections and even the demands of exact grammatical pro-

---

16. Compare Schiffman Bros. v. Texas Co., 196 F.2d 695 (7th Cir. 1952), with Roseland v. Phister Mfg. Co., 125 F.2d 417 (7th Cir. 1942).

17. 322 F.2d 502, 504 (4th Cir. 1963).

priety.' "[18] Remember, in this connection, that Caminetti and Alpers were criminal prosecutions under the Mann Act and the federal obscenity statute, yet in both cases the broader interpretations of statutory coverage were adopted.

Our discussion until now shows, if it shows anything, that the two rules figuring in the Nappier case (the plain-meaning rule and the rule as to penal statutes) as well as other rules encountered along the way, such as ejusdem generis, are not by themselves conclusive. They have qualifications; they may have opposites; they must be considered along with all other relevant factors before the Court's final decision is reached. I shall return to this theme again in the ensuing background note.

B. BACKGROUND NOTE: A FURTHER WORD ON STATUTORY INTERPRETATION; THE SEARCH FOR LEGISLATIVE INTENT OR PURPOSE

Having explored the nature of the interpretation issues that were central in the Nappier case, I should like to now look at the problem of interpretation against a somewhat broader background.

1. You will have noted that the interpreting court generally assumes it is in a subordinate power relationship to the legislature. That is, it plays the subservient role of discovering and effectuating the "legislative intent."

I am not talking now of those cases where the legislature itself has made rather clear that the *court* is to exercise the dominant role. This happens, for instance, where a legislature deliberately enacts a vague provision — perhaps because it feels it doesn't know enough about the subject to be precise, or because conditions are expected to change too rapidly for a rigid standard, or because legislative compromise phrased in

---

18. State v. Firemen's Ins. Co., 164 S.C. 313, 162 S.E. 334, 338 (1931), quoting 25 Ruling Case Law 1085 (1919).

indeterminate language was the only way to get the statute passed. A statute prohibiting "unreasonable speed" rather than setting a specific maximum is one example. The Sherman Act prohibitions against monopolization and restraint of trade, leaving it to the courts to develop the precise meaning of these standards, are other examples. In these instances, the court's freedom operates within elastic boundaries, although it is still true that the legislature has laid down those boundaries for the court.

2. In this latter type of case as well as in the more common type of case, the overwhelming number of court opinions will be found talking in terms of the overriding goal of effectuating "legislative intent" — though sometimes "purpose" is used instead of, or interchangeably with, "intent." Justice Frankfurter once said he always used "purpose" instead of "intent." Why the distinction?

The reason is this. In the typical appellate case of statutory interpretation, the court is dealing with a specific situation that the legislature never thought of. When Congress passed the Alien Contract Labor Act, it hadn't thought specifically about whether a New York church bringing over a minister from England would be covered; when it passed the Motor Vehicle Theft Act, it had not thought specifically about whether a stolen airplane would be covered; when the South Carolina legislature passed its 1902 law on publication of rape victims' names, it had not thought specifically about whether television broadcasts would be covered that allegedly identified without expressly naming the victim. To speak of a legislative intent in the sense of a conscious desire to have a specific situation treated in a particular way would therefore be to speak of a fiction. To avoid that fictional aspect of the search for legislative intent, a court may regard itself as operating more realistically by asking itself not "Did the legislature intend to cover this situation?" but rather this question: "Considering the *general* policy objective or *purpose* of the statute as shown by its provisions, its history, and other extrinsic aids, what *would* the legislature *probably* have said of the specific situation *if* it had thought of it?" Such a

distinction between "intent" and "purpose" makes some
sense, though, as I've said, you will find some judges using
the terms interchangeably.

Of course if "purpose," in the sense indicated, is to be
pursued thoroughly, the court cannot stop with the key
statutory words being construed. It must look at the entire
statute, its legislative history, its relation to other statutes,
maxims of construction, etc. In that kind of search —
whether the court labels it a search for intent or a search for
purpose — barriers like that erected by the plain-meaning rule
would have to be surmounted. The court might invoke the
1940 Supreme Court cases I have mentioned,[19] to the effect
that "It would be anomalous to close our minds to persuasive
evidence of intention on the ground that reasonable men
could not differ as to the meaning of the words. . . . The
meaning . . . can only be derived from a considered weighing
of every relevant aid to construction."[20] Or the court might
invoke the exception to the plain-meaning rule in terms of
"absurd or wholly impracticable consequences," or — what is
roughly equivalent to the exception — the rule embodied in
the Holy Trinity Church case (sometimes called "the golden
rule"). The search for the underlying statutory purpose or
policy would also be supported by the so-called "mischief
rule" or the rule of Heydon's case in sixteenth-century
England, according to which the court is to interpret any
statute in the light of the "mischief" at which it was aimed,
the judge's duty being to make the interpretation that will
"suppress the mischief and advance the remedy . . . according
to the true intent of the makers of the Act, *pro bono
publico*."[21]

19. Notes 13 and 14 supra.
20. United States v. Dickerson, 310 U.S. 554, 562 (1940).
21. 3 Co. 7a, 7b, 76 Eng. Rep. 637 (K.B. 1584): "[F]or the sure and
true . . . interpretation of all statutes in general (be they penal . . . or beneficial,
restrictive or enlarging of the common law), four things are to be discerned and
considered: 1st, what was the common law before the making of the Act? 2nd,
what was the mischief and defect for which the common law did not provide?
3rd, what remedy the Parliament hath resolved and appointed to cure the disease
of the commonwealth? And 4th, the true reason of the remedy; and then the
office of all the Judges is always to make such . . . construction as shall suppress

3. I have been assuming that when the court makes use of legislative history, rules of construction, and other aids extrinsic to the face of the statute, it is still focused on legislative purpose or intent; it is still playing the subordinate power role, at least in theory. I think you should know, however, that not everyone seems to take this view. Thus one scholar argues this way: a court may apply the plain-meaning rule so as to adopt a plain meaning regardless of how strongly the legislative history shows a *contrary* meaning was *intended.* So too, "such established doctrines as the presumption against repeals by implication, the rules of strict construction, and such canons as *expressio unius* and *ejusdem generis* are not really guides to the legislative will or understanding but rather rules of judicial policy which irrespective of subjective legislative intention, may be given controlling effect in the application of statutes."[22]

I think this view would be more persuasive if it were taken to mean that there is such a lack of effective restraint on a judge's freedom in applying the techniques for ascertaining legislative intent, that in practice he is able to effectuate his own conception of proper policy, though in theory his result is reflective of legislative intent. If, however, the quoted view means that even in theory, judicial application of many rules of construction represents a deviation from the legislative intent standard, I think the view is erroneous. I think the opinions in the cases applying the rules of construction assert overwhelmingly that the court is effectuating legislative intent or purpose. Even where a court is giving weight to official attitudes exhibited long after enactment of the statute — e.g., attitudes of administrators, attitudes of subsequent legislatures in their treatment of proposed amendments or in later statutes — this seems to be based on the idea that

---

the mischief and advance the remedy, and to suppress subtle inventions and evasions for continuance of the mischief, and *pro privato commodo*, and to add force and life to the cure and remedy, according to the true intent of the makers of the Act, *pro bono publico.*"

22. Jones, "Statutory Doubts and Legislative Intention," 40 Colum. L. Rev. 957, 966-967 (1940).

those subsequent attitudes throw light on the original legislative purpose or intent.

However, a number of commentators do urge that courts should shift their focus away from original intent or purpose, and openly recognize that they have a "legislative" role to play; that to continue to speak exclusively of original legislative intent is often to deal in an artificial or incomplete way with a problem that cries for the use of additional criteria for its solution. Thus, even assuming that a court can get a pretty clear idea of what the general legislative policy or purpose was, and is fairly confident that the particular situation, X, fits into that policy, this would be one weighty consideration to be taken into account. Another relevant consideration might be: have socioeconomic conditions changed so radically that if the enacting legislature had foreseen them it would not have wanted to cover X? One commentator puts it in terms of what the enacting legislature would have said "had it the time and the awareness of the problems that hindsight now permits."[23] This second sight might extend not only to changed conditions but also to matters such as these: that the coverage of X would be unfair to a litigant who reasonably claims to have read the statute the other way;[24] that the coverage of X will result in less consistency or harmony with the existing body of the law, including law enacted after the statute in question.

The proposal to determine what would have been said by an *ideal* enacting legislature — one blessed with clairvoy-

23. Cohen, "Judicial 'Legisputation' and the Dimensions of Legislative Meaning," 36 Ind. L.J. 414, 418 (1961).

24. For an emphasis upon the meaning that would be given by a reasonable addressee of the statutory language rather than upon the intended meaning of the legislature, see Holmes, "The Theory of Legal Interpretation," 12 Harv. L. Rev. 417 (1899), reprinted in Holmes, Collected Legal Papers 203 (1920); Curtis, It's Your Law c. 2, esp. at 62-67 (1954). The first volumes of the fourth edition of Sutherland, Statutory Construction, have begun to appear, and in the Preface of vol. 1 (pp. v-vi), the editor, Prof. C. Dallas Sands, states that the implications of the difference between the above two emphases have been elaborated in the forthcoming Part 5 of the treatise and "have been fully incorporated into the treatment of all aspects of statutory construction in the present edition."

ance — goes almost as far as one writer's proposal to guess at what the *current* legislature would have said.[25] Both proposals may seem extreme but can be defended on the ground that they propose doing openly what now is often done surreptitiously. The argument would be that while courts cling to the concept of the enacting legislature's intent or purpose as a monolithic standard, the other considerations I have mentioned influence their conclusion. In fact, though not in theory, legislative intent or purpose is not the exclusive standard.

4. But even if we stick to theory, and think of legislative intent or purpose as the exclusive standard, there is, as you have doubtless already concluded, *no exclusive source or clue for the correct application of that standard* in a particular case. The sources or clues are multiple, e.g.: the key statutory words, the rest of the statute, the legislative history, prior interpretations, related statutes and their interpretations, analogous statutes and interpretations in other jurisdictions, common law meanings and attitudes, the various rules or maxims of construction. We can't explore all of these here. I do want to say something more about the last-mentioned category — which was of course involved in my earlier discussion of the plain-meaning rule and the rule on penal statutes.

You have already seen that each of these rules sometimes carried the day, and sometimes not. When it did not, an opposing rule was available for invocation. These maxims travel in pairs. Professor Karl Llewellyn once illustrated this by presenting a table of 28 "thrusts" and "parries" among the "canons of construction" used by state courts, and another 19 drawn from federal court opinions.[26] Back in 1939, Robert Lynd made an analogous list of contrasting assumptions or values in American culture.[27] Herbert Simon, writing on administrative organization, has made a similar

25. Curtis, "A Better Theory of Legal Interpretation," 3 Vand. L. Rev. 407 (1950).

26. See Appendix C of Llewellyn, The Common Law Tradition 521-535 (1960).

27. Lynd, Knowledge for What? 60-62 (1939).

point about contradiction among some "proverbs of administration."[28]

In my teaching of statutory interpretation I have found
this "proverb" notion fruitful. I have likened the maxims or
canons to folk-sayings. I have gone down a list of "thrusts"
with students, and asked for their "parries." I have found
that if I present "He who hesitates is lost" or "The early bird
catches the worm," someone will come up with "Look
before you leap" or "Haste makes waste." If I say, "A penny
saved is a penny earned," I get back, "Penny wise, pound
foolish." If I say "Out of sight, out of mind," I am told that
"Absence makes the heart grow fonder." While "Faint heart
never won fair lady" and "Nothing ventured, nothing
gained," still on the other hand, "Discretion is the better part
of valor," and "The meek shall inherit the earth."

I also discovered that folk-sayings can change meanings as
the times change. I had suggested that the saying "A rolling
stone gathers no moss" could be counterpointed by "Variety
is the spice of life." I had always supposed that the "moss" in
the saying represented something good — stability or matu-
rity — and hence the saying was frowning on the rolling
stone. But I found that about half the class viewed the
gathering of moss as undesirable, and the saying was
therefore praising the rolling stone: if one would savor the
spices of life, one did not stay in one place and be a
mossback. To these people my thrust and parry were
synonomous: it was good to be a rolling stone and gather no
moss, it was good to seek variety as the spice of life. I confess
that nothing that has happened in class in a quarter-century
of teaching has had such an unsettling or aging effect upon
me. While I found authorities to support my understanding
of the saying in various quotational encyclopedias, I'm afraid
the sources could not be described as contemporary: Tusser's
sixteenth-century work, *Five Hundred Points of Good
Husbandry*, or Mrs. Jameson's nineteenth-century volume,
Detached Thoughts.

28. Simon, Administrative Behavior 20-36 (2d ed. 1957).

Folk-sayings are a particularly illuminating analogy to the construction maxims because we readily discount a folk-saying as being only sometimes true. We recognize that it is not a complete and balanced assessment of its subject. The construction maxims too are simply reminders of relevant, not conclusive, bits of experience. I well remember an oral argument in the Second Circuit, with Judge Learned Hand presiding, in which a lawyer was unsophisticated enough to say: "Your honor, this case is governed by the fundamental principle of American law that a penal statute is to be strictly construed." Judge Hand responded, "Young man, that is not a fundamental principle of American law, it is just one of the maxims of construction. We might end up construing this statute strictly, but if we do it won't be because we were compelled by that maxim to do so."

In short, you can at this point appreciate, I am sure, why two acute legal scholars have said: "The hard truth of the matter is that American courts have no intelligible, generally accepted, and consistently applied theory of statutory interpretation."[29]

5. Finally, what is the hope for reducing the complexities and perplexities of statutory interpretation? To begin with, the many sources of statutory ambiguity are not likely to be much reduced. There may be some reduction in the avoidable ambiguities attributable to bad draftsmanship, but most sources of ambiguity will remain: the prevalence of ambiguity in language generally; the unintended but almost inevitable ambiguities that may be introduced by amendments in the course of passage — particularly in amendments from the floor, but sometimes in committee amendments — that are not carefully integrated with the rest of the bill and with other statutes; the introduction of deliberate ambiguities (because the legislature doesn't know enough about the subjects and wants to delegate broad authority to court and/or administrative agency; or because more abstract

29. Hart and Sacks, The Legal Process 1201 (tentative ed. 1958).

language was necessary in order to get the statute passed); the impossibility of the legislature's foreseeing and making provisions for all the situations that might come up.

As for improvements in the process of interpretation: proposals for the creation of usable legislative history materials on the state level comparable to those on the national level may eventually be adopted. Proposals for a specific legislative code of interpretive rules are not likely to meet with success. Some statute books go part of the way by presenting, as applicable to all statutes, definitions of recurring words, and some interpretive rules with respect to gender, tenses, singular and plural, computation of time, etc. The Wisconsin statute book does this with the caveat, "unless such construction would produce a result inconsistent with the manifest intent of the legislature." A more general rule of construction often found in statute books is: "all general provisions . . . shall be liberally construed in order that the true intent and meaning of the legislature may be fully carried out." A rule of this kind is not specifically helpful; and its relation to the classical rule on penal statutes is not clear. Assuming that such rules of construction were not ignored by courts, as they often have been, they too may have to be interpreted. And if formulated very precisely in an attempt to avoid interpretation, they can well prove too rigid and hence too inequitable for some situations.

When we have the ingredients of a formula for a chemical product but no precise weight for each ingredient, perhaps the best we can do is rely upon a skilled chemist to produce the end product that he senses to be the best one for the known purposes of the product. A similar last-ditch reliance upon the quality of the human beings assigned to a baffling task was expressed by Justice Frankfurter at the close of his valuable essay on interpreting statutes. After saying that "perfection of draftsmanship is as unattainable as demonstrable correctness of judicial reading of legislation," he says, "Fit legislation and fair adjudication are attainable. The ultimate reliance of society for the proper fulfillment of both these august functions is to entrust them only to those who are equal to their demands."[30]

This emphasis on the quality of judges also calls to mind an observation once made by Judge Learned Hand. Since a judge must pass upon fundamental issues of power and justice, he must have, said Hand, "at least a bowing acquaintance with Acton and Maitland, with Thucydides, Gibbon and Carlyle, with Homer, Dante, Shakespeare and Milton, with Machiavelli, Montaigne and Rabelais, with Plato, Bacon, Hume and Kant." This has perhaps a purplish tint, but you can see the valid point here. "The words he must construe," Hand continued, "are empty vessels into which he can pour nearly anything he will." His "outlook [must not be] limited by parish or class. [He] must be aware that there are before [him] more than verbal problems, . . .aware of the changing social tensions in every society . . ." Hand was thinking at the moment of constitutional interpretation, but his remarks apply, though with somewhat less force, to statutory interpretation. He was of course aware of the inevitably creative role of a judge in construing a statute and of the statesmanship, wisdom, and integrity needed to keep that creativity within bounds. As he further said:

When a judge tries to find out what government would have intended which it did not say, he puts into its mouth things which he thinks it ought to have said, and that is very close to substituting what he himself thinks right. Let him beware, however, or he will usurp the office of government, even though in a small way he must do so in order to execute its real commands at all.[31]

C. BACKGROUND NOTE: INTERRELATIONS OF COMMON LAW AND STATUTE

As you know, the common law represents nonstatutory, judge-made law. When a statute is passed, it typically changes the law — either the preexisting common law or the preexist-

---

30. Frankfurter, "Some Reflections on the Reading of Statutes," 47 Colum. L. Rev. 527, 546 (1947).

31. Dilliard, ed., The Spirit of Liberty — Papers and Addresses of Learned Hand 81, 108 (2d ed. 1953).

ing statutory law. When South Carolina passed its 1902 statute making criminal the publication of rape victims' names, it changed the preexisting legal situation. For until this statute, such a publication could be made without criminal penalty. Conduct generally is not punishable unless a statute has previously made it punishable.

I say "generally" because while this is true on the federal level and in many states, the doctrine of "common-law crimes" still exists in some states. Even under that doctrine, however, in order to permit prosecution for conduct that has not been made punishable by statute, the conduct would have to strike the court as clearly falling within some residual broad category of conduct whose "criminality" seems unmistakable. Conduct like that of the Nappier defendants wouldn't seem to fit.

But remember that the only legal change expressly made by the statute was the imposition of a criminal penalty. The litigation we are concerned with was not a criminal prosecution by the state; it was a damage suit by private parties claiming invasion of privacy. The court of appeals concluded that "the plaintiff may sue under the common law as fortified by the statute." Why "fortified by the statute"? Because the common law recognized a defense to a privacy action where, as in this case, "the incident was a matter of public concern and record"; and the statutory policy had, in effect, eliminated this defense, though the statute hadn't explicitly addressed itself to the common law right of privacy. As the court of appeals put it, "the statute states an exception to the exemption. No matter the news value, South Carolina has unequivocally declared the identity of the injured person shall not be made known in press or broadcast."

The case thus illustrates one facet of an important phenomenon: the intermeshing of common law and statute. I want now to sketch some features of that phenomenon for you — including but not confined to the problem of civil rights and remedies in relation to criminal statutes.

---

1. In order to gain some perspective, consider first the

situation where a statute contains *no* remedy, criminal or civil, to enforce the standard of conduct it lays down. The statute simply prohibits the doing of certain things or simply declares a right to do certain things. In this situation, courts have sometimes viewed the statute as merely "hortatory," i.e., urging people to act in a certain way, but not providing a sanction to back up the urging. However, in recent years, the Supreme Court has been inclined to take a "where there's a right there's a remedy" approach.

For instance, the federal civil rights law of 1866, which has been held to be authorized by the enabling clause of the Thirteenth Amendment (antislavery), declared simply that "All citizens of the United States shall have the same right in every State and Territory, as is enjoyed by white citizens thereof to inherit, purchase, lease, sell, hold and convey real and personal property."[32] The Supreme Court decided in the 1969 case of Sullivan v. Little Hunting Park, Inc. that in spite of the lack of a specific provision for a remedy, a plaintiff claiming discrimination in private housing could sue for damages. "The existence of a statutory right implies the existence of all necessary and appropriate remedies . . . 'A disregard of the command of the statute is a wrongful act and where it results in damage to one of the class for whose especial benefit the statute was enacted, the right to recover the damages from the party in default is implied . . .' "[33] (An analogous case is one where, without any implementing statute, the constitutional prohibition in the Fourth Amendment against unreasonable searches and seizures was held by the Supreme Court in 1971 to imply a damage remedy against federal narcotics agents who allegedly violated the amendment.[34])

A case like the Sullivan case, then, is a case of implying from a statute which is *silent on remedies* that the *legislature intended that a right it has created* should be enforced by *preexisting common-law remedies*.

32. 42 U.S.C. §1982.
33. 396 U.S. 229, 230 (1969).
34. Bivens v. Six Unknown Federal Narcotics Agents, 403 U.S. 388 (1971).

2. The situation gets more complex where the statute is not silent on remedies, but rather specifies some, e.g., a criminal penalty and perhaps a private remedy as well, and the plaintiff seeks still a different one. You can see how natural it would be to conclude that the legislature wanted to allow only those remedies that were specified.

And this is what courts often do conclude, where the legislature has itself created the right involved — though the decisions are not completely uniform.[35] In the federal field, the statute under which there has been the broadest development of remedies not included in those specified in the statute is the Securities and Exchange Act. Here there has been an outpouring of cases by private investors pursuing remedies not mentioned in the act, for violations of corporate or broker duties under that act and regulations thereunder.[36] But the phenomenon is found under many other statutes too, and has been rationalized in a variety of judicial theories and distinctions.[37]

35. In 1967, the Supreme Court held that under the Lanham Act, which specified particular compensatory remedies for trademark infringement, the further remedy of recovering reasonable attorney's fees should not be implied. The Court said: "When a cause of action has been created by a statute which expressly provides the remedies for vindication of the cause, other remedies should not readily be implied." Fleischmann Distilling Corp. v. Maier Brewing Co., 386 U.S. 714, 720 (1967).

Note that the Court said "not readily" rather than "never." Indeed, in the same year it found there was good reason to imply a further remedy under the Rivers and Harbors Act of 1899. The act declared that one who sank a vessel in a navigable waterway was subject to (1) criminal penalties for a negligent sinking; (2) a requirement that he remove it *or* forfeit his interest in the vessel and cargo; (3) a risk that if the government removed the vessel, it could sell vessel and cargo and retain the sales proceeds. The Court held that in one of the two cases, the government could properly sue to hold the sinkers of the vessel responsible for *removing* it; and in the other case, where the government had already removed it, it could sue for *reimbursement of removal expenses*. The Court found that the specified statutory remedies "were not intended to be exclusive." Wyandotte Transp. v. United States, 389 U.S. 191 (1967).

36. See generally 3 Loss, Securities Regulation 1757-1797 (2d ed. 1961).

37. O'Neil, "Public Regulation and Private Rights of Action," 52 Calif. L. Rev. 231 (1964); Note, "Implying Civil Remedies from Federal Regulatory Statutes," 77 Harv. L. Rev. 285 (1963); Note, "The Use of Criminal Statutes in the Creation of New Torts" 47 Colum. L. Rev. 456 (1947); Morris, "The Relation of Criminal Statutes to Tort Liability," 46 Harv. L. Rev. 453 (1933).

3. The category in which the Nappier case falls is different from both of the categories mentioned above. In this third category, a plaintiff is not asserting a right of action created by the statute or invoking an implied statutory remedy. He is asserting a preexisting *common-law right of action and remedy*, and pointing to the defendant's statutory violation as *proof* that the plaintiff has a good case under the common-law right of action. The most common and well-established example of this is in the negligence field. Suppose the plaintiff claims his injuries were caused by the defendant's driving his car at a negligently high rate of speed. Suppose further that defendant's rate of speed violated the penal statutes on speeding. That violation of a penal statute would furnish at least evidence (and in most states conclusive evidence) that defendant's conduct was negligent, i.e., violated the standard of care of a reasonable man. Thus, the statutory violation *influenced the determination of whether the common-law right* (of freedom from injury caused by negligence) *had been violated.*

The Nappier case is analogous. In South Carolina the plaintiffs had a common-law right not to have their privacy violated by someone not in an excepted category (e.g., the category of newsman making legitimate comment on a newsworthy event or figure), and had a common-law damage remedy for the privacy invasion. The South Carolina criminal statute *influenced the determination of whether the common-law right had been violated.* This is so because the statutory policy against news comment identifying a rape victim influenced the court in refusing to recognize that kind of news reporting as coming within the exception to the common-law right. Notice that the statute had its impact on the common-law right even though the statute said nothing specifically about common-law rights.

This process — by which a judge handles a common-law problem in the light of whatever policy clues he can derive from a statute that operates in a related area but doesn't address itself to the specific common-law problem — has been called "applying a statute by analogy," or using statutes "as principles," "as premises," or "as precedents." Distinguished legal scholars and judges — including Roscoe Pound,[38] James Landis,[39] Chief Justice Stone of the Supreme Court,[40] Justice Schaefer of the Illinois Supreme Court,[41] former Chief Justice Traynor of the California Supreme Court[42] — have all broken some lances in behalf of the practice, and deplored the reluctance of judges to engage in it.

Sometimes of course there is legitimate reason for the reluctance. A judge may regard the legislative policy in the related field as inappropriate for transplantation to the common-law field. Or he may think that the legislature has in effect *forbidden* the transplantation. Suppose, for instance, a statute says that "bastards shall be regarded in the same way as legitimate children, for purposes of determining inheritance from a mother who dies intestate [i.e., without a will]." A case comes up in which a mother had left a will, making certain bequests to her "children." Does "children" include her illegitimate children? This is a common-law problem, i.e., neither the quoted statute nor any other statute, let us assume, addresses the problem specifically. But you can see how the court might feel it desirable to apply, to the common-law problem, the legislative policy on illegitimacy shown in the quoted statute. This some courts have done. But you can also see one barrier to doing that: the court may feel that the statute showed a deliberate choice that in the law of the state, the approach to illegitimacy taken in the statutory rule should apply *only* to cases of intestacy; so that interpreting "children" in a will to cover bastards would be impliedly *forbidden* by the legislature.

---

38. Pound, "Common Law and Legislation," 21 Harv. L. Rev. 383 (1908).

39. Landis, "Statutes and the Sources of Law," in Harvard Legal Essays 231 et seq. (Pound ed. 1934).

40. Stone, "The Common Law in the United States," 50 Harv. L. Rev. 4 (1936).

41. Schaefer, "Precedent and Policy," 34 U. Chi. L. Rev. 3, 18-22 (1966).

42. Traynor, "Statutes Revolving in Common Law Orbits," 17 Catholic U.L. Rev. 401 (1968).

(This would be a case of applying the maxim of "express mention, implied exclusion" that we have encountered before.)

In short, legislative silence about an area related to that which it is covering may mean it wants to leave that *open* for determination either way by courts as a common-law problem — in which case the "statutes by analogy" approach would be permissible. But it *may* mean — on the basis of an "express mention, implied exclusion" approach — that the legislature has decided the related area should *not* be treated in the same way. In such event, the court would have to bow to the legislative will. Often, of course, it will seem that the legislature had no definite intent with respect to the related area, so that the court has to ask itself: what would the legislature have said if it had turned its collective mind more definitely to it; would it have left the matter open to the court, or would it have forbidden the extension of the statutory policy to the related area?

As I've said, some courts did take their cue from the intestacy statute in handling the illegitimacy issue in a will case. And there are, in cases on other subjects, many instances of this approach.[43] Let me illustrate by two cases in divergent fields. One is a 1961 Wisconsin case in the field of real property. Four University students, who had entered into a nine-month lease for a furnished house and moved out after a month, were suing to get back their security deposits plus a sum for their labors in putting the house into a habitable condition. The students were arguing against application of a common-law rule that the landlord makes no implied warranty of habitability of leased premises. In ruling for the plaintiffs, the court said:

Legislation and administrative rules, such as the safe-place statute,

43. See illustrations given in the articles in notes 38-42 supra; also in Page, "Statutes as Common Law Principles," 1944 Wis. L. Rev. 175; Gellhorn, "Contracts and Public Policy," 35 Colum. L. Rev. 679 (1935); Note, "The Uniform Commercial Code as a Premise for Judicial Reasoning," 65 Colum. L. Rev. 880 (1965); Note, "Reasoning by Analogy from Statute in Pennsylvania," 43 Dick. L. Rev. 234 (1939); United States v. Lennox Metal Mfg. Co., 225 F.2d 302, 318-319 (2d Cir. 1955), and cases cited therein.

building codes, and health regulations, all impose certain duties on a property owner with respect to the condition of his premises. Thus, the legislature has made a policy judgment — that it is socially (and politically) desirable to impose these duties on a property owner — which has rendered the old common-law obsolete. To follow the old rule of no implied warranty of habitability in leases would, in our opinion, be inconsistent with the current legislative policy concerning housing standards.[44]

The other case is a 1906 New York case in the field of injuries to employees. The American Express Company had included in its employment contracts a clause absolving the company of any liability for injuries that might be suffered by employees while on the job, including injuries caused by negligence of the company or its officers or employees. The common law of course imposed liability for negligent infliction of injury, but also recognized a certain amount of freedom of contract. The highest court of New York decided that the "release from negligence liability" clause was void. One reason was its inconsistency with the statutory policy of the state as evidenced in laws safeguarding workers by imposing various health and safety requirements upon employers — "the course of legislation framed for the purpose of affording greater protection to the class of the employed." Such a release clause "defeats the spirit of existing laws of the state."[45]

Another reason given by the court illustrates another concept you should be familiar with. The court said the clause was also against "common-law public policy." The policy of the common law in imposing liability for negligent infliction of injury was based on "the conservation of the

44. Pines v. Perssion, 13 Wis. 2d 590, 595-596, III N.W.2d 409, 412-413 (1961). Analogous to this case is Dickhut v. Norton, 45 Wis. 2d 389, 173 N.W.2d 297 (1970), where legislative policy in the urban renewal field was carried over not to a common-law problem but to a problem under a different statute, i.e., the eviction statute. The case recognized the defense, in a landlord suit to evict the tenant, that the eviction was wholly "retaliatory" — i.e, was provoked by the tenant's having complained to health authorities of the landlord's housing code violation. This defense was implied into the eviction statute in the light of the public policy shown in urban renewal legislation and its implication that violations should be reported.

45. Johnston v. Fargo, 184 N.Y. 379, 386, 77 N.E. 388, 390-391 (1906).

lives and of the healthful vigor of . . . citizens, and if employers could contract away their responsibility at common law, it would tend to encourage on their part laxity of conduct in, if not an indifference to the maintenance of proper and reasonable safeguards to human life and limb." You will find a variety of situations in which courts have found contracts to be in whole or part contrary to common-law public policy.[46]

You should also know that among the cases dealing with the impact of a statute on a contract are many involving statutes that are more closely related to the contract than was the New York labor legislation to the negligence-release contract, and hence are even more likely to affect the contract adversely. Thus a contract might be entered into requiring the performance of certain acts which a statute has subjected to a criminal penalty, though it hasn't prohibited the contract itself. Typically, in a suit at common law to enforce the contract, the contract will be held wholly or partly void, but there are exceptions.[47]

4. The fact that common law and statute interrelate with each other has an effect, of course, on your operations as a lawyer. Suppose a client comes in with a case that appears to be a common-law case; i.e., you know of no legislation on the subject. You would be foolish to research immediately into the court cases. For contrary to your faulty memory, there may just be a statute that nullifies what earlier court cases had decided on a purely common-law basis. Furthermore, statutes, even if not applicable to the specific legal problem in your case, may be grist for your mill. They may be pertinent to a subsidiary aspect of the case. Or they may prohibit some acts, the legality of which you have assumed in framing the legal problem in the case. They may be pertinent, moreover, as embodying in a related field a policy analogous to the policy that you want to have the court apply to your

46. See 6A Corbin on Contracts pt. 8 (1963).
47. See Annot., "Validity of Contracts in Violation of Statute Imposing Criminal Sanction but not Specifically Declaring Contract Invalid," 55 A.L.R.2d 481 (1957).

common-law problem. Finally, if you find the common-law clearly adverse to the position of your client and wish to urge the court to overrule itself, again statutes are relevant: You will have to think about how to convince the court that it, rather than the legislature, is the better vehicle for the change in common law. (See 108-110). And you may point to statutory rules in other jurisdictions as a possible model for the changed common-law rule.

Conversely, if it is a case arising under a statute, and you are therefore primarily concerned with that statute, with analogous statutes, and with court interpretations of the statutes, you are still interested in common-law attitudes. For instance, light may be thrown on ambiguous statutory words by referring to their common-law meanings. There is also a maxim to the effect that "statutes in derogation of the common law are to be strictly construed."[48] That is, statutes changing the common law — and few statutes don't — are to be construed as making the narrower of two alternative changes. The maxim was born in the period when statutes were viewed as intruders in the house of the common law. It is not as much cited as it used to be, but still can be found in modern opinions, buttressing a conservative statutory interpretation. It remains a weapon in the advocate's armory, along with other maxims that advise strict construction of certain kinds of statutes, and thus a fuller preservation of the common law.[49] Knowledge of the preexisting common law is therefore pertinent.

48. See Fordham and Leach, "Interpretation of Statutes in Derogation of the Common Law," 3 Vand. L. Rev. 438 (1950).
49. See, e.g., Sutherland, Statutory Construction § §5501-5506, 5301-5305 (3d ed., Horack, 1943; and latest pocket supplement).

CHAPTER 4

Further Aspects of the Case: The Precedents

A. COURT TREATMENT OF THE PRIOR RELEVANT COURT DECISIONS; ASPECTS OF JUDICIAL PROCESS

You have seen, in the Nappier opinions, the disagreement between the trial judge and two court of appeals judges, and between these two judges and their dissenting colleague. You may wonder why it is that a legal system which is supposed to operate on a "precedent" basis can give rise to such disagreement. It may seem to you that a legal decision ought to emerge with all the inevitability of the conclusion of a logical syllogism. For does not the proposition of law derived from the precedents constitute the major premise of a syllogism, and does not the proposition stating the crucial facts in the instant case constitute the minor premise?

It is true that the reasoning in a judicial opinion can be cast into such syllogistic form, and once the premises are formulated, the conclusion flows inevitably therefrom. The trouble — i.e., the uncertainty about the result of a case — lies in the fact that the court has a certain amount of freedom in the choice of premises. There can very often be a reasonable difference of opinion about what this "proposition of law derived from the precedents" is, or should be; and about what should be viewed as the "crucial facts in the instant case."

1. *THE ALTERNATIVE SYLLOGISMS*

To illustrate the judicial freedom in choice of premises in the Nappier case, let me first cast the reasoning of the court of appeals majority on the one hand, and the reasoning of the dissenting judge on the other, into two different syllogisms:

Syllogism of court of appeals majority

Major premise: On the basis of the precedents, a person's right of privacy is violated by news reportage of *intimate facts that are not of legitimate public interest.*

Minor premise: In this case, the facts from which the identity of the plaintiff rape victims could be learned, which were broadcast on defendants' television news program, constituted *intimate facts that were not of legitimate public interest* — since the statute should be construed as making punishable, and hence not of legitimate public interest, all publications by private parties of facts from which the identity of a rape victim can be learned (rather than merely publication of her actual name).

Conclusion: Therefore, defendants' broadcast violated plaintiffs' right of privacy.

Syllogism of court of appeals minority

Major premise: On the basis of the precedents, a person's right of privacy is *not* violated by "publication of *matter of public concern and record.*"

Minor premise: In this case, the defendants' TV broadcast of facts from which the identity of the plaintiff rape victims could be learned constituted "publication of *matter of public concern and record*" — and the statute does not make it any less a matter of public concern, since it should be construed as applying to publication of the rape victim's actual "name" rather than to facts from which her identity can be learned.

Conclusion: Therefore, defendants' broadcast did not violate plaintiffs' right of privacy.

Let me now examine more closely the sources of freedom in formulating the alternative premises of the judicial syllogism.[1]

---

1. I shall be treating these sources of freedom in a rather general way. There have been some elaborate analyses of particular intellectual techniques through which courts make use of this freedom, e.g., Llewellyn, The Common Law Tradition, pt. 1 (1960); Stone, Legal System and Lawyers' Reasonings, cc. 7, 8 (1964). I have tried, in Jurisprudence and Statecraft 84-103 (1963), to show, in more compact fashion, that the same complexities of the process can be delineated even within a narrow field of law in a single state.

2. FORMULATION OF THE MAJOR PREMISE

I want to distinguish two different kinds of freedom here. One is in determining what any particular precedent stands for. The other is in choosing between competing precedents.

a. Determining What a Precedent Stands For; "Ratio Decidendi," Holding, and Dictum

Both the majority and the minority opinions in Nappier cited, as the primary precedent on the South Carolina law of privacy, the 1956 case of Meetze v. Associated Press.[2] This was a case where a girl had married at age eleven and produced a child at age twelve. Newspaper publicity about the birth, featuring the mother's age, was held not to violate the parents' privacy — with the court acknowledging that, in general, the right of privacy existed in South Carolina common law.

How did the Nappier majority and minority opinions differ in their treatment of the Meetze precedent? The minority cited it after making the observation that the privacy right in South Carolina "is not an absolute right, and where the alleged invasion of privacy is the publication of matter of public concern and record," it does not give rise to tort liability. The Meetze opinion had indeed made observations that supported this treatment of it. The opinion had said:

There are times when one, whether willingly or not, becomes an actor in an occurrence of public or general interest. When this takes place, he emerges from his seclusion, and the publication of his connection with such occurrence is not an invasion of his right of privacy . . . The law does not recognize a right of privacy in connection with that which is inherently a public matter. . . . The facts in this article do not show an unwarranted invasion of the right of privacy. It is rather unusual for a twelve year old girl to give birth to a child. It is a biological occurrence which would naturally excite public interest. Moreover, it was an event which the law required to be entered as a public record . . .

The majority, on the other hand, quoted some other observations in the Meetze opinion. Thus, it quoted a

2. 230 S.C. 330, 95 S.E.2d 606 (1956).

definition of actionable invasion of privacy that included "the publicizing of one's private affairs with which the public has no legitimate concern." It might also have quoted a further observation in the Meetze opinion that "newsworthiness is not necessarily the test . . . 'Revelations may be so intimate and so unwarranted in view of the victim's position as to outrage the community's notions of decency.' " This as well as the previous quotation would make it easier to make an argument, based on the South Carolina statute, as to how the common law should apply here. One could say (as I think the majority rather inexplicitly said) as follows: the statute showed that news reportage that revealed a rape victim's identity was not on a matter of "legitimate" public concern, and constituted "revelations . . . so intimate and so unwarranted . . . as to outrage the community's notions of decency," hence the common-law right of privacy had been violated.[3]

My point is that *the language of the Meetze precedent did not compel a subsequent court to go in one direction rather than another.* In the first place, the above-quoted language of the opinion was not altogether consistent. Some of it seemed to suggest an unqualified right to make news comment on matters of public concern and record; some recognized qualifications in terms of "illegitimate" concern and "unwarranted" revelations. Secondly, there is plenty of room for interpretation by the subsequent court, in applying such terms as "illegitimate," "unwarranted," and "public concern"; and in determining whether the precedent value of the case should be restricted to a situation where the facts revealed by the news comment are not only a matter of public concern but also a matter of public record. In other words, the court looking back at the Meetze precedent can

3. The majority did not emphasize the legitimacy element in the first quotation, and, as I say, did not call attention to the second quotation at all. However, it was implying, I think, the line of argument I have suggested, when it said in reply to the argument that news comment on "matter of public concern and record" was exempt from privacy violation: "the statute states an exception to the exemption. No matter the news value, South Carolina has unequivocally declared the identity of the injured person shall not be made known in press or broadcast."

view the "rule" of that case broadly or narrowly (and thus include or exclude the facts before the subsequent court) because of the ambiguity of the categories in which the elements of the rule are framed.

Is it inevitable that ambiguities will be introduced into the formulation of the rule of the precedent? *Some* ambiguity seems inevitable because of the necessity of putting the facts of the precedent into categories, if the rule is to function as a precedent at all. If the rule of the Meetze case were formulated very narrowly in terms of the proposition that a newspaper identifying a twelve-year-old wife who had become a mother does not thereby violate the mother's right of privacy, the rule would have no explicit force as a precedent for the Nappier case or almost any other case, because the facts of that case wouldn't fit into such a narrow formulation. When the Meetze rule is formulated *broadly*, into categories — in terms of *any news agency* reporting a matter which is of *legitimate public concern as well as a matter of public record,* or (more broadly) a matter of *legitimate public concern,* or (still more broadly) a matter of *public concern* — there is at least a possibility that the Nappier facts would be governed by the Meetze precedent. They *will* be so governed if the subsequent court resolves the ambiguities in the categories in a way that brings the subsequent situation within the rule.

In the Nappier case it happened that the key ambiguity to be resolved was in the statutory word "name." If the majority and minority had agreed on that, they would apparently have agreed on whether the elements of the Meetze precedent had been satisfied. But in other cases there could be great uncertainty as to the meaning and application of the indicated possible categories of the Meetze rule. Thus, would the concept of legitimate public concern cover additional news comment revealing intimate facts that were about the person involved in the current event but were not related to the current event? How intimate or embarrassing must the facts be? How far could a magazine story on a former infant mathematical prodigy reveal embarrassing facts on his present activities?[4] Is a movie company publicizing a matter of legitimate public concern when its movie depicts the history and present identity of a reformed prostitute who had some years before been a defendant in a notorious murder trial?[5] These and many other actual cases attest to the ambiguity of the categories in precedent rules on the kind of privacy violation we have been considering: the allegedly unwarranted public disclosure of private facts.

A graphic representation of the point I am making can be found in an analysis by Julius Stone. He was responding to a theory that the rule or "ratio decidendi" of a precedent was to be determined by looking at the facts deemed important by the court which decided it, and then formulating the rule in terms of those facts, e.g.: when such-and-such facts occur, the plaintiff is (or is not) entitled to recover for the loss inflicted by defendant. Stone pointed to a number of difficulties. He said that you often can't tell from the precedent opinion which facts were deemed significant by the court and which were not, and there are often inconsistent indications of significance. More important still, the facts have to be categorized and the opinion may be unclear as to the *breadth* of the fact-category that is deemed significant. He illustrated this by showing the varying breadth that could be assigned by a later court to each of the factual elements in the 1932 House of Lords decision in Donoghue v. Stevenson.[6]

This was a case that imposed liability upon the manufacturer of an opaque bottle of ginger beer found to contain a dead snail, for injury (shock and gastroenteritis) to the plaintiff. She was a Scottish widow who drank from the bottle given her by one who purchased it from a retailer who in turn purchased it from the manufacturer. Stone analyzed the possible future breadth of the constituent fact-categories as follows:

4. See Sidis v. F-R Publ. Corp., 113 F.2d 806 (2d Cir. 1940).
5. See Melvin v. Reid, 112 Cal. App. 285, 297 P. 91 (1931).
6. A.C. 562 (H.L. 1932).

(a) *Fact as to the Agent of Harm*. Dead snails, *or* any snails, *or* any noxious physical foreign body, *or* any noxious foreign element, physical or not, *or* any noxious element.

(b) *Fact as to Vehicle of Harm*. An opaque bottle of ginger beer, *or* an opaque bottle of beverage, *or* any bottle of beverage, *or* any container of commodities for human consumption, *or* any containers of any chattels for human use, *or* any chattel whatsoever, *or* any thing (including land or buildings).

(c) *Fact as to Defendant's Identity*. A manufacturer of goods nationally distributed through dispersed retailers, *or* any manufacturer, *or* any person working on the object for reward, *or* any person working on the object, *or* anyone dealing with the object.

(d) *Fact as to Potential Danger from Vehicle of Harm*. Objects likely to become dangerous by negligence, *or* whether or not so.

(e) *Fact as to Injury to Plaintiff*. Physical personal injury, *or* nervous or physical personal injury, *or* any injury.

(f) *Fact as to Plaintiff's Identity*. A Scots widow, *or* a Scotswoman *or* a woman, *or* any adult, *or* any human being, or any legal person.

(g) *Fact as to Plaintiff's Relation to Vehicle of Harm*. Donee of purchaser, from retailer who bought directly from the defendant, *or* the purchaser from such retailer, *or* the purchaser from anyone, *or* any person related to such purchaser or other person, *or* any person into whose hands the object rightfully comes, *or* any person into whose hands it comes at all.

(h) *Fact as to Discoverability of Agent of Harm*. The noxious element being not discoverable by inspection of any intermediate party, *or* not so discoverable without destroying the saleability of the commodity, *or* not so discoverable by any such party who had a duty to inspect, *or* not so discoverable by any such party who could reasonably be expected *by the defendant* to inspect, *or* not discoverable by any such party who could reasonably be expected *by the court or a jury* to inspect.

(i) *Fact as to Time of Litigation*. The facts complained of were litigated in 1932, *or* any time before 1932, or after 1932, *or* at any time.[7]

One more example. This one is from the presidential address of Herman Oliphant to the Association of American Law Schools in 1927:

7. Stone, "The Ratio of the Ratio Decidendi," 22 Mod. L. Rev. 597, 603 (1959). An outstanding legal scholar, Stone is professor of jurisprudence and international law at the University of Sydney, Australia.

A's father induces her not to marry B as she promised to do. On a holding that the father is not liable to B for so doing, a gradation of widening propositions can be built, a very few of which are:

1. Fathers are privileged to induce daughters to break promises to marry.
2. Parents are so privileged.
3. Parents are so privileged as to both daughters and sons.
4. All persons are so privileged as to promises to marry.
5. Parents are so privileged as to all promises made by their children.
6. All persons are so privileged as to all promises made by anyone.[8]

Karl Llewellyn made a similar point when he referred to the "strict" view of precedent as against the "loose" view. A court taking a strict view would veer away from the broader propositions in the prior opinion, addressed to situations other than that which was actually before the precedent court. It would tend to favor one of the narrower formulations. Sometimes its choice would be so narrow as to "confine the precedent to its precise facts," which would be a polite way of saying the precedent had been overruled; it had been deprived of any precedent value. Usually, of course, a court needn't make its formulation that narrow in order to say that a case is not a precedent for the present case.

Llewellyn described the narrower formulations as those made for an "unwelcome" precedent, and the broader formulations as made for the "welcome" precedent. Each approach, he emphasized, is legitimate and part of the going judicial practice. Addressing Columbia Law School freshmen more than forty years ago, he said:

What I wish to sink deep into your minds about the doctrine of precedent, therefore, is that it is two-headed. It is Janus-faced. That it is not one doctrine, nor one line of doctrine, but two, and two which, *applied at the same time to the same precedent, are contradictory of each other.* That there is one doctrine for getting rid of precedents deemed troublesome and one doctrine for making use of precedents

8. Oliphant, "A Return to Stare Decisis," 14 A.B.A.J. 71, 72 (1928).

that seem helpful. That these two doctrines exist side by side. That the same lawyer in the same brief, the same judge in the same opinion, may be using the one doctrine, the technically strict one, to cut down half the older cases that he deals with, and using the other doctrine, the loose one, for building with the other half. Until you realize this you do not see how it is possible for law to change and to develop, and yet to stand on the past. You do not see how it is possible to avoid the past mistakes of courts, and yet to make use of every happy insight for which a judge in writing may have found expression . . .

Nor, until you see this double aspect of the doctrine-in-action, do you appreciate how little, in detail, you can predict *out of the rules alone*; how much you must turn, for purposes of prediction, to the reactions of the judges to the facts and to the life around them . . .[9]

At this point you may be thinking: "Granted that when the precedent opinion leaves open the possibility of a choice of interpretation of its rule by the later court, the later court is free to choose. But suppose the prior court has written the unusual opinion in which it indicated *precisely* the fact-category *breadth* that it deemed desirable for the rule it was applying. Would the later court still be free to choose a different breadth?" There is some difference of opinion here, but many would still say yes. In this view, if the Meetze case had clearly formulated a rule allowing news reportage of private facts "on any matter of public interest," a later court could say: "We are not overruling that decision but we think the rule was formulated too broadly in relation to its facts. The facts indicated a matter of *legitimate* public interest, and the rule should have been qualified in that way. We don't feel bound by any prior formulation of a rule whose breadth (1) went unnecessarily beyond the type of situation presented, and (2) would produce, when applied to the present case, an unreasonable result." A textbook put it this way, in 1961:

True, the rule of the prior court — announced or otherwise — must necessarily go beyond the precise facts before it [e.g., beyond covering cases of newspaper publicity to the birth of a baby to a twelve-year-old wife] and thus has relevance for later courts operating under a precedent system. But assuming even that the prior court has a definite

9. Llewellyn, The Bramble Bush 68 (Oceana ed. 1951).

breadth of rule in mind which is ascertainable by the later court, is not the *later* court best able to decide whether the rule should be conceived broadly enough so as to apply to the particular "beyond" area brought before *it* for decision? The later court must determine whether the principles or policies underlying the prior decision are also applicable to the later case — i.e., whether the facts of the two cases are "similar" enough (or the differences without sufficient significance) to justify giving the explicit or implicit "rule" of the earlier case sufficient breadth to "apply" to the later case. To allow that breadth to be *fixed* by what was said in a prior court's opinion without the present situation before it, would be to stultify the process of wise decision. The precedent supplies guidance lines, not a straitjacket.[10]

What I have been talking about up to now in terms of the "ratio decidendi" or rule of decision can also be talked about in terms of the "holding" of a case. First, a word of background explanation.

In the early days of the English precedent system, the opinion in a relevant prior case used to be treated like a textbook; everything in it had precedent value. At the end of the seventeenth century, the courts began thinking of precedent value in terms of the court's observations which were relevant to the specific situation before the court. The distinction came to be made, in other words, between "holding" and mere "dictum." A case was a precedent for what it "held," not for its "dicta." The latter were observations in the opinion that were "not necessary" to the decision.

The "not necessary" way of putting it has its difficulties. One pitfall is in its application to a decision which decides more than one issue. Suppose the facts presented two issues, and both were ruled on for the appellant, and the judgment of the lower court was reversed. Is the ruling on the second issue mere dictum? Does it have little or no weight because it was not "necessary" — i.e., the reversal would have occurred because of the first ruling anyway? Courts have been known to fall into the trap of thinking in this way. But the mere fact that the second ruling wasn't necessary for reversal doesn't

10. Auerbach, Garrison, Hurst, and Mermin, The Legal Process 65 (1961).

mean that it is unnecessary in the sense that a dictum is said to be unnecessary. What is that sense?

Apparently the reference is to observations in the opinion that are directed at *facts not present in the case.* In the case I have supposed, the two rulings were directed at issues presented by the facts in the case, so that each was a holding. Both rulings also met a supplementary test sometimes used for distinguishing holding from dictum: the *judgment* (of reversal) *logically followed from* the ruling. I said the rulings favored the appellant; hence the judgment logically following from such rulings would be reversal.

Getting back to a single-issue decision: the "facts not present" test is generally easy to apply. Thus, suppose the Nappier court of appeals had included, in its opinion holding there had been a privacy violation, the following additional observation: "If the girls' assailant had attempted unsuccessfully to rape them our decision would be different." Such an observation would be dictum. It was not "necessary" to the decision. It would not have the force of precedent for a subsequent court faced with a case like the Nappier case except that it involved only an attempted rape.[11]

It is not always so easy to spot a dictum. My example of the Nappier court addressing itself to a hypothetical issue not presented by the facts is a clear case. But suppose the court had said: "*We hold* that whenever a woman has been subjected to sexual assault, and publicity is given to it in a manner that identifies her, so that she suffers embarrassment, mental anguish, and possible damage to her social relations, she may recover damages for violation of her right of privacy; hence these plaintiffs may recover." Here the court has done what is not usually done: it has itself formulated what it conceives to be the holding of the case. And it has included in that purported holding some facts not present in the case,

11. I'm not saying the subsequent court wouldn't decide the case the same way; it probably would, in view of the "assault with intent to ravish" clause of the statute. I'm merely saying the observation in the prior opinion wouldn't have the force of a holding.

i.e., sexual assaults other than actual rape. In addition, the judgment for plaintiff logically follows from the court's generalization on who may recover (judgment for plaintiff would *not* have logically followed from the previously imagined dictum that certain plaintiffs could not recover).

In this situation, you will find some difference of opinion. Some will say that since the court determination with respect to facts not before the court was included in what it labeled its holding, that determination has the force of precedent for the subsequent court (e.g., a court faced with a case involving attempted rape). Others would disagree, saying that insofar as the court's statement of the holding covers facts not before the court, the statement is mere dictum.[12]

This difference of view corresponds of course to the difference previously discussed, when I posed the situation of a court indicating precisely the fact-category breadth that it deemed desirable for the rule it was applying. I asked whether the later court would still be free to choose a different breadth, and said that contrary answers are given to this question. The same conclusion applies here. To talk of determining the "ratio decidendi" or rule of a case is to talk, in other terms, of determining its "holding." And talking, as I'm doing now, about whether a rule of law is addressed to the "facts before the court" and hence is a holding raises the question: *what breadth* of facts before the court?

No matter which of these alternative terms is used, I think it fair to say that scholars nowadays tend to the view that there is *no single, authoritatively correct "ratio" or holding* for a particular judicial decision considered in isolation from how a later court views it; that there are many logical possibilities open to the later court, depending on how broadly or narrowly it classifies the facts of the prior case, and how independent in this respect it wishes to be of the prior opinion's own classification. I expect to return to this subject at a later point.

12. See, e.g., Levi, An Introduction to Legal Reasoning 2-3 (1948; Phoenix ed. 1961).

b. Choosing Between Competing Precedents

I have been discussing the court's leeway in formulating the major premise of the syllogism — and have expounded upon the first aspect of that leeway, the freedom to determine what a particular precedent stands for. The second aspect is the choice between competing precedents. Again, the Nappier opinions furnish illustrations.

Thus, the district court cited five South Carolina cases for the proposition that the statute, being penal, should be narrowly construed. But the court of appeals majority was able to cite two South Carolina cases for the proposition that "the penal aspect of the statute does not require an interpretation so rigid as to strip its wording of its plain connotation."

On the question whether a description can serve the same legal purpose as actual naming, the court of appeals opinion referred to two competing lines of precedent. It cited with approval some libel cases to the effect that "a libelee is nonetheless libeled though his name be not mentioned." And it cited, in order to distinguish them, some cases (arising under a statute prohibiting unauthorized use of a personal name, portrait, or picture in advertising) holding that certain descriptions or references would *not* qualify as naming. These the court of appeals distinguished by saying: "For advertising, only the name, pseudonym or picture of the person — usually because of his prominence — is significant. Any other description is of no value. Consequently the object of the law is not impinged unless the publication embodies the name, portrait or picture. That is not so in the statute now in review."

3. *FORMULATING THE MINOR PREMISE*

So far the discussion of the legal syllogism has been in terms of formulating the major premise. Formulating the minor premise affords the court another area of choice.

The court must determine whether it is reasonable to categorize the facts of the case in such a way as to bring them within the categories of the major premise. When I say this, I don't mean that in the actual chronology of a court's deliberations the major premise comes first. It probably doesn't, usually. But when a court formulates its final, formal opinion, the principle of law functioning as the major premise will generally be presented first, and the categorization of the case will fit into the categories in the major premise. This was true of the two syllogisms formulated earlier about the Nappier case.

You will note that in the Nappier syllogisms, the two different minor premises fitted into two *different* major premises, with different conclusions resulting. But there are plenty instances of a difference in conclusion resulting from using different minor premises and the *same* major premise. For instance, assume that both the majority and minority of the court of appeals subscribed to the same major premise, e.g.: "a person's right of privacy is violated by news reportage of intimate facts that are not of legitimate public interest." There might still have been a difference of opinion between judges on whether that part of a news report which identified the rape victims was on a matter of "legitimate public interest."

The question of what is a matter of "legitimate" public interest involves a value judgment. But sometimes, of course, a difference in minor premises results from a difference in the fact-findings — i.e., as to what actually happened in the case.

B. BACKGROUND NOTE:
MORE ON THE PRECEDENT SYSTEM

1. *HOW FREE IS THE APPELLATE JUDGE, AND HOW UNPREDICTABLE HIS DECISION?*

When you add up all the areas of freedom I've been discussing — determining what a precedent stands for, choosing between competing precedents, and formulating the minor premise — you may conclude that the precedent system leaves an appellate court completely free to move in whatever direction it pleases. I think this would be an

erroneous conclusion. I once summarized some of my reasons
as follows:

One barrier to undue judicial freedom comes from language. That is,
some words of prior judicial rules, of statutes, and of the constitution
strike in most of us a common chord of meaning, so that judicial
repudiation of that meaning without solid basis in context or current
need would strike most of us as arbitrary, and no judge wants to be
considered arbitrary.

We must remember also the check on arbitrariness which comes
from the *group* process of decision. If a judge holds capricious or
ill-considered views, these must run the gauntlet of colleagues' critical
reactions; if a court majority is inclined to arbitrary judgment, the
judges must brook the critical reactions of the profession as a whole.
Even when the maverick judge is unpersuaded by his colleagues, the
tradition is for him to go along with the majority, except where strong
convictions compel that he register dissent.

Efficacy of the group process of deliberation in influencing the
individual case determinations of United States Supreme Court justices
has been questioned by Thurman Arnold. But, however apt his
skepticism may be as applied to some individuals and some issues of
fundamental judicial philosophy, those who have participated in
meetings of corporate boards of directors, of committees of unions,
university faculties, churches, fraternal societies; of law partners, of
government commissions, of parole boards, or other groups charged
with decisions, can surely attest to occasions when group discussion
moderated, modified, or reversed the views of participants. More than
one Supreme Court justice indeed, has acknowledged that such changes
of mind have occurred even after draft majority and minority opinions
have circulated within the court.

Moreover, a tradition embodied in Canons 20 and 21 of the [old]
Canons of Judicial Ethics counsels suppressing the expression of
personal value judgments that are opposed to community value
judgments, and suppressing a personal approach to decision that is not
"the usual and expected method of doing justice." "Justice," says
Canon 21, "should not be molded by the individual idiosyncrasies of
those who administer it." Cardozo's observation in this connection was
that the judge "is to regulate his estimate of values by objective rather
than subjective standards, by the thought and will of the community
rather than by his own idiosyncrasies of conduct and belief."

True, judges do not always adhere to traditions. But these traditions
of responsible decision are coupled with another — the judicial duty
and desire to do justice — and with the tendency for relatively
disinterested minds to agree on the just policy for the situation in hand.
That courts do not usually depart from all these traditions and

tendencies is perhaps suggested by the fact that predictability of the result of the case is . . . high . . .'[13]

On the last-mentioned point of prediction let me add this:

[E]ven those scholars who have done most to detail the complexities and uncertainties in decision see a high rate of accurate prediction. Some have conceded that prediction could be at least eighty percent accurate. If this seems high, remember this: they are talking about a prediction of what side will win (rather than the particular rationale that will be used), and about a prediction by a disinterested, trained lawyer familiar with the particular court. Moreover, they are talking about prediction not just on the basis of precedent rules and facts and past attitudes, but also on the basis of subsequent developments — including those contemporary "felt necessities" and "intuitions of public policy" which tend to pull the malleable rules, facts and attitudes into a particular shape.[14]

Finally, a caveat: what I have suggested about the tendencies of current jurisprudential scholarship on the subject of the precedent system does not apply to all writers or to all judges. Many judges are likely to view their powers more narrowly, or at least to talk that way. They seem to be deferential to what they think is the prior court's view of the proper level of breadth or generality for the rule, "ratio," or holding of the prior case. These judges, in short, don't sound as though they are exercising the full freedom that the scholars tell them they have.

2. THE BINDING FORCE OF A PRECEDENT; THE PROBLEMS OF WHEN AND HOW TO OVERRULE

(a) You may wonder whether a decision's binding force on later courts varies with the relationship between the later court and the court that rendered the decision. It does. As you might expect, a higher court decision, within either the state or federal hierarchy, will bind the lower court within the same hierarchy, but not vice versa.

---

13. Mermin, Jurisprudence and Statecraft 111-112 (1963).
14. Mermin, "Computers, Law and Justice," 1967 Wis. L. Rev. 43, 85.

A state court is not bound by the decisions of other states' courts. Suppose a state court has to decide a federal issue, e.g., arising under a federal statute or the Federal Constitution, and a federal court below the United States Supreme Court has already decided the issue. The decision may have persuasive force but is not binding, though it would be if it had been rendered by the Supreme Court.

Suppose now a federal district court is deciding a federal issue, and the same issue has been decided by: a state court; or another federal district court; or by the federal court of appeals of another circuit. The precedent in none of these courts is binding. But it would be if it had been decided by the court of appeals of the circuit in which the now deciding district court is located (assuming there is no contrary Supreme Court decision on the issue).

Finally, suppose an issue of state common law or statute is presented to a federal court because of the parties' diversity of citizenship. The federal court is bound to follow the state's decisions on the issue. (Recall the discussion of the famous Erie R.R. v. Tompkins case at pages 167-168.[15])

(b) The kind of judicial freedom I discussed earlier occurs within the process of "following" favorable precedents and "distinguishing" unfavorable precedents. But there is also the possibility of breaking with precedent altogether — acknowledging that an unfavorable precedent cannot be reasonably distinguished and should be overruled. In the American precedent system, this drastic step is allowable but is not to be taken lightly. It is to be justified only by the strongest kind of reasons. The English system has been more rigid. Not until 1966 did the House of Lords decide that it had power to overrule its own decisions.[16]

There are a number of aspects of overruling that I should touch on, at least briefly:

15. For documentation of the assertions in the preceding three paragraphs, see 1B Moore, Federal Practice par. 0.402, pp. 51-67 (2d ed. 1961).

16. See Dias, "Precedents in the House of Lords — A Much Needed Reform," 1966 Camb. L.J. 153; Leach, "Revisionism in the House of Lords," 80 Harv. L. Rev. 797 (1967).

(1) Militating in general *against* overruling are the overall reasons for having a precedent system at all: the greater stability and certainty and integrated quality of the law; the greater assurance that different people who find themselves in similar situations will be treated by law in the same way; the saving of human energy and time that comes from building on past analyses of possibly similar problems. It is true that some of these virtues are diminished by the flexibility or leeway with which, as I've tried to show, the precedent system operates. But I suppose the virtues would be still less in evidence if a court operated under a system which did not consult precedent at all.

(2) The court may feel that the legislature, if it has failed to adopt proposals to change the existing judicial doctrine, has in effect approved or ratified the doctrine, so as to preclude the change by court overruling. Courts are less apt to take this attitude than they used to be. You may recall an earlier discussion of the attitudes of various state courts on the overruling of certain tort immunities.[17] They were willing to say that an immunity doctrine that they had themselves created, they could themselves abolish. Legislative failure to make the proposed change was not determinative. It is true, however, that a specific rejection of the proposal by unfavorable vote of the whole legislature weighs more heavily with the court than legislative inaction or death of the bill in committee, or unfavorable committee vote.

(3) Some courts have adopted another kind of legislative ratification argument. They have said that if the precedent in question consists of a decision *interpreting a statute*, then it cannot be judicially overruled because the interpretation becomes part of the statute; so only the legislature can change it. Even courts that have announced such a principle have sometimes, I have noticed, changed their statutory

---

17. A survey of the scope of overruling in tort cases in recent years is in Keeton, "Judicial Law Reform — A Perspective on the Performance of Appellate Courts," 44 Tex. L. Rev. 1254, 1255-1259 (1965); Keeton, Venturing to Do Justice 169-170 (1969).

interpretations, without saying anything one way or the other about the principle. The United States Supreme Court, be it noted, has not adopted the principle. It has many times changed its interpretations of federal statutes.

(4) The Supreme Court has, however, recognized this principle: It will be more prone to overrule its decision on an issue of *constitutional* interpretation than it will be to overrule its decision on other issues. The reason is that if there is great dissatisfaction with the Court's decision on a federal nonconstitutional issue, Congress can rather readily change it. But it cannot change the Court's interpretation of the Constitution; only the cumbersome process of constitutional amendment can do that. Hence, the Court feels it should be more ready to overrule. It observed in 1944 that while it was "not unmindful of the desirability of continuity of decision in constitutional questions," in such questions, "where correction depends upon amendment and not upon legislative action, this Court throughout its history has freely exercised its power to reexamine the basis of its constitutional decisions."[18]

(5) Courts are much less likely to overrule where to do so would work hardship on those who substantially and reasonably *relied* on the previous state of the law. In fact, in an extreme case, such an upsetting of reliance could be unfair enough to be unconstitutional, as a violation of "due process of law." An occasional case, for instance, has had this pattern: a man does something, e.g., sells intoxicating liquor in 1908, after a state supreme court decision declaring that the statutory prohibition against such conduct is unconstitutional. In 1909 the court changes its mind and holds the statute valid. Later in 1909 the state successfully prosecutes the seller for his 1908 sales. The state supreme court reverses the conviction. The defendant's reliance on the earlier decision gives him a good defense as a matter of criminal law; courts generally would probably go further to say that the conviction violated his due process rights. If Congress or a state *legislature* made criminal what was not criminal when it

18. Smith v. Allwright, 321 U.S. 649, 665 (1944).

was done, this would run afoul of the "ex post facto" clauses of the Constitution. Those clauses don't apply to courts, but the due process clauses do. Unduly harsh retroactivity — on the part of courts or any other agency of government, and whether in a criminal or civil suit — may be held to violate due process of law.

In the tort immunities cases referred to in paragraph (2) above, some courts hesitated about overruling the tort immunity of, say, a charitable hospital, or of a city, precisely because of the reliance element. The defendant hospital or city, in reliance on the existing state of the law, had not taken out insurance for tort liability. *After* the decision it could of course do so, to cover contingencies arising in the future. But sudden imposition now of tort liability for past occurrences that were, on reasonable grounds, not covered by insurance, would be harsh — even if not unconstitutional. It would also be harsh on all other defendants in similar cases that were either pending in court or might yet be filed because the claims (while arising out of events in the period prior to the overruling decision) were not yet barred by the statute of limitations. These were largely the reasons why some courts chose to leave the change to the legislature. Legislative decisions are typically *prospective*; judicial decisions are typically retroactive.

(6) But I said "typically." Just as legislation is occasionally retroactive, and validly so when judged not so harsh as to violate the ex post facto or due process clauses,[19] judicial decisions have sometimes been prospective. Indeed, the last decade or so has witnessed the flowering of judicial decision prospectivity.[20]

These very cases on tort immunities have had much to do with this development. They have dealt with the problem of

19. See, e.g., Hochman, "The Supreme Court and the Constitutionality of Retroactive Legislation," 73 Harv. L. Rev. 692 (1960).

20. See Annot., 10 A.L.R.3d 1371 (1967); Annot., 22 L. Ed. 2d 821 (1969); Schaefer, "The Control of 'Sunbursts': Techniques of Prospective Overruling," 42 N.Y.U.L. Rev. 631 (1967); Mishkin, "Foreword, The Supreme Court, 1964 Term," 79 Harv. L. Rev. 56 (1965); Schwartz, "Retroactivity, Reliability and Due Process: A Reply to Prof. Mishkin," 33 U. Chi. L. Rev. 719 (1966).

harsh retroactivity of judicial overruling decisions by introducing some kinds of prospectivity into them. A parallel
development, occurring simultaneously, was the Supreme
Court's introduction of prospectivity into its overruling
decisions in the area of constitutional rights of criminal
defendants.

The major techniques departing from complete retroactivity have been these:

(i) *Complete prospectivity of the decision*

This means the decision doesn't apply to past situations,
not even to the past situation which is the subject of the
decision. It applies only to situations arising after the
decision. This had been the approach taken in a famous
Sunburst Oil case, in which the Montana Supreme Court
overruled a rule of law, but applied the old rule to the case
before the court, declaring that the new rule would apply
only to transactions occurring after the decision. Justice
Cardozo's opinion for the United States Supreme Court
declared that the Constitution did not stand in the way of
the Montana court's doing this if it wanted to.[21]

But it is worth noting that the Supreme Court had not
used this technique in overruling its *own* decisions. In the
decade of the 1960s when the Warren Court was overruling
so many constitutional decisions on criminal procedure, the
Court for the first time gave frontal consideration to the
problem. And it concluded in the 1967 case of Stovall v.
Denno that complete prospectivity in a federal court decision
would be contrary to "the command of Article III of the
Constitution that we resolve issues solely in concrete cases or
controversies." Merely to announce a rule, and not apply it
to the parties in the concrete case before the court, would be
to announce a "mere dictum." And such a practice would
have a possibly adverse "effect upon the incentive of counsel
to advance contentions requiring a change in the law," since

21. Great Northern Ry. v. Sunburst Oil and Refining Co., 287 U.S. 358
(1932).

he would know that the court would not reward his efforts by applying the change to his case.[22] Two years later, a sentence in a 1969 opinion suggested that complete prospectivity would be "most unusual."[23]

(ii) *Partial retroactivity*

One technique of partial retroactivity was applied in a number of the state cases abolishing tort immunities[24] — i.e., the new rule was to apply not only to similar situations arising in the future but also *to the case before the court* (not, however, to other similar situations arising prior to the decision). Sometimes the additional device of postponing the effective date of the decision was used, in order to exclude injuries occurring after the date of actual decision but before potential defendants have had time to adjust by getting insurance.[25] Such a postponement can of course be added to a completely prospective decision, too.

The Supreme Court has also used this partial retroactivity technique. Stovall v. Denno, supra, in which the Court dealt with the right to counsel at police lineups, is an example. The Court had just ruled in some other cases that such a right to counsel existed. But in Stovall the Court said the decision applied only to the defendants in those cases, and to future litigants — not retroactively to Mr. Stovall. It defended this "inequity. . . . to other litigants similarly situated in the trial or appellate process who have raised the same issue" by

22. Stovall v. Denno, 388 U.S. 293, 301 (1967).

23. "Formulation of a rule of law in an Article III case or controversy which is prospective as to the parties involved in the immediate litigation would be most unusual, especially where the rule announced was not innovative." Simpson v. Union Oil Co., 396 U.S. 13, 14 (1969).

24. See, e.g., Molitor v. Kaneland Community Dist. No. 302, 18 Ill. 2d 11, 163 N.E.2d 89 (1959), cert. denied, 362 U.S. 968 (1960); Kojis v. Doctors' Hospital, 12 Wis. 2d 367, 107 N.W.2d 131, supp. opinion 12 Wis. 2d 373, 107 N.W.2d 292 (1961); Holytz v. City of Milwaukee, 17 Wis. 2d 26, 115 N.W.2d 618 (1962).

25. See Holytz opinion, supra note 24; Widell v. Holy Trinity Catholic Church, 19 Wis. 2d 648, 121 N.W.2d 249 (1963); Spanel v. Mounds View School Dist. No. 621, 264 Minn. 279, 118 N.W.2d 795 (1962) (postponement to adjournment date of the then current legislative session).

pointing to: first, the above-mentioned reasons against the alternative of complete prospectivity; second, other reasons against the alternative of complete retroactivity.

These latter reasons showed the Court's attitude to be substantially as follows: *Some* overrulings should be, and have been, made completely retroactive — e.g., the Gideon v. Wainwright decision[26] recognizing the right of an indigent defendant to free counsel at trial was later applied to cases of prisoners who had been convicted years before, who were now bringing habeas corpus cases to get the benefit of the new rule. The relative impact of the right involved upon the "integrity of the truth-determining process" is one of the relevant factors. It is a matter of degree; the unfairness to defendant of not having counsel present at the lineup was not as great as not having counsel at trial. Thus the nature of the particular ruling can make a difference. Second, when "the extent of the reliance by law enforcement authorities on the old standards" is substantial, as here, it can make a difference. Third, when retroactive application will have a "disruptive" effect on the "administration of justice" by throwing a possibly intolerable burden of reopened cases on the courts, it can make a difference. So the nature of the ruling and its probable effect on the truth-determining process "must be weighed against the prior justified reliance upon the standard and the impact of retroactivity upon the administration of justice."

It is further worth noting that in some instances of partial retroactivity, the Court has taken a position somewhere between the Stovall position and complete retroactivity. That is, the new rule has sometimes been applied not only in the case in which it was announced but also in *some* similar cases whose facts occurred prior to the overruling decision. Sometimes, for instance, the standard was in terms of cases which, at the time of the overruling decision, had not yet been brought to trial;[27] sometimes, more broadly, it covered

26. 372 U.S. 335 (1963).
27. See, e.g., Johnson v. New Jersey, 384 U.S. 719 (1966), taking this approach to the famous Miranda decision concerning the right of a person in

all cases not yet so "finalized" that further decision on direct review was precluded.[28]

3. *THE LIGHTER SIDE*

The vagaries of the precedent system have their lighter aspects, too. What do you do if you're asked by the court for precedents to support your position and you've so far been unable to find any? Well, if you're the ingenious Rufus Choate, you might come up with this: "I will look, your Honor, and endeavor to find a precedent, if you require it; though it would seem to be a pity that the Court should lose the honor of being the first to establish so just a rule."[29]

If you're a judge announcing an overruling, you could take a lesson in gracefulness from a concurring opinion of Justice Jackson that was supporting a position contrary to one he had taken in an earlier case as attorney general:

> I concur in the judgment and opinion of the Court. But since it is contrary to an opinion which, as Attorney General, I rendered in 1940, I owe some word of explanation. 39 Ops. Atty. Gen. 504. I am entitled to say of that opinion what any discriminating reader must think of it — that it was as foggy as the statute the Attorney General was asked to interpret . . .
>
> Failure of the Attorney General's opinion to consider the matter in [the light of indicated history] is difficult to explain in view of the fact that he personally had urged this history upon this Court in arguing Perkins v. Elg, 307 U.S. 325, 83 L. Ed. 1320, 59 S. Ct. 884. Its details may be found in the briefs and their cited sources. It would be charitable to assume that neither the nominal addressee [of the Attorney General opinion, Secretary Stimson] nor the nominal author of the opinion read it. That, I do not doubt, explains Mr. Stimson's

---

custody to receive police warnings concerning his right to counsel and his privilege against self-incrimination.

28. See, e.g., Linkletter v. Walker, 381 U.S. 719 (1965), taking this approach to the Mapp v. Ohio (367 U.S. 643 (1961)) rule excluding unconstitutionally seized evidence from the trial; and Tehan v. Shott, 382 U.S. 406 (1965), taking this approach to the Griffin v. California (380 U.S. 609 (1965)) rule against a prosecutor or judge making adverse comment on the defendant's failure to testify.

29. 1 Brown, Works of Choate 292 (1862), quoted by Justice Gordon in Niedfelt v. Joint School District, 23 Wis. 2d 641, 648, 127 N.W.2d 800 (1964).

acceptance of an answer so inadequate to his questions. But no such confession and avoidance can excuse the then Attorney General.

Precedent, however, is not lacking for ways by which a judge may recede from a prior opinion that has proven untenable and perhaps misled others. See Chief Justice Taney, License Cases, (U.S.) 5 How. 504, 12 L. Ed. 256, recanting views he had pressed upon the Court as Attorney General of Maryland in Brown v. Maryland (U.S.) 12 Wheat. 419, 6 L. Ed. 678. Baron Bramwell extricated himself from a somewhat similar embarrassment by saying, "The matter does not appear to me now as it appears to have appeared to me then." Andrews v. Styrap, (Eng.) 26 [L.T. (n.s.)] 704, 706. And Mr. Justice Story, accounting for his contradiction of his own former opinion, quite properly put the matter: "My own error, however, can furnish no ground for its being adopted by this Court. . . ." United States v. Gooding, (U.S.) 12 Wheat. 460, 478, 6 L. Ed. 693, 699. Perhaps Dr. Johnson really went to the heart of the matter when he explained a blunder in his dictionary — "Ignorance, sir, ignorance." But an escape less self-depreciating was taken by Lord Westbury, who, it is said, rebuffed a barrister's reliance upon an earlier opinion of his Lordship: "I can only say that I am amazed that a man of my intelligence should have been guilty of giving such an opinion." If there are other ways of gracefully and good naturedly surrendering former views to a better considered position, I invoke them all.[30]

Justice Jackson would doubtless have included in his illustrations a Supreme Court of Minnesota gem had it come into being by then rather than two years later. It seems that that court had changed its position on a legal issue within a period of three months without referring to the prior case, because it had apparently forgotten about it! When the same issue came up in a third case, in which this sad situation was brought to light, the court straightened things out by overruling the second case, and observing: "Upon [this] issue, this court has displayed extraordinary impartiality by aligning itself on both sides of the question."[31]

---

30. McGrath v. Kristensen, 340 U.S. 162, 176-178 (1950).
31. Knuth v. Murphy, 237 Minn. 225, 54 N.W.2d 771, 774 (1954).

CHAPTER 5

Further Aspects of the Case: The Constitution

A. THE CONSTITUTIONAL ISSUE THAT
DEFENDANTS MIGHT HAVE RAISED
BUT DIDN'T

You may recall from the previous discussion of the constitutional law of privacy (pages 197-202) that the Nappier defendants might have raised a constitutional issue. They might have argued that they had a First Amendment right to make a news report on the identity of the plaintiff rape victims — since the facts reported were not intentionally or recklessly false, indeed were not false at all.

A First Amendment constitutional argument *was* made, and was rejected, in the 1948 Wisconsin case of State v. Evjue.[1] The case arose under a statute similar to the South Carolina one except that its prohibition was broader; it was against publishing the "identity of a female who may have been raped or subjected to any similar criminal assault." The Wisconsin Supreme Court first pointed to United States Supreme Court language in the 1942 case of Chaplinsky v. New Hampshire for the proposition that First Amendment rights of free speech and press are not absolute:

> Allowing the broadest scope to the language and purpose of the Fourteenth amendment, it is well understood that the right of free speech is not absolute at all times and under all circumstances. There are certain well-defined and narrowly limited classes of speech, the prevention and punishment of which has never been thought to raise any constitutional problem. These include the lewd and obscene, the profane, the libelous, and the insulting or "fighting" words — those which by their very utterance inflict injury or tend to incite an immediate breach of the peace. It has been well observed that such utterances are no essential part of any exposition of ideas, and are of such slight social value as a step to truth that any benefit that may be derived from them is clearly outweighed by the social interest in order and morality.[2]

---

1. 253 Wis. 146, 33 N.W.2d 305 (1948). On remand, and after a plea of not guilty and a nonjury trial, the defendant was found not guilty, and the Wisconsin Supreme Court held that a statute permitting state appeals in criminal cases didn't apply in this situation. 254 Wis. 581, 37 N.W.2d 50 (1949).

2. 253 Wis. 146, 160-161, 33 N.W.2d 305 (1948). The quotation appears in the Chaplinsky case at 315 U.S. 568, 571 (1942).

The same point applied, said the Wisconsin Supreme Court, to the kind of publication prohibited by the statute. The statute

is intended to protect the victim from embarrassment and offensive publicity which no doubt have a strong tendency to affect her future standing in society. In addition to that it is a well-known fact that many crimes of the character described go unpunished because the victim of the assault is unwilling to face the publicity which would follow prosecution. . . . It is considered that there is a minimum of social value in the publication of the identity of a female in connection with such an outrage. Certain it is that the legislature could so find. At most the publication of the identity of the female ministers to a morbid desire to connect the details of one of the most detestable crimes known to the law with the identity of the victim. When the situation of the victim of the assault and the handicap prosecuting officers labor under in such cases are weighed against the benefit of publishing the identity of the victim in connection with the details of the crime, there can be no doubt that the slight restriction of the freedom of the press prescribed by [the statute] is fully justified.[3]

Circumstances can be imagined in which the court might have come to a different conclusion. Thus, a commentator observed:

When identity is essential to a complete understanding of the story, the arguments for privacy, gallantry and law enforcement, are as strong, but the public's interest in knowing the identity increases. No longer can it be dismissed as curiosity or morbid desire, since it is part of the body of relevant information about a news event. Suppose a newsman hears that a rape suspect has been badly beaten in the jail to which he was taken. Authorities contend that the suspect fell down a flight of stairs. The suspect claims he was beaten by the sheriff. It is only by reporting that the alleged victim of the rape was the sheriff's daughter that the story can be fully understood. If an absolute statutory bar were to be upheld in such a case, the newspaper would be confronted with an unenviable choice: either omit the story completely or report only the details permitted by the statute, thereby providing an incomplete and possibly misleading account. Neither alternative is consistent with traditional notions of a newspaper's freedom to print a meaningful account of what is acknowledged to be news.[4]

But even in the absence of such special circumstances, the

3. 253 Wis. 146, 161, 33 N.W.2d 305 (1948).
4. Franklin, "A Constitutional Problem in Privacy Protection: Legal Inhibitions on Reporting of Fact," 16 Stan. L. Rev. 107, 134-135 (1963). Copyright © 1963 by the Board of Trustees of the Leland Stanford Junior University. Reprinted by permission.

United States Supreme Court today might strike down a
statute of this type. My earlier discussion of the case of Time,
Inc. v. Hill (pages 200-201) suggested the Court is today
inclined to let the First Amendment side of the scales
outweigh the privacy side. The point is in some doubt since,
as I cautioned earlier, the Court in the Hill case has a
footnote observation leaving open for decision the Nappier
type of problem: "This case presents no question whether
truthful publication of such matter could be constitutionally
proscribed." By "such matter" it was referring to "revelations . . . so intimate and so unwarranted in view of the
victim's position as to outrage the community's notions of
decency."[5]

B. BACKGROUND NOTE: SOME
BASIC FEATURES OF OUR
CONSTITUTIONAL JURISPRUDENCE

1. *JUDICIAL REVIEW OF CONSTITUTIONALITY*

We've seen that the Wisconsin court considered (and the
South Carolina federal courts would have considered had the
issue been raised) the question whether the court should
strike down the statute as unconstitutional. Such a power,
exercised by one branch of government against a coordinate
branch, is an awesome power. (a) You may wonder whether
the Constitution clearly authorizes it, and do governments
really have to be run this way? Couldn't the legislature be
allowed to be its own judge of whether its enactments will
violate the Constitution? (b) Wouldn't that be more democratic, since the legislature is popularly elected, whereas some
state courts and all federal courts are not? (c) Finally you
may wonder whether there are any recognized limits on the
court's exercise of this power. I'll take these points up, in
order.

(a) In fact, some countries of the world do *not* recognize
such a power in the courts. England, for instance, does not.
What was distinctive about English constitutional history was

5. Time, Inc. v. Hill, 385 U.S. 374, 383 n.7 (1967).

the development of an independent Parliament and independent courts, formerly subservient to the king. But as between these two independent bodies — the Parliament and the courts — the courts were never clearly recognized as supreme, in the sense of being empowered to hold a statute unconstitutional. Parliament is the sole judge of whether a proposed statute is in conformity with the usages and traditions embodied in England's unwritten constitution.

There were of course some written documents in English constitutional history that asserted certain basic rights, and certain barriers to legislative and executive domination. There was for example, the Magna Carta of 1215; Cromwell's "Instrument of Government" of 1653; Parliament's "Bill of Rights" of 1689. But none of these documents suggested that the *courts* could strike down statutes for infringement of a specified right — and rarely did any court opinion assert such a power. One instance was a 1610 dictum of Lord Coke in Dr. Bonham's Case,[6] as follows: "When an Act of Parliament is against common right and reason, or repugnant, or impossible to be performed, the common law will control it and adjudge such act to be void." But the alleged precedents cited by Coke did not support such a broad proposition, and his dictum was never accepted in England.

It did, however, take root in America. There were some early manifestations of the idea even in the period prior to the 1787 Constitutional Convention. The colonial legislatures were well aware that their legislation was subject to review and invalidation by the British Privy Council. There were a few judicial dicta in the colonial courts that the Stamp Act was unconstitutional. There were a few state court decisions in the 1780s holding a law invalid as violating a state constitution. The latter eighteenth century was, moreover, a period in which "natural law" was in the ascendancy — a "higher law" against which enacted law must be measured. And the courts must have seemed the most objective external agency to do the measuring. Particularly after the Declaration of Independence and its talk of natural and inalienable rights,

6. 8 Eng. Rep. 118a (C.P. 1610).

there was much feeling that certain rights were so fundamental and inherent that no law could take them away.

As for the 1787 Constitutional Convention itself, the topic of judicial review wasn't fully discussed. It came up as a side issue, and opinion on it was divided, though probably a majority assumed the power existed. In the course of arguments in the various states over ratification of the Constitution, the power was assumed. The power was also strongly defended by Alexander Hamilton in Number 78 of the *Federalist* papers. In the decade or so after ratification, the power was defended in congressional speeches and university lectures, it was exercised in dozens of lower courts; and even a few Supreme Court cases assumed the existence of the power without any full analysis or actual invalidation of a law.

Finally, in 1803, the Supreme Court in the famous case of Marbury v. Madison[7] authoritatively established the power of judicial review.

Essentially, the point of view expressed in this case was that the power was *implied* in the Constitution: A judge has a duty to decide what the law is; in case of actual conflict between a statute and the Constitution, he must have the power and duty to resolve the conflict in favor of the higher authority, the Constitution, in accordance with his oath to support the Constitution.

(b) Those who have continued, from time to time, to raise the issue of constitutional authorization of the judicial review power have generally coupled this with an attack on the allegedly *undemocratic* character of the power.

The response to the democracy argument is that the American system is not one of pure democracy; it is a system of checks and balances, designed to safeguard against undue concentration of power in any one branch. Judicial review of constitutionality is one check on the legislature — and indeed on unconstitutional executive acts as well. It does not give the Supreme Court unrestrained supreme power, since the

---

7. 5 U.S. (1 Cranch) 137 (1803).

legislature and other departments have certain checks on the courts: (1) The people's elected representatives in the Senate have to approve the presidential appointments of federal judges, and in extreme cases Congress may impeach federal judges. (2) Congress furthermore has, as we have seen (pages 111-112 supra), a certain limited power to control the appellate jurisdiction of the Supreme Court, and hence to withdraw some classes of cases completely from the Court's power to decide — as well as power over jurisdiction of the lower federal courts. (3) Court decisions that are resisted cannot be effective without executive enforcement. (4) When the public dislikes a court decision heartily enough, it has been known to defy it, with little or no steps being taken to enforce it — e.g., a 1965 survey showed that about one-fourth of the American high schools were continuing to hold the kind of classroom religious observances that the Court had held unconstitutional a few years before. (5) Or the public may protect itself still further by voting for a constitutional amendment to overcome the Court decision, as it has sometimes done. Indeed the public is free to abolish altogether, by constitutional amendment, the power of judicial review of constitutionality.

The indirectness of such public participation is probably not too high a price to pay for the benefits of judicial review. Unlike the legislature, the Court can devote itself in a principled way, relatively removed from the pull of special interests, to the analysis, exposition, and integration of constitutional policy. In so doing, it can symbolize and dramatize for the American people the fundamental moralities to which law must be subject. Most observers would probably agree with these sentiments of Cardozo:

The great ideals of liberty and equality are preserved against the assaults of opportunism, the expediency of the passing hour, the erosion of small encroachments, the scorn and derision of those who have no patience with general principles, by enshrining them in constitutions, and consecrating to the task of their protection a body of defenders. By conscious or subconscious influence, the presence of this restraining power, aloof in the background, but none the less always in reserve, tends to stabilize and rationalize the legislative judgment, to infuse it with the glow of principle, to hold the standard aloft and visible to those who must run the race and keep the faith. I do not mean to deny that there have been times when the possibility of judicial review has worked the other way. Legislatures have sometimes disregarded their responsibility and passed it on to the courts. [And courts have sometimes made disastrous decisions in exercising this power. —Ed.] Such dangers must be balanced against those of independence from all restraint, independence on the part of public officers elected for brief terms, without the guiding force of a continuous tradition. On the whole, I believe the latter dangers to be the more formidable of the two.[8]

(c) We've already encountered some limits on the process of judicial review of constitutional questions — e.g., reluctance to decide a constitutional issue unless absolutely necessary (so that if a statute can reasonably be construed so as to avoid a constitutional doubt, that will be done); the idea that a constitutional ruling is not to be formulated any more broadly than is required by the precise facts; and the principles of standing and justiciability discussed in Chapter 2 (pages 174-187).

What I wish to add here is the restraint imposed by the principle that legislation is *presumptively constitutional.* By this principle the Court gives weight to the expressed judgment of a coordinate and popularly elected branch of the government. It means the burden of proof is on the person attacking the constitutionality of the statute. Suppose he claims the statute violates "due process of law": he carries the burden of showing that the legislative judgment was an arbitrary one — as to the existence of the evil at which the statute was aimed, or the reasonableness of the means it was using to combat the evil. There was a time (in the decades

8. Cardozo, The Nature of the Judicial Process 92-93 (1921). For discussions of the legitimacy of judicial review — including its constitutional authorization and its democratic character — see Levy, ed., Judicial Review and the Supreme Court (1967); Berger, Congress v. The Supreme Court, cc. 1-8 (1969); Gunther and Dowling, Cases and Materials on Constitutional Law 15-23 (8th ed. 1970); Bickel, The Least Dangerous Branch, c. 1 (1962).

On judicial review in other countries, see McWhinney, Judicial Review (4th ed. 1969); Cappelletti, Judicial Review in the Contemporary World (1971); Cappelletti and Adams, "Judicial Review — European Antecedents and Adaptations," 79 Harv. L. Rev. 1207 (1966).

preceding 1937 when the Supreme Court seemed to be giving only lip-service to this principle of presumptive validity. This was the period when it was invalidating social legislation such as statutes governing maximum hours of labor, minimum wages, and maximum prices. The Court seemed to be in fact acting as a super-legislature and substituting its own judgment as to reasonableness of the legislation, instead of asking merely whether reasonable men could have arrived at the legislative judgment.

In 1937, however, this trend was reversed, and the presumption of constitutionality is now more uniformly observed in fact, as well as announced in the opinions — i.e., in cases involving statutes regulating economic matters. When it comes to statutes restricting civil liberties, the Court has been willing to examine the statute more closely. Thus in many cases involving attacks under the due process or equal protection clauses, if the statute is curbing a First Amendment free speech right or other personal right deemed "fundamental," or is creating a "suspect classification," e.g., through racial discrimination, the Court seems to be either assuming that *no* presumption of constitutionality applies, or that a presumption of *un*constitutionality applies.

In fact the Court under Chief Justice Earl Warren had been so vigilant in its efforts to protect civil liberties, that much criticism was heard to the effect that the Court was unduly stretching the meaning of constitutional phrases in order to impose its own views of good policy. In other words, the same criticism that was made of the Court prior to 1937 — that it was acting as a super-legislature in the field of economic regulation — was being made of the Court's role in the field of civil liberties. The response to the criticism might be that in this field — where we are dealing with rights like the rights to freedom of speech and religion, or the rights of those accused of crime — we are dealing with minorities, who lack the political power in the legislature to protect their interest in fair treatment. The courts may be virtually their only hope. At any rate, the Court under Chief Justice Warren Burger has somewhat altered the Warren Court trend, so that criticism is starting to come from those supporting a more "activist" Court.

You may wonder how the case upholding the Wisconsin statute fits in with what I've said. Let me repeat two sentences from the previously quoted language: "It is considered that there is a minimum of social value in the publication of the identity of a female in connection with such an outrage. *Certain it is that the legislature could so find.*" (Emphasis added.) This illustrates what I've said about the presumption of constitutionality. The Wisconsin Supreme Court, while apparently in agreement with the legislative judgment, was reminding us that the question was not what the court would have found or said if it were the legislature, but rather whether a reasonable legislature could have found and said what it did.

But is the case inconsistent with what I've described as the United States Supreme Court attitude in civil liberties cases? Since the case involved the defendant's freedom of expression, wouldn't the Supreme Court have recognized no presumption or a reverse presumption? Probably not. Even assuming that the corporate defendant's freedom of publication was the equivalent of a personal liberty, the defendant's liberties here were confronted with a *competing* personal liberty – the female victim's right to privacy, which the legislature was trying to protect. Such a situation makes inapplicable the rule-of-thumb preference for civil liberties or human rights as against property rights, and requires a choice among the nonproperty rights. This is analogous to another problem currently confronting the courts: determining the extent to which the news media's First Amendment rights to publicize the facts relevant to court proceedings can be curbed in the interest of protecting a defendant's right to a fair trial.

2. *THE FOURTEENTH AMENDMENT AND THE BILL OF RIGHTS*

The Constitution formulated at the 1787 convention was ratified by the necessary number of states in 1788, and the new Congress began functioning in March 1789. Because of considerable apprehension that the rights of states and individuals were not sufficiently protected against abuses by the new federal government, a Bill of Rights was adopted soon after the Constitution, and became effective in November 1791. These were the first ten amendments to the Constitution. They established certain rights *against the federal government* — including freedom of speech, press, and religion, freedom from unreasonable searches and seizures, the privilege against self-incrimination, right to jury trial, right to counsel, etc. Here is the text:

AMENDMENT I

Congress shall make no law respecting an establishment of religion, or prohibiting the free exercise thereof; or abridging the freedom of speech or of the press; or the right of the people peaceably to assemble, and to petition the government for a redress of grievances.

AMENDMENT II

A well-regulated militia being necessary to the security of a free State, the right of the people to keep and bear arms shall not be infringed.

AMENDMENT III

No soldier shall, in time of peace, be quartered in any house without the consent of the owner, nor in time of war, but in a manner to be prescribed by law.

AMENDMENT IV

The right of the people to be secure in their persons, houses, papers, and effects, against unreasonable searches and seizures, shall not be violated, and no warrants shall issue but upon probable cause, supported by oath or affirmation, and particularly describing the place to be searched, and the person or things to be seized.

AMENDMENT V

No person shall be held to answer for a capital, or otherwise infamous crime, unless on a presentment or indictment of a grand jury, except in cases arising in the land or naval forces, or in the militia, when in actual service in time of war or public danger; nor shall any person be subject for the same offense to be twice put in jeopardy of life or limb; nor shall be compelled in any criminal case to be a witness against himself, nor be deprived of life, liberty, or property, without due process of law; nor shall private property be taken for public use without just compensation.

AMENDMENT VI

In all criminal prosecutions, the accused shall enjoy the right to a speedy and public trial, by an impartial jury of the State and district wherein the crime shall have been committed, which district shall have been previously ascertained by law, and to be informed of the nature and cause of the accusation; to be confronted with the witnesses against him; to have compulsory process for obtaining witnesses in his favor, and to have the assistance of counsel for his defense.

AMENDMENT VII

In suits at common law, where the value in controversy shall exceed twenty dollars, the right of trial by jury shall be preserved, and no fact tried by a jury shall be otherwise re-examined in any court of the United States, than according to the rules of the common law.

AMENDMENT VIII

Excessive bail shall not be required, nor excessive fines imposed, nor cruel and unusual punishments inflicted.

AMENDMENT IX

The enumeration in the Constitution of certain rights shall not be construed to deny or disparage others retained by the people.

AMENDMENT X

The powers not delegated to the United States by the Constitution, nor prohibited by it to the States, are reserved to the States respectively, or to the people.

The Constitution makes no similar list of protections against the *state* governments. But the Fourteenth Amendment, adopted after the Civil War, does, among other things, prohibit a state from depriving any person of life, liberty, or property without "due process of law," or denying to any person the "equal protection of the laws." So the question then came up in a number of cases whether this very broad "due process" language should be interpreted to include the same protections against the state government that the specific provisions of the Bill of Rights gave against the national government.

The Court's answer was that the due process clause does not automatically incorporate all of the Bill of Rights; it incorporates only those provisions which must be regarded as fundamental or essential to a free democratic society. Some were regarded as essential, others were not. However, the Court has gradually changed its mind about whether particular rights were essential, so that now almost all parts of the Bill of Rights are regarded as incorporated into the Fourteenth Amendment due process clause and hence applicable to the states.[9] A large number were thus incorporated in just the last decade or so. Not yet incorporated are the Fifth Amendment provision for grand jury indictments in the case of major crimes, and the Seventh Amendment provision for jury trial in civil cases.

In what way was the freedom of expression issue, which was raised in the Wisconsin case and which might have been raised in the South Carolina case, rooted in the Constitution? The key language was in the First Amendment: "Congress shall make no law . . . abridging the freedom of speech or of the press . . ." This restriction has been liberally construed to apply to other agencies of the federal government besides Congress; and the Fourteenth Amendment due process clause has been held, at least since 1925,[10] to incorporate the restriction so as to apply to agencies of state government.

3. *ROLE OF THE TENTH AMENDMENT*

You will note from the constitutional text quoted above that the first eight amendments are in the form of specified restraints on government activity, whereas the last two take a different form. In fact, those who refer to the Bill of Rights have often been referring just to the first eight amendments. The Ninth Amendment, however, has a greater similarity to the first eight than does the tenth. The ninth specifies no restrictions on the federal government, but it does call

9. See Annots., 18 L. Ed. 2d 1388 (1967); 23 L. Ed. 2d 985 (1969).
10. See Gitlow v. New York, 268 U.S. 652 (1925).

attention to the possibility of restrictions other than those that have been enumerated. And, in fact, the Supreme Court in the case of Griswold v. Connecticut[11] construed its broad language to encompass at least one specific restriction. It found that the Ninth Amendment together with policy emanations from other amendments in the Bill of Rights protected a right of privacy of married persons — sufficient to invalidate the Connecticut prohibition against their use of contraceptives.

The Tenth Amendment, on the other hand, seems to have a different focus: the distribution of power between state and federal governments. It seems to be saying that if a power has not been granted by the Constitution to the federal government, then it is a power which the states can exercise — unless the Constitution has prohibited the states from exercising it.

In spite of the relative clarity of this provision, considerable confusion has developed over it. A striking example of confusion is the following colloquy on the floor of the Senate by two Southern senators who were critical of the Supreme Court's 1954 decision invalidating state school segregation laws:

Mr. Thurmond. I should like to ask the distinguished Senator a question or two. Is it not true, speaking of the segregation decision, that in the first 10 Amendments to the Constitution, known as the Bill of Rights, which were drafted by a great citizen of the Senator's state, George Mason, the 10th Amendment to the Constitution provides that all powers not specifically delegated to the Federal Government are reserved to the states?

Mr. Byrd. The Senator is correct.

Mr. Thurmond. Is it not further true that the word 'education' is not even to be found in the United States Constitution?

Mr. Byrd. That is correct.

Mr. Thurmond. Is it not further true that since the field of education was not delegated to the Federal Government, therefore it was reserved to the States and should remain reserved to the States and to the people thereof?

Mr. Byrd. The Senator is correct.[12]

11. 381 U.S. 479 (1965).
12. 103 Cong. Rec. 10,676 (July 16, 1957).

The first confusion here is the assumption that when the Tenth Amendment refers to powers not delegated "to the United States," the quoted phrase includes the Supreme Court as well as the legislature and executive. As far as I know, the cases under the Tenth Amendment are concerned with the scope of nonjudicial powers of the federal government, typically the powers of Congress. But even if we were dealing, in this segregation situation, with an exercise of congressional power rather than of Supreme Court power to interpret the Constitution, the following fallacies would be present in the quoted colloquy:

(a) The mere fact that the word "education" isn't mentioned in the Constitution wouldn't mean that Congress had no power over it. Congress has specific power, for instance, to spend money for the general welfare (which surely includes education). Further, Congress has specific power under Section 5 of the Fourteenth Amendment to enforce the Fourteenth Amendment prohibition against a state's depriving people of the equal protection of "the laws." No exception is made, in this prohibition, for education laws.

In the context of judicial rather than congressional powers, the colloquy argument is even more inept. For to say that a federal court has no power to decide a case whose subject matter (such as education) hasn't been specifically mentioned in the Constitution as coming within federal judicial power is to virtually eliminate the federal judicial power. This is because, as we have seen in Chapter 2, virtually all of the judicial power is stated not in terms of specific subject matter, but rather in terms of the nature of the parties and whether the case arises under the Constitution, federal laws, or treaties.

(b) Under the language of the Tenth Amendment, in order to qualify as a reserved state power, the power must not only have been (1) not granted to the federal government but also (2) "not prohibited to the States." And the Fourteenth Amendment *does prohibit* states from depriving people of equal protection of "the laws," including, of course, education laws.

(c) In any event, the Tenth Amendment, as currently interpreted, does not itself operate as a limitation upon federal power. In applying it, a court is not supposed to decide first whether the subject matter has been reserved to the states, and if so, declare that the exercise of federal power violates the amendment. Rather, a court faced with a federal statute on a particular subject first determines (by looking at the Constitution, its history, current conditions, etc.) whether power over the subject has been granted to the federal government by the Constitution. If so, then the power has not been reserved to the states; if not so granted, then the power has been reserved to the states. The reserved power is a *residual* power; it is not a limitation on the scope of federal power. As the Supreme Court said in 1941, the Tenth Amendment "states but a truism that all is retained which has not been surrendered."[13] It instructs us that no power which the Constitution fails to allocate to the federal government exists in a no-man's-land free from both federal and state power; rather, it is a power reserved to the states (unless specifically denied to the states).

This was the original view of the Tenth Amendment as well as the present view — though between the early period and 1937 the Supreme Court did sometimes take the view that Tenth Amendment considerations could invalidate what was otherwise an authorized exercise of congressional power.[14]

4. WHETHER CONSTITUTIONAL RESTRAINTS CAN APPLY TO PRIVATE AS WELL AS GOVERNMENT ACTION

I've referred more than once to the fact that the major constitutional protections are restraints against government: the federal government in the case of the Bill of Rights, and

13. United States v. Darby, 312 U.S. 100, 124 (1941).

14. The history is summarized in Corwin, The Constitution and What It Means Today 235-240 (11th ed. 1963).

the state government in the case of the Fourteenth Amendment. The conduct of private parties is, in general, not covered by these restraints.

You should know, however, that there are some exceptions to this general proposition. I'll touch briefly on the following categories of exception: (a) situations in which the executive or legislative governmental element is so intertwined with the private conduct as to make the private party a kind of "government instrumentality"; (b) situations in which a court decision backing up the conduct is viewed as providing the necessary governmental element (a "judicial enforcement theory" of government action); (c) situations governed by the unusual kind of constitutional restraint which is itself directed at private parties as well as government (e.g., the Thirteenth Amendment).

(a) One situation illustrating the government instrumentality theory is that of *government aid to the private party, through some form of economic connection or encouragement.* A well-known Supreme Court case is one in which a private restaurant's racial discrimination was held to have violated the Fourteenth Amendment — because of its economic connection with the state.[15] A state agency running a parking facility had leased space to the restaurant, which was an integral part of the state's plan to operate the building as a self-sustaining unit.

This case was distinguished by a 1972 Supreme Court decision involving the refusal of a Moose Lodge, located on private property, to serve food and beverages to a black guest of a Caucasian lodge member. The Supreme Court ruled that the fact that this private club received a liquor license from a state board and was subject to certain record-keeping and other regulations of the board did *not* "sufficiently implicate the State in the discriminatory guest policies of Moose Lodge so as to make the latter 'State action' within the ambit of the Equal Protection Clause of the Fourteenth Amendment."[16]

---

15. Burton v. Wilmington Parking Authority, 365 U.S. 715 (1961).
16. Moose Lodge No. 107 v. Irvis, 407 U.S. 163 (1972).

The Court found lacking here "the symbiotic relationship between lessor and lessee that was present in" the parking facility restaurant case. It also noted that the board was not encouraging discrimination; and that the club was not in a liquor monopoly situation. (The Court did authorize enjoining a board regulation requiring club licensees to abide by their constitutions and bylaws — since the result, however unintended, was to put the force of the state behind bylaws requiring racial discrimination against guests.)

The Moose Club case involved *a government grant of authority* to a private party — through a license. But *some* such grants of authority might be treated as more significant. Consider, for instance, the case of a labor union which was certified under the Railway Labor Act as sole bargaining agent of certain workers, including blacks, and which discharged its bargaining function in a racially discriminatory manner. Because of the government certification for discharge of statutory obligations vitally affecting the workers, it could be argued that the union had been given a grant of authority to act as virtually a government agent; hence its discriminatory conduct could be treated as a violation of the due process clause of the Fifth Amendment, just as direct federal government discrimination would be. This was the view taken by the Supreme Court of Kansas in 1947.[17] A couple of years earlier, the United States Supreme Court in a similar case had found the union conduct violative of the *statute*, and strongly intimated that if the statute were interpreted otherwise, *it* would be unconstitutional.[18]

Somewhat related to the "grant of authority" cases are those in which the private party is carrying on *a function of a governmental nature*, i.e., one which is typically carried on by government. Here there are the so-called "white primary" cases, which found racial discrimination by political parties or political clubs unconstitutional because — even where operating without specific statutory authority — they were

17. Betts v. Easley, 161 Kan. 459, 169 P.2d 831 (1946).
18. Steele v. Louisville & N.R.R., 323 U.S. 192 (1944).

part of the total election machinery and hence discharging a function governmental in nature.[19] Similarly, the refusal of a town manager in a "company town" to grant a permit for distribution of religious literature was treated as state action. His functions were analogous to those of an official of an ordinary town; he was discharging a function governmental in nature.[20]

(b) Turning now from the "government instrumentality" theory to the "judicial enforcement" theory: the landmark case here is the Supreme Court's 1948 decision in Shelley v. Kraemer,[21] which I've referred to before. This was the case involving the black purchasers of houses that were subject to racial covenants. These covenants embodied *private* discrimination. Hence, viewed by themselves they were not subject to the Fourteenth Amendment's prohibition against a state's depriving people of the equal protection of the laws. But when one of the covenantors tried to enforce the discriminatory covenant by going to court — in one case to oust the black purchaser, and in the other to restrain him from taking possession — the court's granting the injunction would constitute the state action violating the Fourteenth Amendment. So the Supreme Court held.

But the Shelley case is still something of an enigma. If *any* private discrimination (or other possibly unconstitutional action) becomes state action once a court backs it up by granting or denying relief, wouldn't this in effect eliminate the private vs. governmental distinction? Suppose a black man in a mixed housing project had a party in his apartment to which he did not invite a white neighbor because he preferred not to socialize with him, and the white neighbor asks the court for an injunction requiring either an invitation or the payment of damages for the failure to invite. Should the court's denial of relief be treated as state action that would make the private discrimination legally effective, and

19. Terry v. Adams, 345 U.S. 461 (1953); Rice v. Elmore, 165 F.2d 387 (4 Cir. 1947), cert. denied, 333 U.S. 875 (1948).

20. Marsh v. Alabama, 326 U.S. 501 (1946).

21. 334 U.S. 1 (1948).

hence would be unconstitutional — thus requiring the granting of the requested relief? This would strike most people as
close to absurdity. People must be free to give rein to *some*
preferences in their social relations, if only for reasons of
"psychic health," as Edmund Cahn put it.[22] So it becomes
relevant to ask *what kind* of private discriminatory conduct
are we talking about, and to balance the interest and freedom
of the discriminator against the substantiality of the impact
on the victim and the society.

The *kind* of discrimination is relevant in still another
respect: was the discrimination in effect prior to the court
action, or was it the *court's determination that brought the
discrimination into actual effect*? The language of the Shelley
case itself seemed to emphasize that the judicial action in the
form of an injunction would create or make effective a
discrimination that previously didn't exist or was ineffective.
Remember that prior to court action these defendants were
not being effectively discriminated against. In spite of the
covenants, they had actually purchased the properties.

These are cases in which the purposes of the agreements were secured
only by judicial enforcement . . . It is clear that but for the active
intervention of the state courts, [defendants] would have been free to
occupy the properties without restraint. These are not cases . . . in
which the States have merely abstained from action, leaving private
individuals free to impose such discriminations as they see fit . . .[23]

Thus, there are limits on the Shelley doctrine. Indeed, the
Supreme Court has not pushed the decision beyond the racial
covenant situation presented in that case. There are plenty of
theories about the proper scope of the doctrine, and about
the "state action" concept generally,[24] but it will take more

---

22. Cahn, "Jurisprudence," 30 N.Y.U.L. Rev. 150, 156 (1955).

23. 334 U.S. 1, 13, 19 (1948). The case was discussed earlier at 181-182.

24. See Comment, "The Impact of Shelley v. Kraemer on the State Action
Concept," 44 Calif. L. Rev. 718 (1956); Pollak, "Racial Discrimination and
Judicial Integrity," 108 U. Pa. L. Rev. 1 (1959); Van Alstyne and Karst, "State
Action," 14 Stan. L. Rev. 3 (1961); Henkin, "Shelley v. Kraemer: Notes for a
Revised Opinion," 110 U. Pa. L. Rev. 473 (1962); Haber, "Notes on the Limits of
Shelley v. Kraemer," 18 Rutgers L. Rev. 811 (1964).

Supreme Court cases to furnish authoritative clarification of this "judicial enforcement theory."

(c) Up to now I've been talking about the possibilities of private conduct running afoul of constitutional restraints purporting to apply to government rather than private conduct: restraints on states under the Fourteenth Amendment and on the federal government under the Bill of Rights. But the government action requirement is not included in every constitutional provision granting rights or protections. Thus it has been held that no such requirement is in the Thirteenth Amendment, prohibiting slavery or involuntary servitude. The amendment had authorized Congress to enforce it, and in the 1968 case of Jones v. Mayer[25] the Supreme Court declared the amendment was a valid source of authority for the 1866 civil rights law declaring: "All citizens of the United States shall have the same right in every State and Territory as is enjoyed by white citizens thereof to inherit, purchase, lease, sell, hold and convey real and personal property."

Thus, private discrimination in the sale or rental of housing runs afoul of this statute, which has implied injunctive and damage sanctions.[26] The statute was thought, at the time of the Shelley case in 1948, to not apply to private discrimination. If the present interpretation had then been in effect, there would have been no need to wrestle with the "state action" problem under the Fourteenth Amendment.

Finally, I suggest that of the various theories canvassed, the potential for profound future impact on our society lies mainly with the "government instrumentality" approach: i.e., with the possible extension of constitutional restraints to, e.g., corporate and union centers of private power — on the model of the cited Kansas court decision on union responsibility.[27]

25. 392 U.S. 409 (1968).
26. Sullivan v. Little Hunting Park, 396 U.S. 229 (1969).
27. Page 286 supra.

POSTSCRIPT

As I look back on these pages, I realize that there is much about the legal system that I have ignored or only hinted at. I intend here to make a partial filling of the gaps, and on only three topics.

A. THE FUTURE OF THE LEGAL PROFESSION

For instance, I have neglected the legal profession, its forms of legal service, and the provocative changes now in ferment. A 1970 ABA committee survey of lawyer opinion on the future of the profession, based on current trends, produced some prognostications (shared, I think, by most independent observers) which I summarize below, occasionally quoting from the chairman's language,[1] and inserting some bracketed comments of my own.

1. *CURTAILMENT OF SOME FORMS OF LEGAL SERVICES*

There will be less involvement of attorneys in personal injury claims, because of the expected spread of "no-fault insurance"; less practice before a jury, because of the expected elimination of jury trials in some classes of civil cases; less practice before a court, because more disputes will be resolved by arbitration and through government administrative procedures; and some areas of practice will be totally surrendered to nonlawyers, i.e., government officials and lay experts, since "uncontested divorces and other aspects of domestic relations problems, such as support, may be handled by direct application to a government official . . . without the assistance or intervention by a private attorney and without the requirement (in many cases) of the proof of fault. Other traditional legal transactions that may be handled by non-attorneys include the routine settlement of small estates, a variety of real estate transactions, simple

1. Fuchs, "Lawyers and Law Firms Look Ahead — 1971 to 2000," 57 A.B.A.J. 971 (1971).

tax problems and phases of so-called pension planning and estate planning."

2. EXPANSION OF OTHER FORMS OF LEGAL SERVICES

Government subsidization of free legal services to the poor — e.g., through Office of Economic Opportunity lawyers (or through the experimental "Judicare" system employed in northern Wisconsin, under which the poor select any lawyer, who is paid somewhat reduced fees by the government) — "may be expanded to include the lower-middle-income groups on a complete or part subsidy basis" [but the Nixon administration in early 1973 seemed to be more interested in retrenchment]. There may be a growth in "group legal services" plans — offered, e.g., by a labor union, fraternal society, etc., for at least some kinds of legal claims at no extra cost to members or at reduced fees, and involving, usually, a limited choice of one's lawyer.[2] [Or the plan may be offered by a cooperative, whether or not attached to another organization, functioning like a health cooperative on a periodic prepayment basis, with a panel of cooperating lawyers; or insurance companies may expand their currently experimental plans for prepaid legal insurance.[3]] Finally, because of the "growing social consciousness" of the new young lawyers, and because the law firms "have become more socially conscious anyway, more and more lawyers and law firms are donating the time and talent of their offices to poverty law and class actions especially in the large metropolitan centers." Some "are sending lawyers into the ghetto areas to help in legal aid offices or to set up the firm's own law office." Some "are holding themselves out as willing to undertake class actions on a *pro bono publico* basis when

2. See, e.g., Note, "Group Legal Services: A Blessing in Disguise for the Legal Profession," 58 Iowa L. Rev. 174 (1972); Committee Report, "Group and Prepaid Legal Service Plans," Wis. B. Bull., Aug. 1972, at 19; Meserve, "Our Forgotten Client: The Average American," 57 A.B.A.J. 1092 (1971).

3. See Goldstein, "Legal-Insurance Plans Pushed by Insurers, Lawyers; INA Announces a Pilot Program," Wall St. J., Oct. 6, 1972.

asked to by government or interested civic groups."[4] [Note, however, that by 1973 the enthusiasm of young lawyers for "public interest law practice" seemed to be waning.]

3. EXPANSION OF TOTAL NEED FOR LEGAL SERVICES

There will be more need for lawyers representing criminal defendants and suspects, in view of the rising crime rate and Supreme Court rulings that any defendant faced with a potential jail sentence has a constitutional right to free counsel if indigent, and that a suspect's right to counsel accrues as early as he is taken into custody. More legal services will be needed as certain new rights and liabilities are generated or expanded: "rights growing out of ecology . . .; consumer's rights; students' rights; welfare and other poverty rights; space rights; communications rights; the right to medical care and the right to receive replacement of human organs; the right to privacy, especially against 'bugging' through the use of electronic devices; and the whole maze of rights growing out of the struggle of the individual against big government, big business, big charities, and big institutions of every kind."

4. LAW OFFICE ORGANIZATION AND OPERATION

Greater use of lay assistants or "paraprofessionals" is highly likely for a number of reasons, perhaps primarily because of practitioners' feeling that they are "pricing themselves out of the market" as legal fees rise from increased office costs and increased salaries for young lawyers. Fees can be brought down by training secretaries, or lay specialists, "to take over and master lower-level legal tasks, such as preparing corporate minutes, probate accounts, deposition notices, interrogatories, simple pleadings and a host of other tasks . . ." Technological improvements are

4. For a symposium of articles on public interest law practice, see 79 Yale L.J. 1005-1152 (1970).

expected to increase office efficiency, in the area of duplicating machines, automatic tape memory typewriters, dictating equipment (which even records dictation to a lawyer's office by telephone from any telephone wherever located), and computers. Computers can help not only for record-keeping, bill preparation, and the like, but for the important task of research into applicable legal authorities for a disputed point. To some extent it is already true, and in the future it will be more true, that an inquiry put to a computer terminal in the law firm or bar association library will be "transmitted by telephone wire to the computer center, which may be in a distant city, and the computer, after scanning the statutes and authorities already programmed, will respond almost instantaneously with a clearly typed list of citations in point, with a brief description of the holding or gist of each citation." [Note, however, that progress in the art has not reached, and will not in the foreseeable future reach, the point where this material will be completely reliable and relevant and in such form as will make the lawyer's exercise of human analysis, judgment, imagination, and wisdom unnecessary.]

Law firms will be bigger, with more specialization within them. The general practitioner who practices by himself, and who now constitutes about half of the approximately 225,000 lawyers in private practice,[5] is on the way out — though his future in rural areas is more secure. He might, instead of becoming part of a firm, become a "satellite" who along with other satellites is "under the wing of a larger city law firm." And the "reciprocal of the small satellite law firm, some other lawyers predict, will be the creation of the national law firm. This giant, like the huge public accounting firms we have come to know, will engage in multistate practice, with branch offices located in major

5. This figure includes an estimated increase over the 200,000 figure given in American Bar Foundation, The Legal Profession in the United States 11 (2d ed. 1970). The same bulletin declares that 75,000 lawyers were *not* in private practice — of which about 30,000 were employed by business concerns, and 40,000 were attached to government institutions, including about 10,000 judges. Id. at 15-16.

cities and state capitals. This firm would represent the maximum in the use of legal specialists, computer research and the newest of communication equipment." Another configuration predicted by some is the "clinic" of legal and business specialists, performing "a full range of professional and business services for the client, running the gamut from business and financial planning to real estate, accounting and legal advice." An alternative is to "place the clinic business specialist under the law firm's roof."

Incorporation of law firms is likely to increase. "Most states permit the incorporation of professional associations, and incorporation makes available most of the tax benefits of qualified profit-sharing and pension plans for business corporations." With attractive retirement benefits thus made possible, lawyers can be expected to retire earlier, "and not, as heretofore, to 'die with their boots on.' "

A factor affecting a lawyer's operations is the increasing complexity and more rapid rate of change in the law. Hence there is greater need for enrolling in the institutes, refresher courses, etc. offered by bar associations, law schools, and others. "More than now, continuing legal education will become part of the daily practice of law in the next thirty years."

B. LEGAL EDUCATION

In regular law-school education, too, change is on its way. In the early 1970s, law school enrollments, and particularly the percentages of women and racial minority students, have been mounting. Law school curricula have been expanding to reflect a general interest in areas posing some pressing contemporary issues: the environment, welfare, poverty, consumer protection, housing, urban problems, communications, space, medical jurisprudence, drugs, racial issues, women's rights, student rights, prison reform. Law schools have been struggling, within grossly inadequate budgets, to afford more "clinical" training — which could include "problem-solving" work in school, but mainly has involved on-the-job training through part-time placements with lawyers, judges, prosecutors, and administrative officials, with faculty attempting (with varying success) to maintain a substantial involvement.

In addition, studies in the early 1970s were suggesting radical changes in law school curricular organization and teaching methodology.[6] A much discussed reform proposal was to make the first degree in law available after two rather than three years. Coupled with this was the suggestion for an advanced curriculum thereafter, to serve the needs of those interested in a career of teaching or research or specialized public service, or those who have had professional experience and wish to acquire a specialty through one or more semesters of study. Still another type of curriculum, to last only one year, was suggested for college upperclassmen or graduates who seek no degree for the practice of law, but wish an understanding of the legal system as part of their general education, or are uncertain about their career goals, or wish to attain professional competence in fields allied to law practice (e.g., counseling in such areas as family welfare, labor, taxation).

In general, it is proposed that in many courses the emphasis be not on doctrinal subject matter but on the development of certain skills and techniques, and understandings about operation of the legal system; that there be more instruction, and more individualized instruction, in research, writing, problem-solving, planning, counseling, advocacy; that there be a greater attempt to incorporate pertinent knowledge from other disciplines, and that more team-teaching be utilized.[7]

---

6. See Packer and Ehrlich, New Directions in Legal Education (1972). This book contains, at 1-91, the report prepared for the Carnegie Commission on Higher Education; and, in an appendix at 95-328, the 1971 Carrington Report prepared for the Association of American Law Schools. The proposals I shall refer to in the text which follows come from the Carrington Report, with the Carnegie Report in agreement on some specific points, and on others willing to tolerate experimentation.

7. For a historical survey of legal education problems, which includes references to the voluminous literature, see Stevens, "Two Cheers for 1870: The American Law School," in Fleming and Bailyn, eds., Law in American History 405 (1971).

How imminent are such changes? One law professor who had thoroughly canvassed the history of legal education to 1970 and was assessing initial reactions to the new proposals was skeptical:

Just as the law faculties were not enthusiastic over the prospect of returning respectability to clinical studies, so the idea of fragmentation of the curriculum and particularly the shortening of the basic law course were not likely to meet with general enthusiasm. The idea of a shorter law course would probably be even less attractive to members of the bar. While some might sneer at law schools as high-grade schools of rhetoric, teaching by methods other than the casebook is probably not congenial to most law professors whose chief and sometimes only skill may be the analytical one associated with the pa[r]sing of cases. There is understandable skepticism about venturing into other fields — "depth research" has frequently been an excuse for inexact analysis and sloppy scholarship . . .

Even assuming a greater willingness than predicted for changes in legal education, would they be possible? Are students interested in changes other than those which take them into a practice situation sooner? Are law professors interested in any change which might impinge upon their well-known independence? Is there any chance of developing a form of legal scholarship which is meaningful both to the profession and the university community? Finally, is there the remotest chance of the type of funding which will allow radical reform of legal education to proceed?[8]

The last-mentioned factor may be the most troublesome one of all. Expansion of small group instruction, of curricular options and specializations, of multi-disciplinary research programs and libraries, are only some of the pressures that would send legal education costs skyrocketing far beyond their presently high levels[9] — though perhaps not beyond medical education costs.

C. LAW AND OTHER DISCIPLINES

I referred to knowledge from other disciplines as a desirable element in legal education. This covers a considerable field.

8. Id. at 546.
9. See Manning, "Financial Anemia in Legal Education; Everybody's Business," 55 A.B.A.J. 1123 (1969).

(1) First, as far as the discipline of historical study is concerned, its relation to law has been relatively neglected in this country, and usually has been studied with unduly narrow focus. Professor Willard Hurst, America's leading legal historian, has said that historical study of American law "adds up to a very limited accomplishment."[10]

He has long counseled a broadening of the historical focus: to cover not only judicial activity (the study of which, moreover, has concentrated on the United States Supreme Court to the relative neglect of other federal and state courts, particularly trial courts), but also the federal and state and municipal legislative, executive, and administrative processes, and the "operating public policy created by the ways in which lawyers and their clients, and laymen working without benefit of counsel, shape affairs with more or less use, avoidance, or evasion of the law emanating from official agencies"; to avoid "the conventional historical preoccupation with formal constitutional law" by paying attention to the "constitutive roles in this society of the market, the business corporation, public utilities, the church, trade associations, trade unions, public and private educational organizations, and welfare and research foundations" and the "aspects of law related to the legitimation and distribution of practical power within and among such institutions"; to study the development of not only the functions and procedures of legal agencies but "the substantive content of public policy," and in doing so, to avoid the overidentification of public policy with regulatory standards of conduct, by including study of the law's direct and indirect "allocation of resources," "indirect compulsion," and "situation structuring"; to avoid exaggeration of the areas of interest conflicts and "directed" use of law, since much of "men's social experience in which the law was involved entailed neither combat nor consent, but merely the mindless cumulation of unperceived, unplanned, unchosen events," i.e., "drift and inertia."[11]

10. Hurst, "Legal Elements in American History," in Fleming and Bailyn, eds., Law in American History 13 (1971).
11. Id. at 6-10.

Not all historical studies have neglected such concerns, as Hurst's footnotes to his above-quoted monograph show, and as his own studies massively demonstrate.[12]

(2) A number of other disciplines devoted to the study of people in society have been found relevant to the law — a fact that should hardly be surprising, in view of the Chapter 1 point on the mutual interaction of law and society. There is a growing research literature into law and psychology,[13] law and psychoanalysis,[14] law and anthropology,[15] law and biology and medicine.[16] The last decade or so has seen a

12. See his Legitimacy of the Business Corporation in the Law of the United States (1970); Law and Economic Growth (1964); Law and Social Process in United States History (1960); Law and the Conditions of Freedom in Nineteenth-Century United States 1956); The Growth of American Law (1950).

13. E.g., Marshall, Law and Psychology in Conflict (1966); the Psychology Today issue on "Psychology and Law," Feb. 1969; Kelso, "Behavioral Psychology: Springboard for Imaginative Legal Educators," 45 Denver L.J. 313 (1968); Singer, "Psychological Studies of Punishment," 58 Calif. L. Rev. 405 (1970); Winick, "A Primer of Psychological Theories Holding Implications for Legal Work," Dec. 1963 Am. Behavioral Scientist; Marshall, Marquis, and Oskamp, "Effects of Kinds of Question and Atmosphere of Interrogation, on Accuracy and Completeness of Testimony," 84 Harv. L. Rev. 1620 (1971); Boehm, "Mr. Prejudice, Miss Sympathy, and the Authoritarian Personality: An Application of Psychological Measuring Technique to the Problem of Jury Bias," 1968 Wis. L. Rev. 734; Walker, Thibaut, and Andreoli, "Order of Presentation at Trial," 82 Yale L.J. 216 (1972).

14. E.g., Ehrenzweig, Psychoanalytic Jurisprudence (1971); Watson, Psychiatry for Lawyers (1968); Halleck, Psychiatry and the Dilemmas of Crime (1967); Goldstein, The Insanity Defense (1967); Glueck, Law and Psychiatry (1962); Bienenfeld, "Prolegomena to a Psychoanalysis of Law and Justice," 53 Calif. L. Rev. 957, 1245 (1965); Goldstein, "Psychoanalysis and Jurisprudence," 77 Yale L.J. 1053 (1968); Shaffer, "Undue Influence, Confidential Relationship, and the Psychology of Transference," 45 Notre Dame Lawyer 197 (1970).

15. E.g., Koch, "Law and Anthropology: Notes on Interdisciplinary Research," 4 Law and Society Rev. 11 (1969); Nader, ed., "The Ethnography of Law," 67 Am. Anthropologist No. 6, pt. II (1965); Nader, Koch, and Cox, "The Ethnography of Law: A Bibliographic Survey," 7 Current Anthropology 267 (1966); Pospisil, The Anthropology of Law: A Comparative Theory (1971); Gluckman, The Judicial Process Among the Barotse of N. Rhodesia (rev. ed. 1967); Hoebel, The Law of Primitive Man (1954); Llewellyn and Hoebel, The Cheyenne Way (1941).

16. See Curran and Shapiro, Law, Medicine and Forensic Science (1970); Freund, ed., Experimentation with Human Subjects (1970) (esp. the contributions from a legal perspective by Freund, Jaffe, Cavers, and Calabresi); Jones, ed., Law and the Social Role of Science (1966) (most of the bibliography at 147-185); Symposium, "Medical, Moral and Legal Implications of Recent Medical

preoccupation of many political scientists with the possibility of sociomathematical or computerized analyses and predictions of judicial decisions[17] (a possibility of which I happen to take, as far as prediction is concerned, a dim view.)[18] Since the early 1960s, a journal now called *Jurimetrics Journal* (formerly called *Modern Uses of Logic in Law*, or *M.U.L.L*) has devoted itself to articles and news items involving use of computers, quantitative methods, and symbolic logic in the law.

More fruitful, I think, has been the surge of empirical research by sociologists and empirically-minded political scientists and legal scholars into the operation of legal institutions. "Sociological jurisprudence" had been one of the banners under which the eminent legal scholar, Roscoe Pound, marched in the first decade or so of this century; and though some bold legal spirits, including the American "legal realists" of the 1930s, marched to the same general tune, the sociolegal research output was sparse. The two or so decades after World War II produced much more. There were, for instance, valuable large-scale research efforts into jury operations, judicial administration, police practices, and compensation in auto accident cases — some of which studies have been cited in Chapter 1. Interest in legal-empirical research mounted sufficiently to justify the founding of the *Law and Society Review* in the mid-1960s. Surveys at that time showed an impressive amount and variety of existing

Advances," 13 Vill. L. Rev. 732 (1968); Symposium, "Medical Progress and the Law," 32 Law and Contemp. Prob. 561 (1967); Symposium, "Reflections on the New Biology," 15 U.C.L.A. L. Rev. 267 (1968); Symposium, "Some Legal Problems in Medical Treatment and Research," 36 Fordham L. Rev. 631 (1968); Symposium, "Health Care," 35 Law and Contemp. Prob. 667 (1970); Dukeminier, "Supplying Organs for Transplantation," 68 Mich. L. Rev. 811 (1970); Wadlington, "Artificial Insemination," 64 Nw. L. Rev. 777 (1970); Caldwell, "Intersections of Medicine and Law: Bases for Future Collaboration," 31 Ohio St. L. Rev. 224 (1970); Symposium on Genetics, 48 Ind. L.J. 527 (1973).

17. E.g., Goldman, "Behavioral Approaches to Judicial Decision-making," 11 Jurimetrics J. 142 (1971); Grossman and Tanenhaus, eds., Frontiers of Judicial Research (1969); Symposium, "Social Science Approaches to Judicial Decision-making," 79 Harv. L. Rev. 1551 (1966); most of the articles in Symposium, "Jurimetrics," 28 Law and Contemp. Prob. 1 (1963).

18. Mermin, "Computers, Law and Justice," 1967 Wis. L. Rev. 43, 72-87.

empirical studies[19] which have been supplemented since then — and all of which take their place with substantial theoretical studies before and since.[20] In 1973 a new Office for Law-Related Research (initially funded by the Ford Foundation and a Massachusetts foundation called the Council on Law-Related Studies), closely affiliated with the Association of American Law Schools, was launched "to develop nontraditional research about law and legal education and to encourage use of modern methods and interdisciplinary resources."[21] Another significant fact was the decision of the University of Chicago Law School to start publishing in 1972 a journal devoted to "the application of scientific methods to the study of the legal system," called *The Journal of Legal Studies.*

This journal includes a strong element of economic analysis in its contributions from various social sciences,[22]

---

19. Skolnick, "The Sociology of Law in America — Overview and Trends" (in "Law and Society," a supplement to the summer 1965 issue of Social Problems); Auerbach, "Legal Tasks for the Sociologist," 1 Law and Society Rev. 91 (1966); Skolnick, "Social Research and Legality — A Reply to Auerbach," 1 Law and Society Rev. 105 (1966).

(Special mention might be made of the continuing interest of political scientists in "impact studies" — i.e., studies of the effectiveness or other consequences of legal decisions. Some useful surveys and analyses are: Becker, ed., The Impact of Supreme Court Decisions (1969); Wasby, The Impact of the U.S. Supreme Court (1970); Symposium, "Impact of Supreme Court Decisions," 23 J. Legal Ed. 77-150 (1970).)

20. E.g., Pound, "Scope and Purpose of Sociological Jurisprudence," 24 Harv. L. Rev. 591 (1911); 25 id. 140, 489; Llewellyn, "Some Realism About Realism," 44 Harv. L. Rev. 1222 (1931); Ehrlich, Fundamental Principles of the Sociology of Law (Moll trans. 1936); M. Rheinstein, ed., Max Weber on Law in Economy and Society (Shils and Rheinstein trans. 1954); Davis, Foster, Jeffery, and Davis, Society and the Law (1962); Evan, Law and Sociology (1962); Stone, Social Dimensions of Law and Justice (1966); Stone, Law and the Social Sciences (1966); Simon, The Sociology of Law (1968); Friedman and Macaulay, Law and the Behavioral Sciences (1969); Schwartz, and Skolnick, Society and the Legal Order (1970); Kalven, "The Quest for the Middle Range: Empirical Inquiry and Legal Policy," in Hazard, ed., Law in a Changing America 56-74 (1968); Rehbinder, "The Development and Present State of Fact Research in Law in the United States," 24 J. Legal Ed. 567 (1972); Zeisel, "Reflections on Experimental Techniques in the Law," 2 J. Legal Studies 107 (1973).

21. Association of American Law Schools, press release, March 6, 1973.

22. The editor's analysis of the first volume states: "Eight of the contributors . . . have academic backgrounds in law, five in economics, three in political

thus adding to other works with an economic focus on law.[23] Another boost for economic analysis came in the following year, with the publication by the *Journal*'s editor of a pioneering book applying the distinctive approach of an economist throughout most of the law's fields.[24]

Incomplete though this picture of the expanding scope of sociolegal research may be, it is enough to make my point. It is the point Cardozo made in a 1930 speech to lawyers: "Nothing in the whole realm of knowledge but is grist for our mill."[25] It is the point made more than once by Holmes. In an 1897 speech to Boston University law students, he said: "For the rational study of the law, the black-letter man may be the man of the present, but the man of the future is the man of statistics and the master of economics."[26] In an 1886 speech to Harvard undergraduates he had said that "a man may live greatly in the law as well as elsewhere; that there as

science, and one each in sociology and psychology, and all the articles by lawyers show the stamp of one or another social science. I regret, and hope in future issues to remedy, the absence of historians and anthropologists. . . ." Posner, "Volume One of the Journal of Legal Studies — An Afterword," 1 J. Legal Studies 437 (1972).

23. The Journal of Law and Economics, published by the University of Chicago since 1957, is the richest single source, but see the voluminous literature cited in Samuels, "Law and Economics: A Bibliographical Survey, 1965-1972," 66 L. Libr. J. 96 (1973); id., "Legal-Economic Policy: A Bibliographical Survey," 58 L. Libr. J. 230 (1965). These bibliographies include books, as well as articles in the more than one hundred law journals of the law schools and the miscellaneous economic and other social science journals. In years past, the legal scholar's concern with economics was confined to such fields as antitrust, business regulation, taxation, and corporations, where the economic theories and economic facts were palpably relevant. Nowadays, one finds a good deal of writing on economic theory and economic fact in fields like judicial administration, tort (including economic aspects of accidents involving automobiles and defective products, theories of negligence and strict liability), contract law and contract damages, property law (including personal and real property, zoning, property restrictions in the interest of environmental improvement), criminal law (including procedure and disposition of offenders), and areas of constitutional law, like "equal protection."

24. Posner, Economic Analysis of Law (1973).

25. Cardozo, "The Home of the Law," in Hall, ed., Selected Writings of Benjamin Nathan Cardozo 405, 408 (1947).

26. Holmes, Collected Legal Papers 187 (1920). The "black-letter" reference is to the darker type in which important legal rules may appear in some legal texts.

well as elsewhere his thought may find its unity in an infinite perspective . . . If your subject is law, the roads are plain to anthropology, the science of man, to political economy, the theory of legislation, ethics, and thus by several paths to your final view of life . . . To be master of any branch of knowledge, you must master those which lie next to it . . ."[27]

(3) In this perspective, more even than social science is relevant. Jurisprudence or legal philosophy has not only its law-in-society phase, but also its "analytical" (law, language, and logic)[28] and ethical (law and values)[29] dimensions. In that same 1897 speech, Holmes, after calling jurisprudence "a study which is sometimes undervalued by the practical-minded," went on to defend it in nonpractical terms as well:

> We cannot all be Descartes or Kant, but we all want happiness. And happiness, I am sure from having known many successful men, cannot be won simply by being counsel for great corporations and having an income of fifty thousand dollars. An intellect great enough to win the prize needs other food besides success. The remoter and more general aspects of the law are those which give it universal interest. It is through them that you not only become a great master in your calling, but connect your subject with the universe and catch an echo of the infinite, a glimpse of its unfathomable process, a hint of the universal law.[30]

27. Id. at 30.

28. E.g., Stone, Legal Systems and Lawyers' Reasonings (1964); Hart, The Concept of Law (1962); Summers, ed., Essays in Legal Philosophy (1968); Summers, ed., More Essays in Legal Philosophy (1971); Hughes, ed., Law, Reason and Justice (1969); Wasserstrom, The Judicial Decision (1961); Kelsen, What Is Justice? (1957); Guest, ed., Oxford Essays in Jurisprudence (1961); Simpson, ed., Oxford Essays in Jurisprudence (2d ser.) (1973); Llewellyn, The Common Law Tradition (1960); Gottlieb, The Logic of Choice (1968); Raz, The Concept of a Legal System (1970); Friedrich, ed., Rational Decision (Nomos 7) (1964).

29. E.g., Stone, Human Law and Human Justice (1965); Fuller, The Morality of Law (2d ed. 1969); Hook, ed., Law and Philosophy, pts. 1 and 2 (1964); Shuman, Legal Positivism (1963); Perelman, The Idea of Justice and the Problem of Argument (1963); Freund, On Law and Justice (1968); Rawls, A Theory of Justice (1971); Patterson, Jurisprudence, pt. 4 (1953); Cahn, The Sense of Injustice (1949); Friedrich and Chapman, eds., Justice (Nomos 6) (1963); Pennock and Chapman, eds., Political and Legal Obligation (Nomos 12) (1970); Cohen, Ethical Systems and Legal Ideals (1933).

Some of the works cited in either footnote 28 or 29 could readily be cited in both footnotes. Nor does either footnote purport to present a complete bibliographical coverage.

30. Holmes, Collected Legal Papers 202 (1920).

Most of us who study law and the legal system, in or out of the legal profession, may not tread all the paths that beckon, or hear the "echo" that Holmes heard. But for many it will be true that the study of law and the legal system, if I may alter a Baconian aphorism, "maketh a full person."

APPENDIX

Tips on Some Mechanics of
Law Study

A. SUMMARIZING ASSIGNED CASES

Most law school textbooks reprint the full or partial text of a good many court opinions — typically, appellate court opinions. As a student, you have to make summaries or "briefs" of the assigned cases. (The term "brief" is also used to refer to the printed argument that a lawyer files with a court.) These summaries are useful for you in the class discussion of the cases, and in studying for examinations. Moreover, your understanding of the case is enhanced by your putting the important features of it down on paper in your own words. The process reveals gaps and other aspects of the case that you would otherwise remain unaware of. And it is a bread-and-butter process that a practicing lawyer engages in constantly, for which his skills should be sharpened in law school.

What then should a brief of a case look like? I submit below a sample brief, based on the court of appeals opinions in the Nappier case. (You can look again at the opinions, reproduced at pages 123-132 supra. The facts of the case are reproduced in the district court opinion on pages 125-126.) The letter P is used below to designate plaintiff, and the letter D to designate defendant.

NAPPIER v. JEFFERSON STANDARD
LIFE INSURANCE CO.
322 F.2d 502 (4th Cir. 1963)

Damage action for privacy violation through TV broadcast.

FACTS:

S.C. Stat.: Misdemeanor to publish in newspaper, magazine, or other publication, "name" of female victim of actual or alleged rape, or assault with intent to ravish.

Complaint allegations: The two young women Ps taught dental hygiene in S.C. public schools, using a traveling puppet show involving puppet called "Little Jack," and a state-furnished station wagon bearing prominent inscription: "Little Jack, Dental Division, S.C. State Dept. of Health."

Someone raped Ps at their Kingstree motel and fled with their station wagon, which was found abandoned later that day. D broadcasting co. in two newscasts that day showed pictures of station wagon revealing above inscription and license number, with announcer identifying wagon as "that used by the two young women who had been attacked in Kingstree."

Throughout the state, Ps were spoken of as "The Little Jack Girls." As a result of the broadcasts they became generally known in the state as the victims of the crime, to their embarrassment and humiliation, and in violation of their right of privacy.

Motion to dismiss for failure to state claim on which relief can be granted.

Dist. Ct.: grants motion.

ISSUES:

On basis of fact allegations of complaint, did D's broadcasts violate Ps' privacy right under S.C. law?

HELD (2 to 1):

Yes — under S.C. common law "as fortified by the statute." Reversed and remanded for trial on whether D did *in fact* "name," i.e. identify, Ps.

REASONING:

1. The statutory prohibition against publication of "name" prohibits published *identification* of rape victim rather than merely publication of *proper name.*

   a. Only this interpretation would serve statutory purpose of protecting rape victims from publicity and encouraging them to report the crime to police.

   b. The narrower interpretation: (1) isn't required by fact that statute is penal. That fact "does not require an interpretation so rigid as to strip its wording of its plain connotation" — especially since statute here is being used not in penal suit but to help provide civil redress; (2) isn't required by fact that similar statutes of some other states use "identity" instead of or in addition to "name." "Name" alone can also be enough.

c. Cases on defamation show that an identifying description can be the equivalent of a name: "A libelee is nonetheless libeled though his name be not mentioned."

d. Cases under statutes prohibiting unauthorized use of personal name, portrait, or picture in advertising are not analogous: in advertising, "only the name, pseudonym or picture of the person — usually because of his prominence — is significant. Any other description is of no value."

2. Ps *can recover* for privacy violation *"under the common law as fortified by the statute."*

a. S.C. recognizes a common-law right of privacy — including "the publicizing of one's private affairs with which the public has no legitimate concern, or the wrongful intrusion into one's private activities, in such manner as to outrage or cause mental suffering, shame or humiliation to a person of ordinary sensibilities."

b. The exemption from such common-law liability in cases of news reporting of "matters of public concern and record," doesn't apply here because of the statute. "The statute states an exception to the exemption. No matter the news value, S.C. has unequivocally declared the identity of the injured person shall not be made known in press or broadcast."

3. No constitutional issue has been raised.

DISSENT:

1. Statute doesn't apply: word "name," even on liberal construction, is not equivalent of "identity."

If S.C. legislature had identity in mind, would have used that word, as Wis. legislature did.

2. Under S.C. common law of privacy, exception for "publication of matter of public concern and record" applies here.

———————

A brief of a case doesn't always have the same form, though some features are pretty standard, such as the full name of the case and citation (first three lines of the above brief) and an introductory capsule phrase to orient you in the legal field and situation when you start reading the brief (fourth line). Under the *FACTS* heading, it would not be typical to have a "complaint allegations" subheading, because the typical appellate opinion recites as facts not those alleged in the complaint but those which have been found by the lower court on the basis of the evidence and which are not contested on appeal. Here there was no evidence at any trial, since the defendants had moved to dismiss, and for purposes of that motion the factual allegations of the complaint are assumed to be true.

Another thing: there will be times when you want to write not a full brief but a shorter version, which might omit the reasoning and telescope the facts, issues, and holding into one or two sentences. For the Nappier court of appeals decision it might be something like this:

HELD: (1) S.C. crim. prohib. vs. publishing rape victim's "name" was meant to include prohib. vs. identification without use of her proper name — hence where D's TV broadcast showed picture of victims' auto with license no. and prominent inscription, "Little Jack, Dental Div. S.C. State Dept. of Health" (they being known as "Little Jack Girls" in their travels to pub. schools of state with show featuring "Little Jack" puppet), this violated stat. (2) In victims" c/law dam. suit for privacy viol., fact that this stat. prohibited D's conduct eliminated c/law defense in terms of reporting matters of legitim. pub. concern and record. *Dismissal of complaint reversed.*

Even in this shorter version, you will note that I have included some very specific facts about the particular case. It would not have been sufficient, for instance, to stop before the dash and omit the "hence" clause. To do so would communicate the thought that identification of some kind would fulfill the statutory purpose, but would omit the specific contribution of this case to the determination of what constitutes sufficient identification. It is true that a subsequent court faced with a different form and different area of alleged identification may read the fact categories of this precedent "broadly," and treat it in terms of a precedent for all forms of alleged identification (however different from this type of TV picture) and for any area of alleged identification (no matter how much smaller than the state-

wide area here). But this is up to the subsequent court. It is
not up to you. When you're briefing a case, you're not
engaged in predicting how broadly a subsequent court will
read it. You are treating the fact categories *narrowly*. It is
your record of precisely what happened in this case.

A final thing to remember about briefing is this: don't
brief the case as you go along in your first reading. Read the
opinion all the way through first. Some complex cases you'll
have to read more than once. And in your reading it will be
profitable to stop a moment after you've grasped the facts
and issues, and before the court starts giving its solution to
the problem. You might ask yourself at that point what
strikes you as a wise solution. Of course sometimes your
reaction won't be worth much, especially if the whole subject
matter is entirely new to you. But at other times it can be
valuable, by making possible an original, imaginative response
to the problem instead of letting you fall into the easy groove
of the court's thinking.

Assume now that you have briefed a case. The next step is
not to turn to the next assigned case for briefing. Instead you
are expected to do some thinking about the case you have
just briefed. Consider whether you agree with the court's
reasoning; if not, why not? Does it commit any logical
fallacies? Has the opinion distorted what a precedent said or
held (assuming you are familiar with the precedent)? Does
the result violate your feelings of justice or fairness? Do the
probable social consequences of the decision seem desirable?
Could the losing attorney have done (or argued) better?

Further, consider how the case stacks up with any prior
assigned cases in the same section of the book. Is it consistent
with them? Is it distinguishable? What aspect of the general
problem in that section is *added* by this case? You see, the
cases in a particular section of the book are related to each
other in a special way. After all, on the subject of any
particular section — let us say, "contributory negligence" — there are thousands of cases in existence, and the
editor has selected perhaps only four. Why these four?
Perhaps the first one lays out the whole problem in an

effective way, together with the historical background. Perhaps the second one illustrates an exception to, or limitation upon, the contributory negligence principle, such as the "last clear chance" doctrine. Perhaps the third one presents a borderline situation to which the doctrine has never been applied before but to which it might reasonably be so applied if the court desired. Perhaps the fourth shows the changes that a statute has made in the common law on the subject. So you will gain some perspective on the assigned cases and be more ready for class discussion if you have asked: Why is this case here? What does it add?

You will gain further perspective on the problem of an assigned case or group of cases by consulting a treatise on the problem. Thus, reading the discussion of contributory negligence by Prosser,[1] or by Harper and James,[2] is very likely to enhance your understanding of the subject and of the assigned cases on it. This reading of a treatise, or of relevant law-review articles cited in the casebook, is a much-neglected final step in the proper procedure for doing the assignment and preparing for class. In case you don't have time to do it for a particular assignment, make a note to do it at some later point when time is more free.

Another thing you will find very helpful is a group discussion, with a few of your fellow students, of the problems in a section of the course that has just been completed. If every participant prepares an outline of that section (based on his case briefs, his reading of treatises and articles, and his class notes), you are likely to find the discussion highly rewarding.

I should not have to add, finally, that there is *no painless substitute* for the process I've outlined of briefing the cases, critically evaluating them, and reading and thinking about what the scholars have said about them. It's incredible but true that a certain percentage of students every year is deluded into thinking that an equivalent training in the study of cases can be obtained by simply buying and reading ready-made briefs that someone else has written, sometimes accompanied by comments thereon that some usually anonymous nonscholar (paid on a piecework basis) has ground out. For a future lawyer, this makes just about as much sense as it would for a football team member, expecting to play in an upcoming game, to avoid the practice sessions, allowing a proxy to participate in his place and getting a written report on the sessions from his proxy.

B. CLASSWORK

What are you expected to do in class? First of all, there's a lot that goes on in class that you will want a record of. Your memory alone won't be good enough. But of course it has to be a critical kind of note-taking, a "sifting and winnowing." You will want to jot down not only the significant ideas (a good many won't be) from the other side of the lectern, including significant questions that may remain unanswered, but also the ideas and questions that a classmember may express, and those that occur to you during the discussion.

Secondly, it will benefit you to participate orally in the discussion — by volunteering answers to questions, by asking questions, and by taking issue with expressed ideas that you disagree with. Let me tell you a story about the importance of class work. About twenty-five years ago, I was teaching at the University of Oklahoma Law School in Norman, when a black girl applied for admission and was rejected because of her race, pursuant to state law. The state offered instead to provide *separate* instruction in a room at the state capitol in Oklahoma City by a member of the bar (whose practice apparently left him with some time on his hands). This was at a time when the constitutional doctrine of "separate but equal" was still good law. The state was arguing that the separate facilities in Oklahoma City were equal to those in Norman, and perhaps even superior since the girl would have a private tutor and be free from the distractions of campus life.

In an injunction suit to compel her admission to the law school at Norman, the NAACP lawyers (who included, among others, the present Supreme Court Justice Thurgood

Marshall) rounded up a parade of prominent legal educators as witnesses. There was Dean Griswold of Harvard, Dean Harrison of Pennsylvania, Professor Max Radin of California, Professor Charles Bunn of Wisconsin, Professor Walter Gellhorn of Columbia, and perhaps others I can't remember. The striking thing about these witnesses' testimony, as I recall it, was that they emphasized not the inequality in physical facilities and teaching faculty (though they did point to those inequalities) but the fact that the girl would be deprived of the benefit of a substantial group of fellow students. This was the benefit of experiencing the *different viewpoints* which can be held on the same set of facts by people of varying backgrounds and temperaments. It is an experience which develops an awareness of or sensitivity to the latent richness in any given set of facts — like the variations in sparkle that you get from turning a gem slightly so as to reflect the light differently.

You can see the same thing in comparing the majority and dissenting opinions in some cases: you read the majority opinion and you're convinced; you read the dissent, and it puts such a new slant on the facts — e.g., a different emphasis, or a pointing up of some facts' significance or some reason or argument that was neglected by the majority — that you change your mind completely. Another illustration of the hidden complexities or ambiguities in a set of facts is this: a professor preparing for class may read the same case for the sixth year, and in that reading may see significances that he did not see in any of his prior readings.

By not hesitating to express yourself in class, you not only improve your skill in oral discourse but you contribute to the development in the whole class of a sensitivity to (1) the varying interpretations which may be put on facts, and (2) the varying types of arguments that are possible for the ultimate decision on such facts. The practicing lawyer has to have this sensitivity when he listens to the facts of a client's story, and has to interpret them, relate them to a number of possible conceptual categories and possible legal arguments pro and con.

Not surprisingly, such a sensitivity or flexibility is primarily what is called for in answering questions on the typical law examinations. An example is given below.

C. LAW EXAMINATIONS

Law examinations take various forms. Occasionally there will be an "objective" question (true-false or multiple-choice) where primarily the scope of your information is being tested. Occasionally, also, some "short answer" questions may be included, which may call for information or for something more. The typical question, however, is the "problem" question. This gives the facts of a concrete situation, and expects you to find the issues and deal intelligently with those issues in the light of what you have learned about legal treatment of apparently similar issues. You may be asked to decide the issues, as judge. Or you may be asked to argue one side of the case, for plaintiff or defendant. (The question I shall present below asks you to argue for the defendant-appellant.) The examination may or may not be "open book." And it is not usually a "take-home."

The person reading your examination will start climbing the walls if he or she finds you talking all around the issues, spouting all the law that you have memorized on a particular subject and hoping that some of it will seem relevant to the reader. You are expected to confine yourself to law drawn from reasonably similar concrete situations. Your task is first to spot the issues, in all the areas of the problem where controversy is reasonably possible. Your next task is to indicate the legal principles that might be applied to those areas, by showing the respects in which the policies underlying existing rules or doctrines in apparently similar situations would or would not apply. If you are asked to play the advocate's role, you try consistently to handle those rules and doctrines in a way that puts the best face possible (without intellectual dishonesty) on your side. If you are asked to be a judge, you must not make the mistake of leaving the solution hanging. You must take the plunge and decide the case, indicating why you think the considerations favoring one side outweigh those favoring the other.

I am going to set forth a situation which I once used on an examination. It is relatively simple but calls for some of the skills I've been talking about as well as for skill in logical organization of one's total material. I will follow it with a suggested answer. You would need to have a certain amount of legal education under your belt before you could give an answer like the one suggested. Still, the Chapter 3 material on statutes, together with your common sense, will enable you to anticipate much of the answer. Please think about the problem before you read the suggested answer.

PROBLEM

The "Condemnation" chapter of a state statute book included this provision: "§100. If it be desired at any time to establish a cemetery ... or to enlarge any such already established, and the title to land needed cannot otherwise be acquired, land sufficient for the purpose may be condemned ... [etc.] ."

Subsequently there was added to the "Zoning" chapter of the same book a provision, effective June 1, 1940, reading: "§5. No cemetery shall be established within 250 yards of any house, home, hotel, inn, or other structure without the consent of the owner ... Violations of this section may be prosecuted as misdemeanors, and shall be enjoined at the suit of said owner ..."

Fairlawn Cemetery Corp., needing to enlarge its cemetery, has acquired a large tract of wooded land, through condemnation proceedings. The boundary of this tract is 200 yards from Mr. Will Full's property — the Heavenly Foods Grocery Store, which is a one-story affair, with a back room in which he sleeps and sometimes prepares meals. On May 15, 1940, Fairlawn commenced to improve, cultivate and stake out the tract in contemplation of cemetery operations within it; and the workers so engaged would habitually purchase groceries from Mr. Full for their noontime lunches, joshing him about how much shorter his funeral ride was now going to be, etc.

On July 15, 1940, Mr. Will Burry introduces himself to Mr. Full as being the president of Fairlawn, and says to Mr. Full: "We trust you don't object to these expansion operations of ours." Mr. Full brusquely replies, "You should put your trust in God. I've got you dead to rights." In short, he soon sues to enjoin the operations. He claims that the zoning statute was violated and that it is therefore the court's duty to issue an injunction against the use of the newly acquired tract for a cemetery.

You are the attorney for Fairlawn. Outline, in logically coherent fashion, all the arguments that should go into your brief, in opposition to Will Full's position.

SUGGESTED ANSWER

1. *There Was No Violation of the Zoning Law.*
    a. *The zoning law should be presumed to be prospective.*
    Hence, it shouldn't apply at all to a case where the property is already acquired and preliminary operations have already begun.

Supporting this conclusion are the following considerations:

    (1) There is a well-known *presumption* that substantive, as distinguished from procedural, statutes operate *prospectively* only.[1] This is to avoid an unduly harsh impact of a retroactive requirement — which is precisely what would be involved here, since Fairlawn had already bought, improved, and cultivated the tract prior to the June 1 effective date of the zoning law.

    (2) Another established principle is that if reasonably possible a court should choose, of two alternative statutory constructions, the construction which *avoids a constitutional doubt.*[2] To construe the zoning statute as retroactively affecting Fairlawn's pre-June enlargement activities would raise a constitutional doubt as to its validity under the due process clause. Further, the facts show that

Fairlawn was acting pursuant to a court judgment in condemnation proceedings permitting use of this new tract for a cemetery — so retroactivity of the zoning statute would be of more dubious validity than if Fairlawn were acting without a court judgment.

b. *Anyway, the zoning law doesn't apply to "enlargement" operations.*

Note the contrast in language of the two statutes: *"establish"* in the zoning law, and *"establish . . . or enlarge"* in the condemnation law. There is a "pari materia" principle of construction[1] to the effect that statutes on roughly the same subject — here, the subject of land use — should be construed together. Hence it is a reasonable inference that "establish" in the zoning law doesn't include an enlargement operation. The legislature had in mind, in the zoning law, new cemeteries established thereafter, not old cemeteries enlarged thereafter. (Alternatively, even if "enlargement" operations constitute "establishing," this establishing occurred when the new tract was improved, staked out, etc., so the zoning law would be inapplicable under the retroactivity point, in "a" above.)

c. *The zoning law is further inapplicable because Will Full's property was not a "structure" within the meaning of that law.*

The statutory pattern of specific enumerations followed by a catchall clause ("any house, home, hotel, inn, or other structure") makes relevant the "ejusdem generis" principle of construction.[2] Since all the specific enumerations are used primarily for residence or lodging, the principle would exclude a building that was primarily for selling groceries, with the lodging element a minor or incidental feature.

While such maxims of construction are not controlling, the maxim should be given weight here, where there is nothing strong to rebut it and a particular legislative concern, in this cemetery situation, over *residential* structures would make sense.

d. *The above-urged narrow constructions are particularly appropriate since this is a penal statute.*

The zoning law carries a criminal sanction, and nothing is

better established than the principle that criminal statutes are to be strictly or narrowly construed.[1] It is true that this is not a criminal case, but the question whether the statute has been violated by these operations would probably have to be answered the same way in a criminal suit as in this injunction suit.

e. *Even if the zoning law were otherwise applicable in this situation, there was no violation in view of Will Full's "consent."*

The statute's prohibition applies where the owner has not given his "consent." But here it seems that the owner did consent, since he put up no protest for more than two months after gaining knowledge from the workers of what was going on.

2. *Even If the Zoning Law Was Violated, No Injunction Should Issue.*

Will Full argues that because of the violation the court is under a "duty" to issue an injunction. It is true that there is a contextual argument for mandatory issuance — since the statute uses "may" in speaking of the bringing of criminal prosecutions and "shall" in speaking of the issuance of injunctions.

However, it takes a whole lot to show a legislative purpose to abolish the traditional power of a court of equity to exercise its discretion over whether to issue an injunction. [The Supreme Court so stressed in Hecht Co. v. Bowles, 321 U.S. 321 (1944).][2] There is no strong reason here, shown in any legislative history or otherwise, to overcome the view that the difference in language was inadvertent. There are many cases in which courts have held "shall" to mean "may" in a particular context.

Since, then, a court is still free under the statute to exercise its discretion about issuance of an injunction, it should exercise it here *against* issuance. This could be justified by Will Full's apparent bad faith (one must come into a court of equity with "clean hands") in getting the benefit of the added grocery business while not objecting for over two months.

3. *Even If an Injunction Should Issue, It Shouldn't Grant the Full Relief Requested.*

Will Full requests an injunction "against the use of the newly acquired tract for a cemetery." He thus seeks to enjoin the use of the whole new tract. Yet the most he is entitled to under the statutory "within 250 yards" requirement is that the *closest 50 yards* (the tract is now within 200 yards of his store) be enjoined from use as a cemetery.

There is another possible, but rather weak, argument under "1" (that there was no violation of the zoning law). It would be premised on the continued availability of the condemnation procedure in spite of the zoning law. It would run like this:

The zoning law didn't repeal the authority in the condemnation law to acquire, by condemnation, tracts that "cannot otherwise be acquired." Implied repeals are not favored by the law;[1] the two statutes should be read together in a reconciling way if possible.

So: previously if you wanted to acquire an adjoining tract without condemnation proceedings, all you needed was the tract-owner's agreement; after the zoning law, you have to *also* get agreement of the owner of the "structure" within 250 yards. *If that consent is lacking, the situation would be one of the situations where title "cannot otherwise be acquired" than by condemnation* within the meaning of the "Condemnation" chapter. So you would proceed to condemn. (Here Fairlawn had already instituted condemnation proceedings and acquired the property; it should be in at least as favorable a position as it would have been in if it had waited to condemn the property *after* Will Full claimed to be refusing his consent.)

Note: The foregoing argument has not been included because it seems weak. It is unlikely that the legislature wanted the zoning provision to be so ineffectual — i.e., allowing the new requirement of owner's consent to be so easily nullified, by condemnation.

NOTES TO SUGGESTED ANSWER

p. 318
    1. See p. 104
    2. See p. 171
p. 319
    1. See pp. 212-213
    2. See pp. 205-206, 208-209, 212, 213, 214
p. 320
    1. See pp. 209, 214, 217, 221-223
    2. See p. 210
p. 321
    1. See p. 226

INDEX